"Rich in detail . . . goes far beyond nostalgic, thumbnail sketches of New York City's monuments to capitalism."
—*New York Post*

"A richly textured study of an important American icon that symbolizes the intertwining of capitalism and government entrepreneurship in the United States. A nicely crafted study, certain to be of interest to students of American politics and culture, and to engineers and architects."
—Jameson W. Doig, professor of politics and public affairs, Princeton University

"Mr. Gillespie provides the facts about the center that many of us, who have taken the twin towers as part of the landscape without knowing much about their origins or purposes, will find riveting . . . Mr. Gillespie writes a gripping chapter on the construction of the towers, showing in detail how the monumental problems of engineering and design were solved."
—*The New York Times*

"Well-rounded . . . informed and easily readable."
—*Choice*

"Offers a fascinating section on the engineering challenges faced by [architect] Yamasaki and the Port Authority project managers."
—*The Wall Street Journal*

"Through his numerous first-hand interviews conducted with the people who work there daily, Gillespie vividly portrays the world of bankers, shippers, freight forwarders, and traders. With skill and insight, he captures what happens during a normal twenty-four-hour day in the Twin Towers, starting with early morning food deliveries and ending with the patrols of nighttime security guards."
—*Bulletin of Science, Technology & Society*

"[A] fascinating, and now terribly poignant, story of how the towers were built, what they represented and how they functioned."
—*BookPage*

"Enjoyable . . . the text is rich with authentic dialogue."
—*Technology and Culture*

Twin Towers

THE LIFE OF NEW YORK CITY'S WORLD TRADE CENTER

ANGUS KRESS GILLESPIE

NEW AMERICAN LIBRARY

New American Library
Published by New American Library, a division of
Penguin Putnam Inc., 375 Hudson Street,
New York, New York 10014, U.S.A.
Penguin Books Ltd, 80 Strand,
London WC2R 0RL, England
Penguin Books Australia Ltd, Ringwood,
Victoria, Australia
Penguin Books Canada Ltd, 10 Alcorn Avenue,
Toronto, Ontario, Canada M4V 3B2
Penguin Books (N.Z.) Ltd, 182–190 Wairau Road,
Auckland 10, New Zealand

Penguin Books Ltd, Registered Offices:
Harmondsworth, Middlesex, England

Published by New American Library, a division of Penguin Putnam Inc. This is an
authorized reprint of the hardcover edition published by Rutgers University Press.
For further information contact Rutgers University Press, 100 Joyce Kilmer Avenue,
Piscataway, NJ 08854.

First New American Library Printing, August 2002

10   9   8   7   6   5   4   3   2   1

 REGISTERED TRADEMARK—MARCA REGISTRADA

LIBRARY OF CONGRESS CATALOGING-IN-PUBLICATION DATA

Gillespie, Angus K., 1942–
    Twin towers : the life of New York City's World Trade Center / Angus Kress Gillespie—
Rev. ed.
        p.   cm.
    Includes bibliographical references and index.
    ISBN 0-451-20684-3 (alk. paper)
    1. World Trade Center (New York, N.Y.)   2. Skyscrapers—New York (State)—
New York.   3. City planning—New York (State)—New York—History—20th
century.   4. New York (N.Y.)—Buildings, structures, etc.   I. Title.
NA6233.N5W674   2002b
725'.23'097471—dc21   2002021946

Printed in the United States of America

For my sons,
Neil and Tristan

This edition is dedicated to those who
lost their lives on September 11, 2001, especially:

Roko Camaj

Frank A. DeMartini

Eugene J. Raggio

Contents

Illustrations

FIRST TEN FIGURES COURTESY OF THE PORT AUTHORITY OF NEW YORK AND NEW JERSEY. FIGURE 8.1. CREATED BY JEFF WARD.

Acknowledgments

MY INITIAL fascination with the Twin Towers as the subject of a book stemmed from a lifelong interest in architecture, engineering, and transportation. I am deeply indebted to my teachers for spurring these interests. My thanks to Vincent Scully of Yale University, who turned me on to the study of American architecture when I was an undergraduate, and to Alan Gowans, who further stimulated that interest while I was in graduate school at the University of Pennsylvania. I also had the good fortune early in my career to work as a technical editor at the Electric Boat Division of General Dynamics, which fueled my interest in how things work. In addition, I admired the attitude of the engineers who worked there. Like the engineers at the Port Authority, whom I met years later, they were people who "got things done."

In a real sense this book is a sequel to the earlier work, *Looking for America on the New Jersey Turnpike*, which I co-authored with my good friend Michael Aaron Rockland, who has always nurtured my scholarly ambitions. While that book was about a big road, this book is about a big building, or rather, a pair of big buildings. Many of the underlying ideas are the same. In both cases, we take a monumental work of civil engineering and "tease" it for its cultural implications. Those familiar with the field of American Studies will recognize my debts to Leo Marx, John A. Kouwenhoven, and Alan Trachtenberg. I try to carry on their work of exploring American artifacts as clues to American thought and values.

I approached the Twin Towers not just as an artifact, but as a living social institution. Here I drew heavily on studies in occupational folklore. I was influenced by the work of Benjamin A. Botkin,

Archie Green, Robert H. Byington, Roger D. Abrahams, Robert S. McCarl, Jr., and Jack Santino. Like the oral historian Studs Terkel, I talked to all kinds of people whenever I had the time over the last seven years. I will never forget the help of Robert C. DiChiara, the now-retired assistant director of the World Trade Center. He seemed to know everyone in the building complex, and he spared no effort to introduce me to those with the best stories.

There are countless individuals to whom I am indebted. New Yorkers are supposed to be legendary for their rudeness, but I found many kind and helpful people at the World Trade Center who shared their stories with me. Most of them are acknowledged in the footnotes that appear in the following chapters, but a few deserve special mention here. I thank Richard Leone, who served as chairman of the Port Authority from 1990 through early 1994, for sharing his candid thoughts on the proper role of public authorities in a democracy such as ours. He helped set me straight on the complex political changes that have affected the Port Authority over the years. My thanks to Roger Cohen, executive policy analyst at the Port Authority, for steering me to the invaluable weekly reports of the executive director to the commissioners; Guy Tozzoli for his encyclopedic knowledge of the design of the World Trade Center; Ray Monti for his energetic and enthusiastic stories about the actual building of the complex; Robert Kelley for his ability to explain the mechanics of international trade; Joseph Martella for his detailed background information on the Port Authority police; Sal Marciante for his wonderful stories of after-hours drinking and socializing; Al Pettenati for his remembrances of the early years up on the observation deck; and Jules Roinel for relating the complex story of Windows on the World and what makes it tick.

As I started this project, I consulted the book *World Trade Center: Politics and Policies of Skyscraper Development* by Leonard I. Ruchelman of Old Dominion University in Norfolk, Virginia, published by Syracuse University Press. Though full of useful information, Ruchelman's book is highly specialized, dealing with policy formation and policy implementation. By way of contrast, my book uses the American Studies approach, which is more broadly cultural.

Nonetheless, in writing this book I did have to come to grips with the policy decisions underlying the Twin Towers, which led me to an evaluation of the Port Authority of New York and New Jersey. In talking with people and in going through the literature, I tried to keep an open mind. However, it was not easy to do so because most of those who have studied the matter are of strong opinion. Institutions that set out to "get things done" attract enemies and critics. I began writing this book with an admiration for the World Trade Center, and I came to believe that no one besides the Port Authority could have done the job.

Thus my book stands in contrast to Robert A. Caro's Pulitzer Prize–winning *The Power Broker: Robert Moses and the Fall of New York* (1974). Whereas Caro portrays Moses as the ruthless czar of the Triborough Bridge and Tunnel Authority, I tend to see Austin Tobin, the head of the Port Authority, as a more benign figure, more inclined to build political consensus before proceeding. I was intrigued by Annemarie Hauch Walsh's *Public Business: The Politics and Practices of Government Corporations* (1978). Like Walsh, I find that "public enterprises are loaded with social and political implications" as well as with technical and financial ones; however, I would go further to argue that they also have broad cultural meanings.

My work follows directly in the footsteps of Jameson W. Doig of Princeton University, to whom I am greatly indebted. Doig has written the best account yet on the political strategies used by Austin Tobin to advance the Port Authority. Professor Doig has written a chapter about Tobin in the book that he co-edited with Erwin C. Hargrove called *Leadership and Innovation* (1987). In this chapter, Doig only treats the World Trade Center in passing. However, his analysis of Tobin's overall career strategy was invaluable to me in getting a clear picture of how the Port Authority operated. Doig paints a picture of Tobin that succeeds in capturing the man's tremendous energy and enthusiasm.

I owe a major debt of gratitude to Anthony Robins, who wrote the book *The World Trade Center* (1987), a volume in the Classics of American Architecture series. I relied heavily on the work of Robins in my chapter 5, "Architecture: Beloved by All Except the Experts," which deals with architectural esthetics. Robins makes a significant contribution by explaining why the Port Authority turned away from Wallace K. Harrison, Gordon Bunshaft, and Edward Durrell Stone to the "iconoclastic outsider," Minoru Yamasaki. It would have been difficult, if not impossible, to have completed my chapter on architecture without consulting Anthony Robins.

Early in my research, I was inspired by an issue of *Portfolio: A Quarterly Review of Trade and Transportation*, published by the Port Authority during the winter of 1990–1991, to mark the twentieth anniversary of the Twin Towers. This special issue had four separate articles, all of which proved to be enormously helpful to me. Roger Cohen wrote "Casting Giant Shadows: The Politics of Building the World Trade Center," which inspired my chapter 1, "Political Background: The Uneasy Alliance between New York and New Jersey." Ray Monti wrote "A Tall Order," which was about the engineering design and construction of the World Trade Center akin to my chapter 2, "It Can't Be Done: Overcoming the Obstacles in Building Tall Towers," and chapter 3, "Erecting the Towers: It's One Story after Another." Susan Girardo wrote "Letting the Twins," about attracting tenants which has similarities to my chapter 6, "The World Trade Center Concept: Not Just Another Office Building." Finally, August K. Preschle wrote "One Hundred and Ten Stories," which motivated my chapter 7, "A City within a City; or, A Day in the Life. . . ."

My thanks to the spokespeople in the office of corporate and media relations of the Port Authority. To be sure, it is their job to tell the agency's side of the story. Yet I found them to be responsive rather than hostile when I challenged their views. They answered my questions, returned my phone calls, and went out of their way to set up numerous interviews. I remember talking with spokesman Allen Morrison shortly after the 1993 bombing. I had been favorably impressed with the frequency and thoroughness of his press briefings, and I told him so. He replied, "Well, it's up to us to be forthcoming and complete. Otherwise, reporters will assume the truth lies elsewhere."

Later, Peter Yerkes of media relations made arrangements for me to have access without restriction to the weekly reports of the executive director to the commissioners. These candid reports were an extraordinarily useful resource. Because public agencies can be defensive and suspicious about providing outside researchers with access to archives, I was struck by the unusual openness of the Port Authority. I found myself at times struggling to maintain objectivity. Certainly, I do believe that a policy of openness is in the best interest of the agency, the scholar, and the public. Of course, the Port Authority has made its share of mistakes and missteps, but a policy of candor enables the agency to overcome these errors and move ahead.

My thanks to Rutgers, the State University of New Jersey, for a small research council grant in 1992, which enabled me to hire journalist Richard Skelly to go through the *New York Times Index,* providing me with an essential baseline of valuable information. Rutgers also provided me with a sabbatical leave from teaching duties during the fall semester of 1994, which gave me a wonderful period of uninterrupted time to focus on the research for this book.

As I worked on this project, I attended a number of academic conferences where I was able to present early drafts of material in order to solicit constructive (mostly) criticism and feedback. In 1995 I gave a talk on the architecture of the World Trade Center at a meeting of the American Culture Association in Philadelphia. My panel was chaired by Professor Gaylord Richardson of the Architecture and Urban Design Department of the University of Kansas. Professor Richardson and other colleagues there made numerous helpful suggestions. In 1996 I gave an updated and revised talk on the architecture of the Twin Towers at a meeting of the American Culture Association in Las Vegas. Again, many colleagues had interesting and useful things to say. Professor David M. Sokol of the College of Architecture and the Arts of the University of Illinois at Chicago was unusually helpful. Finally, in 1996 I gave a talk on collecting the folklore of international trade at a meeting of the American Folklore Society in Pittsburgh. Some of the information in this paper found its way into my chapter 6, "The World Trade Center Concept: Not Just Another Office Building." Especially generous with his time and encouragement at that session was folklorist Nicholas Burlakoff of Ossining, New York.

Robert Blake Truscott and Robert Santelli, both professional writers and authors, deserve special thanks for serving as writing coaches when I first tried to put my ideas on paper for a book proposal to my publisher. This book was enormously improved by the advice of several colleagues at Rutgers. Michael Aaron Rockland,

Leslie Fishbein, William Barillas, Louise Duus, and Frank Popper read portions of my first drafts, giving much valuable advice. A word is also in order concerning people at Rutgers University Press. My wholehearted thanks to director Marlie Wasserman for her encouragement and support. Along the way I received much editorial advice from Marilyn Campbell, Doreen Valentine, and Helen Hsu. Without these individuals, this book would not have been possible. Near the very end of the editorial process, author and folklorist Tad Tuleja went patiently through the entire manuscript. Special recognition must go to him for offering important tips on style and organization.

Finally, I thank my wife, Rowena Cosico Gillespie, who already leads a busy life, for helping me make the time to work on this book. I depended on her patience, forbearance, love, and encouragement.

Twin
Towers

Introduction

In democracies, nothing is more great or more brilliant than
commerce: it attracts the attention of the public, and fills
the imagination of the multitude; all energetic passions are
directed towards it.

—ALEXIS DE TOCQUEVILLE, *DEMOCRACY IN AMERICA*

HORROR HAS the power to rivet our attention. Why would anyone want to bomb the World Trade Center? This was the question
on everyone's mind on February 26, 1993. It was lightly snowing
on a Friday afternoon when suddenly, at 12:18, a massive explosion shook the foundation of the Twin Towers of the Trade Center
in lower Manhattan—the tallest buildings in the region and a magnet for tourists and business travelers alike. A bomb hidden in a van
had exploded, causing an immense shower of glass and concrete debris to fall. Shrill screams of innocent victims followed, and then
the piercing wails of sirens from ambulances, police cars, and fire
engines resounded in all of downtown Manhattan. Experts called it
the most destructive act of terrorism ever committed on U.S. soil.[1]

Who? Why? At first all that was known was that a bomb set
off the blast. Though weeks and months would go by before federal
authorities could figure out *who* did it and wrap up the case, the
question of *why* the World Trade Center was chosen was never in
doubt. The very next day, a reporter from the *New York Times*

interviewed Bruce Hoffman, a terrorism specialist with the Rand
Corporation and the author of several surveys of terrorism in the
United States. Hoffman said, "A car bomb in a street in New York
doubtless would have killed more people. But the World Trade Cen-
ter is a symbol of Wall Street and the Manhattan skyline and the
United States itself, and I think that is very important."[2]

Hoffman's remarks intrigued me. A core mission of American
Studies is to identify and interpret American symbols. In our 1989
book, *Looking for America on the New Jersey Turnpike*, Michael
Aaron Rockland and I had argued for consideration of the turnpike
as an American icon. We had a difficult argument to put forth because the turnpike is not beautiful; to most scholars it is even ugly.
We argued for a new perspective that would allow for an esthetic
appreciation of the turnpike and its stripped-down, no-frills look.[3]

A similar problem confronts me in a consideration of the
World Trade Center as an icon. The building has won no architectural awards. Architectural critics, if they look at it at all, dismiss
the Twin Towers as square, steel shafts clad in aluminum rising from
a low cluster of steel-and-glass buildings. There are no architectural
embellishments or decorative windows. The only spire is a 330-foot
television mast. As one of my colleagues said, "The buildings are
tall—and that's about it."[4]

All true, yet somehow the Twin Towers have symbolic meaning. Interpreting an artifact is akin to interpreting a poem. There
may be more than one meaning, perhaps a cluster of meanings. At
the level of experience, the Twin Towers, because of their height, are
regarded as sublime—as noble, grand, and majestic. This experience of sublimity can be captured in two ways, either by looking up
from below or looking down from above. Either way, the view is
dizzying and overwhelming.[5] But what do the Twin Towers mean?
Certainly, they may be taken to symbolize the Manhattan skyline,
or the City of New York, or perhaps the Port of New York and New
Jersey. But on a somewhat higher plane, the Twin Towers may be
taken to symbolize American exceptionalism, or American capitalism, or even America itself. Indeed, the World Trade Center is a
global symbol, instantly recognized to stand for America, just as
the Eiffel Tower or Big Ben stand for their respective countries. In
the chapters which follow, I will show that this audacious symbol
did not come about by chance. Its origins can be found in the mind

of Austin Tobin, the high-powered executive director of the Port Authority. Often, whether addressing suburban luncheons in New Jersey or national conventions in New York, Tobin would recall the words of Daniel H. Burnham, the early twentieth-century Chicago architect who built New York's first great skyscraper, the Flatiron Building. "Make no small plans," Tobin quoted Burnham. "For they have not power to stir the blood."[6]

The Twin Towers of the World Trade Center started with an extraordinarily bold plan. In the first place, it called for clearing a thirteen-square-block site. How in the world would anyone go about holding public hearings and obtaining the approvals and permits for even the first phase of the project? The key to the problem was the nature of the sponsor—the Port Authority, which had been set up in 1921 with far-reaching powers. The Port Authority, as a government corporation, was a hybrid creature, with some of the characteristics of private firms and some of public agencies. For better or worse, it was precisely the kind of organization that was needed to get the job done.

Taken together, the Twin Towers, completed in the early 1970s, are not just a pair of skyscrapers but a preeminent symbol. The builders intended to make a statement about the importance of the Port of New York and New Jersey. They argued that the region's geography, history, and economics made building the World Trade Center inevitable. The Towers complex rises like Emerald City around a carefully groomed, five-acre elevated plaza with fountains and sculptures from what was once a dilapidated area of half-abandoned stores. Today the Twin Towers make up the foremost souvenir postcard subject of the city. Stop at any retail store in the city that places revolving metal racks of postcards out on the sidewalk and examine the selection. What do you find? Along with the obligatory cards of the Statue of Liberty, there are cards of various museums and attractions and the overall New York skyline by day and by night. And always there is the World Trade Center with its Twin Towers. A trip to New York is not validated until one purchases that card, because it shows the one structure that people back home will instantly recognize as standing for New York.

When people heard that the title of my next book was to be *Twin Towers*, they often asked, "Oh, is it all about the bombing?" I explained over and over again that it was not *primarily* about the bombing, but that certainly I would deal with that. Instead, my book was intended to be more broadly cultural. Indeed, I began my study of the World Trade Center in earnest in 1991, two years before the bombing even took place. When that tragic event occurred, I did have the sobering thought that the bombers and I had one important area of agreement: we both felt certain that the World Trade Center had tremendous symbolic significance. While I was trying to understand its importance to our culture, they were trying to destroy it.

In fact, there already is a comprehensive book about the bombing called *Two Seconds under the World* by Jim Dwyer and David Kocieniewski, Deidre Murphy, and Peg Tyre. The authors, all reporters at *New York Newsday* and *Newsday*, carefully trace the events surrounding both the bombing and the subsequent investigation. I can add little to what they have already written.[7]

However, I should point out that for the Port Authority, the challenge of rebuilding the Trade Center after the bombing was, in a strange way, an exciting and invigorating time for the agency. If we accept the notion that institutions have personalities, then we might say that the Port Authority at its best is a paramilitary engineering agency that thrives on adversity. The agency was full of seasoned military veterans who loved to build things and fix them if they were only given a chance to do so. Now they had that chance.

The 1993 bombing recovery effort gave the seventy-two-year-old agency a stunning opportunity to show what it could do. Engineers and managers put in sixteen-hour days for many weeks. It is doubtful that any commercial landlord could have summoned the talent and the resources to repair the Twin Towers with such energy and determination. The bill in the end would be staggering. The explosion cost $300 million for repairs to the basement and its mechanical systems, and another $225 million for cleaning the smoke damage on each story of both towers.[8]

Totally aside from the bombing issue, I noticed something very curious as I began my research. As I talked about my project with family, friends, colleagues, and students, I came to realize that very few had much knowledge about the Towers. Most knew that it was a pair of very tall office buildings, but that was about it. They did not know who built it or why. Eager to quantify this insight, I devised a short informal questionnaire: (1) Have you ever heard of the World Trade Center in New York City? (2) Would you recognize it if you saw a picture of it? (3) Have you ever visited it? (4) Do you know who is the owner-builder-landlord of the complex? I gave this questionnaire to hundreds of students at Rutgers University, most of them New Jersey residents quite familiar with New York City. Nearly all of them had heard of the World Trade Center, and said that they would recognize a picture. About half had visited the place, but only very few (a tiny percentage) could identify the owner-builder-landlord. Most people did not have a clue and were unwilling to venture a guess. Those who did guess were usually wrong. Some said it was the Rockefeller family; others said it was the city of New York; still others thought it was a group of Japanese investors.

The correct answer, of course, is the Port Authority of New York and New Jersey. Quite puzzled at the ignorance, I discussed my findings with the media-relations people at the agency. They told me that they had commissioned a similar, albeit formal and scientific study that had come up with the same basic conclusions. It wasn't just Rutgers undergraduates who were in the dark. Most people in the region, both young and old from both states, had no idea that the owner-builder-landlord was the Port Authority.

So the Port Authority became the subject of my first chapter. Here I discuss the origins of that unique bistate agency, its early growth as a nonpolitical engineering agency, the development of the idea for a World Trade Center, and the political maneuvering to make it happen. I then look at the unusual problems in preparing the foundation for the Twin Towers as well as the technological innovations required for the elevatoring and structural systems in chapter 2. Once the foundations are in place, I discuss the erection of the Towers in chapter 3. In chapter 4, I show how the Twin Towers, through a combination of rational planning and plain good luck, overcame the objections of its critics and won a place in the hearts and minds of people everywhere. In chapter 5 I show why, despite its popularity with the people, the Twin Towers fell out of favor with architectural critics. The idea of the Twin Towers as a specific place to facilitate international trade with the right mix of tenants is the subject of chapter 6. Finally, in chapter 7 I look at a typical twenty-four-hour cycle of activities in the complex. This final chapter in its narrative form is different from all the others. An inherent difficulty with telling the story of one day is that the account is necessarily highly selective. From the tens of thousands of possible individual stories, I had to select a few dozen to paint a representative picture. To avoid wrenching transitions as I go through the daily cycle, I have divided that chapter into bite-size segments, each preceded by a subheading. My hope is to capture a sense of the frenzy of activity that swirls through the complex on a daily basis.

Despite my attempt in these chapters to discover larger meanings for the Twin Towers—the ideas and values of which it is emblematic—the World Trade Center is also, of course, just there, part of the landscape, and I try to describe it accurately, to capture its flavor. However, the World Trade Center is a constantly changing institution. During the period of time that I was working on this book, most of the 1990s, I had the sense of someone who was trying to hit a moving target. To borrow a shopworn expression, the World Trade Center of today is not the same as it was yesterday and it will not be the same tomorrow. This problem was particularly noticeable with respect to the two rooftop attractions.

For some time, Windows on the World atop the North Tower was one of the highest-grossing restaurants in the world. In 1985, it made $21.5 million; in 1986, $22 million; in 1987, $24.7 million; in 1988, $25.4 million. But by 1989, Windows on the World had started to slip. In fact, Windows actually lost money in 1993, the year the bombing took place. No one knows exactly what went wrong, but the decline was apparently due to a combination of poor management of the property along with a downturn in the U.S. economy in general and the Manhattan economy in particular.[9]

The bombing took place in February 1993, and Windows was forced to shut down. Most of the physical damage from the bombing took place on the lower levels. Windows on the World, located high up on the 106th and 107th floors, suffered only a light coating of dust over everything. In theory, it might have been possible to reopen the facility in three or four weeks. But the contracted operator, Inhilco, decided not to reopen. The bombing gave Inhilco the chance to part company with the Port Authority. Since the facility was losing money, both sides were unhappy with the contract, which was due to expire in a few years anyway.[10]

In March 1993, the restaurant at the top of the North Tower was thus empty. The Port Authority had to move quickly to find a new operator. A consultant was hired to frame the criteria that would be used to request proposals from qualified bidders. The final selection process was to take into account not only the financial strength of the bidder, but also the bidder's reputation and competence in food preparation. Out of a field of eight respondents, the final choice was the team of Joe Baum, Michael Whiteman, and Dennis Sweeney. It was the same team that had originally planned and staffed Windows on the World in 1976.[11]

Shortly after these changes took place at Windows on the World, the observation deck atop the South Tower was renovated. Although the deck had been run quite well under Port Authority management for nineteen years, it was decided in 1995 to bring in a private company with plans to spend $5.8 million to make the deck into a high-tech "experience" to attract tourists in any weather. Ogden Entertainment Services agreed to lease the deck for eleven and a half years. Ogden hired designers with ties to the Disney Company in the hope of creating a "world's fair" atmosphere. Under the terms of the lease, Ogden agreed to pay the Port Authority at least $5.5 million per year for the deck plus 10 percent of its revenues over $10 million. When the agency itself ran the deck, it grossed about $9 million and netted between $5 million and $6 million. So there was at least the potential of harvesting greater revenue from the deck.[12]

Though in recent years changes have been made in both rooftop attractions, the Twin Towers' height at least has been constant. One World Trade Center, with 110 stories, is fixed at 1,368 feet; Two World Trade Center, also with 110 stories, is fixed at 1,362 feet. Though the height of the Twin Towers never changes, their relative place in the record books keeps slipping downward.

In chapter 3 I explain that in 1973 the Twin Towers briefly held the title of "The World's Tallest Building," taking the honor away from the Empire State Building, which had held the record for forty years. But the following year, in 1974, the title was taken by the Sears Tower in Chicago, with 110 stories at 1,454 feet. As this is written, first and second place goes to the two Petronas Towers at 1,476 feet each in Kuala Lumpur, Malaysia, pushing the Sears Tower into third place. Next, at fourth place, comes the Jin Mao

Building in Shanghai at 1,379 feet. The Twin Towers currently have thus dropped into fifth and sixth place. The official records for this sort of thing are kept by the Council on Tall Buildings and Urban Habitat at Lehigh University in Bethlehem, Pennsylvania.[13]

Historically, the tall skyscraper was an American invention, spurred on by competition between New York and Chicago. Now, at the close of the twentieth century, it is clear that the real competition is taking place in Asia. What are the implications for the World Trade Center? Though prediction is always risky, I believe it will always be *the last tallest skyscraper in New York*. For several reasons, it is very unlikely that such a tall building will be constructed in New York ever again. In the first place, local neighborhoods have been empowered to block projects they do not want. In the second place, environmentalists can and do raise valid objections to large-scale projects. But the most important factor of all is that the culture was changing in the early 1970s just as the World Trade Center was being completed and dedicated.

Nowhere was that change of attitude shown more clearly than in Ernst F. Schumacher's influential book *Small Is Beautiful: A Study of Economics as If People Mattered* (1973). Here the author challenged the prevailing Western assumption that bigger is always better. "Man is small and, therefore, small is beautiful," he argued. "To go for gigantism is to go for self-destruction."[14] The gradual but widespread acceptance of Schumacher's argument meant that skyscrapers started to fall out of fashion. They were seen as symbols of monumental ego, corporate extravagance, and terrible waste.

The corporations of today outdo themselves in trying to keep a low profile in the green fields of exurbia. At Microsoft's headquarters outside of Seattle, the tallest building is three stories high, outclassed by the surrounding firs. Asked about the possibility of a tall building, the company's spokesperson Erin Carney said, "Oh, no. For us, what's truly important is the products and software you produce, not a flashy, tall building."[15]

The Port Authority found itself on the wrong side of history. It should be remembered that the World Trade Center project was born in a period of expansive national optimism, but it was completed during a period of national gloom and retreat. It was in the early 1960s that John F. Kennedy was elected president of the United

States. It was the beginning of the Camelot era, when Americans were fascinated with the prospect of a newly imperial, globally engaged, internationalized America. In 1961 the Port Authority issued a report recommending the establishment of a World Trade Center. Kennedy took office, and soon announced plans to send an American to the moon. It was an era of big plans and big dreams.

In the early 1970s, as construction of the World Trade Center neared completion, the mood of the country had changed. The United States was exhausted by the divisive Vietnam War and shocked by the Watergate scandal. The World Trade Center, begun in the rosy glow of Camelot, was completed just as the Nixon administration was collapsing. The fact that this large quasi-governmental project was finished at a time when government itself was being questioned has colored all subsequent discourse about the building. During the post-Nixon seventies, new questions arose about the wisdom of large-scale projects. There were questions that had never seriously been asked before about environmental protection, historical preservation, and community participation.

Over the last twenty-five years, since the first tenants moved into the World Trade Center, many people have had their say about the project. It has attracted the attention of politicians, columnists, academics, writers, and citizens at large. Much of what has been said and written has been negative. What I have tried to do in this book is to take a fresh look at the Twin Towers, using a nonjudgmental, non-chip-on-the-shoulder approach.

I began talking with my friends, and I quickly discerned a pattern. I found that the World Trade Center, the most controversial project of the Port Authority, can serve as a kind of political litmus test. My colleagues at Rutgers were mostly liberals who tended to favor the expansion of government. Most of them, with the exception of the architectural historians, thought that the project was a neat idea. My friends in the business community were mostly conservatives who were suspicious of government. Most of them, with the exception of the tenants, wanted the government out of the private sector and thought the project was a dumb idea.

The trouble with talking with friends (I hope they will forgive me for saying this) was that usually they had very strong opinions but not much insight. Some of them felt that the Port Authority could do no right; others, that the Port Authority could do no wrong. It was time to go to the library to find out what the experts had to say on this matter. There I read with keen interest the work of Jameson W. Doig of the Woodrow Wilson School of Public and International Affairs at Princeton University. Here at last was a scholar who managed a balanced portrait of executive director Austin J. Tobin and the Port Authority. For the most part, Professor Doig praises the agency for its accomplishments, yet he maintains an ability to point out the places where it stumbles.

Let us turn to Doig's analysis to examine the four strategies for action developed by Austin Tobin in the postwar years. During that period, the agency focused its attention on developing airports and marine terminals. First, there was the "self-supporting" criterion. Since the Port Authority had no power of taxation, all of its projects had to pay their own way by generating enough revenue to cover all of the costs. Second, there was a need for "regional balance." If a project were built in New York, a parallel project of equal importance would have to be found in New Jersey. There did not have to be a dollar-for-dollar balance in any given year, but there had to be roughly equal treatment over a period of time. This was elementary politics for a bistate agency. Third, the Port Authority always took a "passive stance." The agency pretended not to take the initiative in developing new ideas for projects. Instead, they would try to get others to make "requests." Such ideas might come from business associations, civic groups, mayors, governors— anyone but the Port Authority. This strategy allowed the agency to keep a low profile. Finally, there was the need to "deflect political pressure" for reducing bridge-and-tunnel tolls. The prewar toll on bridges and tunnels was fifty cents, but there was always pressure— especially from the New Jersey side—to reduce it. Meanwhile, the agency was counting on these surplus funds to bankroll new projects. The idea was to make the projects so attractive that people would continue to accept the tolls.[16]

Throughout the late 1940s and on through the 1950s, Tobin brilliantly pursued these entrepreneurial strategies. He and his staff continued to identify new projects for the Port Authority. They built a vast marine terminal on the Jersey side for Port Elizabeth and Port Newark, three airports, a bus terminal in midtown Manhattan, and two large truck terminals. The list of Tobin's accomplishments is truly impressive, and it certainly helped that the Port Authority paid for its own projects at no expense to either state.

In retrospect, there were serious problems for the Port Authority in taking on the World Trade Center project. The agency was indeed stretching the limits of its charter, which called for "improving commerce and trade." Because the Twin Towers project had such a high profile, it attracted a great deal of criticism. In general, it is a bad idea for the government to get into the private real estate market. But in this particular case, it turned out to be beneficial. It was a government subsidy by the diversion of resources into the construction of the building, yet it contributed to the subsequent boom of the downtown area. It made a difference, just like building a bridge or power plant or a military base stimulates a local economy.

The Port Authority was always proud of itself and its ability to take on large projects. It now seems clear that the World Trade Center was the last great project that the agency would undertake, at least in our time. Because of the sheer size and scope of the Twin Towers project, all subsequent proposals have been viewed with suspicion and hostility. In the past, the Port Authority had the luxury of a great surplus. The agency was resented because it was perceived as having vast amounts of money and an arrogant attitude. Those days are over now because the Port Authority has become more politicized. It has become much harder for the agency to take on large-scale projects that take time and require huge amounts of money. There is more resistance now to government spending, and there is more focus on short-term results.

On the positive side, one can argue that the Port Authority in the last twenty-five years has become more open in its dealings with the public. The agency has become more responsive to comments from citizens and their representatives from both sides. The downside is that it is much harder to get things done in a democracy. The agency has drifted into a deep-rooted inertia because the easiest way to avoid criticism is to do nothing new, to maintain the status quo. As one Port Authority executive said, "Give us a big project and then the Port Authority can rise to the occasion. Without big projects, we become dull and sluggish, just maintaining what we have already built."[17]

In recent years, the Port Authority has suffered. When Austin Tobin retired in 1971 after forty-five years of service, the agency lost its regional focus. Today, there is a preoccupation with maintaining an absolute balance between New York and New Jersey, tit for tat. So it has become much more difficult to carry out a truly great project in one place or the other. It has become the pattern to do two small projects, one in New York and one in New Jersey. There is a terrible hidden cost to the Port Authority's current pattern of inaction. To pick the most obvious example, difficult and controversial decisions relating to dredging the harbor and deepening the shipping channels have been postponed and delayed. Meanwhile, the port that created New York City and once was the busiest in the world now handles less cargo than Houston or the Port of Southern Louisiana.[18]

As the final chapters of this book were being written, the Port Authority had spent three years and $4.5 million to study whether the World Trade Center should be turned over to the private sector. In September 1998 the commissioners finally reached a decision to look for someone in the private sector to lease the five buildings in the complex, including the Twin Towers, for ninety-nine years. Under the plan, the Port Authority will continue to own the sixteen acres of land, but a lessee will assume control of the ten million feet of office space and the seventy-eight-store mall. It will be up to the lessee to collect rents and maintain the property. The decision came about in large part because of a unique set of historical circumstances. With George Pataki serving as governor of New York and Christine Whitman serving as governor of New Jersey, the decision did not surprise political observers. Since both states were led by Republican governors committed to the notion that government should step aside and let the private sector take over wherever possible, the decision seemed inevitable.[19]

As this book goes to press, it is difficult to know how this momentous decision will play out in the years ahead. It is possible that the Port Authority will be empowered to devote the proceeds of the sale to improve the transportation infrastructure of the region. At this time, the Port Authority is like a sleeping giant, but the day may yet come when New York and New Jersey will put aside their bickering and ask the agency to do great things. To see what the agency can do, we need look no further than the construction of the Twin Towers.

Introduction to the Paperback Edition

FOR ME, TUESDAY, September 11, 2001, was a day that started much like any other. I was at home in New Brunswick, getting ready for an appointment later that morning in Princeton. I was sipping coffee and reading the newspaper. Then I got a call from my older son from his car phone. He said that an airplane had crashed into the World Trade Center. I turned on the television and saw smoke billowing out of the North Tower. I watched with rapt attention. I assumed it was an accident, at least up until the moment that a second airplane crashed into the South Tower. Then I knew that it was terrorism, but I wasn't overly worried because I assumed that the firemen would come along and put out the fire and the damage would be repaired and life would go on as usual. I turned off the television and went down to Princeton. On my way back, I heard on the radio that both towers had collapsed.

In a state of shock and disbelief, I returned home just past noon. I checked my telephone answering service. A mechanical voice said, "You have sixty-seven messages." Then it hit me: my obscure book was getting attention. That book asked the question: What do the Twin Towers mean? I argued that, on the most basic level, they might be taken to symbolize the Manhattan skyline, or the City of New York, or perhaps the Port of New York and New Jersey. But on a higher plane, the Twin Towers might be taken to symbolize American exceptionalism, or American capitalism, or even America itself. I wrote, "Indeed, the World Trade Center is a global symbol, instantly recognized to stand for America, just as the Eiffel Tower or Big Ben stand for their respective countries."

Reporters all over the country, reading a summary of my book on the Internet, put two and two together. If the World Trade Center was a symbol of America, then it was the perfect target for enemies of America. I had no time to grieve. I just started answering the phone. While I was on the phone answering one reporter's questions, my answering service stacked up two more requests for help.

There were calls from all the major newspapers, the wire services, and the television networks. I talked with reporters from the *New York Times,* the *Washington Post,* the *Boston Globe,* the *Dallas Morning News,* the *Los Angeles Times,* and countless others. An old friend called to tell me that my book was now number one on Amazon.com. CBS sent a car service to New Brunswick to take me to their midtown studio to do a live interview with Bryant Gumbel. Others sent camera crews to my home near Douglass College. Despite my shock and grief, I had a sense of great empowerment. This process went on, hour after hour, day after day, until Saturday morning. Then, just as suddenly as it started, the phone stopped ringing.

Now came the hard part. I was all alone with my feelings. On the one hand, I was proud of the book. It contained much useful information. Perhaps, I told myself, it could serve as a tribute to the victims. On the other hand, I was profoundly upset that it took a tragedy of this magnitude to draw attention to the book. I had always dreamed of a wider readership, and now I had it. But I was reminded of the Chinese proverb "Beware of what you wish for."

On Sunday morning, I woke up crying. The realization of the human loss finally hit me. Many of those I had interviewed had become friends, and now they were gone. I realized that during the entire previous week, I had been living a dream. I had been the indispensable commentator, the man of the hour. I was especially embarrassed and guilty that, during the intense hours of answering the phone, I had never thought to inquire after the fate of my younger son Tristan, who had commuted every day from his home in Hoboken to his office in lower Manhattan by means of the PATH, passing underneath the World Trade Center. What was I supposed to do next? Now I was just plain old me, with laundry to do and bills to pay, like everyone else.

On Monday morning at the office, a friend asked me, "How does it feel to have written a book about something that no longer exists?" It felt awful, and it was sickening. I had a difficult time getting in touch with my emotions. Being brought up in a WASP family, I had always held back rather than displayed my emotions. The whole thing seemed like a formulaic disaster movie, with the explosion and the fireball and the collapse of the two towers. I experienced a drop in my energy and my enthusiasm for teaching and research. As the days went by, horrific images were published, and I fell into a state of introspective withdrawal. I was hard hit by the funerals of the firefighters. I began to feel the impact of the tragedy, dimly sensing my own mortality.[1]

It is still hard for me to speak of the Twin Towers in the past tense. When I first began to research the building in the early 1990s, I assumed that the World Trade Center would last forever. When the first edition of this book came out in 1999, I felt that I had done my part to tell the story of the life of the World Trade Center and to lend some respectability to an important structure that had not received serious respect from intellectuals and architectural critics. Now that the Twin Towers are gone, I have noticed a shift. Previously ignored, the building now is getting some serious and sympathetic attention from pundits and scholars.

In this edition, I have gone through the entire book, trying to take full advantage of this opportunity to revise the text. I have corrected all the errors of spelling and dates and names and facts that I could find. When important new information came to light, I included it. A number of historic photographs have been added. But most important, at the urging of my editor, I have included a final chapter, "Destruction: The Terrorist Attack and Its Aftermath." Here I describe the attack on the World Trade Center and its rapid collapse. I review the response of the firefighters and other emergency service personnel. I follow the story of the rubble removal and the important investigation into why the Towers collapsed. From a human standpoint, the most important stories are those that chronicle the lives of both the victims and the survivors. Finally, I examine the short- and long-term significance of this catastrophic event on American culture.

My debts are many, and I hope they have been properly acknowledged in the footnotes. Among the many people who have helped me with the revisions for this new edition, I feel that I need to give special thanks to Richard C. Sullivan, who kept in touch with letters and phone calls, freely offering information and advice. Sullivan joined the Port Authority in 1951 as a management trainee and, after several assignments, in 1960 became assistant to Roger Gilman, who was director of port development. Sullivan worked with Gilman in early discussions with the Downtown–Lower Manhattan Association. Subsequently Sullivan was assigned to lead the study group that produced the March 1961 Port Authority report on the World Trade Center. In February 1962, when Austin Tobin created the World Trade Office with Guy Tozzoli as director, Sullivan was named concurrently as Tozzoli's deputy. Dick Sullivan, with his firsthand knowledge of the early period of the project, provided many useful insights and clarifications.

I am similarly grateful to Carl K. Panero, who worked for the Port Authority for eight years from 1959 to 1967. Panero worked his first three years as an architectural designer in the Aviation Department and then five years from 1962 to 1967 as a planning architect for the World Trade Center. In this capacity, he was involved from the inception of the project to the start of steel erection. Panero offered numerous suggestions and generously shared his observations on how the project took shape. I should also acknowledge the help of David Curran, Allen Cohen, Robert DiChiara, Paul Goldberger, Nicholas Humez, David Keim, Philippe Petit, and Philip Wearne.

Finally, I wish to dedicate this edition to the memory of three extraordinary friends who lost their lives on September 11, 2001, at the World Trade Center—Roko Camaj, Frank A. DeMartini, and Eugene J. Raggio. I could not hold back the tears when I read in the newspaper of their passing. Roko was a window-cleaning machine operator who had spent hours patiently explaining things to me. Frank was an architect who knew and loved the Trade Center. Frank and I had worked together with the producers of the History Channel show detailing the life of the Twin Towers. Gene was a general operations supervisor who would often let me tag along with him as he went about his duties, giving me a good overall picture of what it took to run the place. They all held positions of trust, and they died, as they had lived, carrying out their duties. I, and their many friends, will miss them. I extend to their families my deepest sympathy.

—A.K.G

1
Political
Background

The Uneasy Alliance Between New York and New Jersey

Make no small plans. For they have no power to stir the blood.

—Daniel Hudson Burnham (1846–1912), American architect
(cited in *Portfolio*, Winter 1991–1992)

AUSTIN TOBIN, the high-powered and hard-charging executive director of the Port Authority of New York, arrives for work early in the morning in his chauffeured Cadillac limousine. A small and solid man with a full head of silver-gray hair, handsome and clean shaven with a square jaw, Tobin is wired into power, and power seems to radiate out from his presence. He wears a conservative blue-gray, two-button, single-breasted suit. It is not far from his apartment on East 66th Street to his headquarters building at 111 Eighth Avenue. The building, a reddish fortress that was formerly the Union-Inland Terminal No. 1, built in 1932, occupies an entire city block extending east to west between Eighth and Ninth Avenues and south to north between West Fifteenth and West Sixteenth Streets. So cavernous is this warehouse building that heavily loaded tractor-trailers can pull in off the street and drive right onto massive freight elevators and be lifted to upper floors.

When Tobin arrives, he is driven through the whole building right to the nearest door. Advance notice comes in, and the elevator operators put on white gloves. Tobin gets out of the car and squares his shoulders. His posture is terrific. He is whisked to the executive offices on the fifteenth floor. It is practically like the admiral of the fleet has arrived. As he takes his place in his spacious, mahogany-paneled office with its commanding view of the Hudson River, he reviews plans for generating more revenue from his glorious bridges and colossal tunnels. Next there is an early staff meeting. Tobin never has more than eight staff members reporting to him, and he never goes around them. Everyone walking into his office knows the agenda in advance; they are all well prepared. But this morning a few staff members are in disagreement. Tobin, the quintessential autocrat, asks them to leave and return when they are in agreement. This arrangement will guarantee advance coordination among the various departments next time. Tobin does not like to waste time on lengthy discussions. A few minutes later, a young aide comes in with the schedule for the rest of the day. There is a high-level meeting over on the New Jersey side later that morning, so Tobin is escorted up to the roof to a waiting helicopter. As he flies over the harbor, he looks down at the Statue of Liberty—the exact center of his empire, the port district, which extends in a radius of twenty-five miles from the statue, in the states of New York and New Jersey, including more than 750 miles of water frontage.[1]

To understand the World Trade Center, we first have to understand the Port Authority, the organization which built it. It is a complex story of money and politics, law and engineering, public service and personal pride. To build a monument requires a powerful builder. The scale of the World Trade Center was so massive that no other entity—public or private—could have built it. Constructing the Twin Towers involved packaging a unique blend of political, financial, and human resources that only the Port Authority could muster.

The Port Authority got started in the 1920s as a sleepy bridge-and-tunnel outfit, and it evolved over the following fifty years to become a master builder. Unrestrained by civil service salary caps, the agency was able to recruit and retain the very best talent. It had real estate specialists to assemble large parcels of land, top lawyers to draw up airtight contracts, engineers who were master builders, and (most important) accountants to make sure the bondholders were always paid on time. From this pool of talent, leaders were developed and brought up through the ranks. During this period—through the Great Depression, World War II, and other crises—the Port Authority acquired vast wealth and virtually unchecked power in its own domain. In the process, the Port Authority made both friends who helped to push its projects forward and enemies who put up fierce resistance.

The Port Authority, as it grew, cultivated an institutional "personality" much as people do. It developed an institutional way of doing things that encouraged people to get results rather than just "operate by the rules." Of course, the organization—like other bureaucracies—valued hard work, loyalty, and a sense of duty. In short, the Port Authority developed the personality of a New Yorker—not of old Dutch New York or even of moneyed WASP New York, but of immigrant New York with hustle and ambition. The agency was led by people who were hard driving and fast talking. They may or may not have been smarter than other Americans, but they were second to none in self-promotion. They took pride in being New Yorkers. The Port Authority's view of the world was not unlike that of the famous Saul Steinberg drawing on the cover of the *New Yorker* magazine which showed New York City dwarfing in importance the rest of the country and the rest of the world. In fact, it was not until 1972, more than fifty years after its founding, that the aloof and elite agency changed its name from the Port of New York Authority to the Port Authority of New York and New Jersey.

The agency unabashedly took a masculine outlook on the world. It favored the functional over the decorative, the vernacular over the genteel. Its public works projects were created unselfconsciously, with thought only to whether they would work, not on how they would look. Its bridges and tunnels were all business; they put form after function. The agency developed ladders of promotion that, while taking seniority into account, mainly rewarded initiative. It favored male recruits with backgrounds in engineering or law. Though it was never made explicit, a tour of duty in the military—especially in the U.S. Navy—helped to place a newcomer on the fast track to promotion. Engineers especially found the Port Authority to be a place that was a manly environment rewarding the brave and the courageous. At the same time, they found it to be intellectually stimulating and engaging. The best way to be promoted was to get appointed to a challenging project with an element of risk and to make a success of it. Not just an engineering success, but a financial success as well. As the Port Authority enjoyed success after success, it became a proud organization. Pride ultimately fueled the ambition to build the world's tallest building.

The architectural design and engineering construction of the World Trade Center were very much a human process reflecting the personalities of those involved. The key figures had grit, determination, and a willingness to shoulder risk. Most of all, we shall show that the successful completion of the project was not a foregone conclusion to its contemporaries. The history of the period reveals that the Twin Towers had numerous obstacles and a few implacable enemies. A favorable outcome, far from being inevitable, might have been blocked at any of a number of steps along the way.

The Port Authority was founded in the 1920s in an unusual burst of cooperation between two age-old rivals, the states of New York and New Jersey. From colonial days, there had been boundary disputes between the two states. At one point, things got so bitter that state policemen actually exchanged shots in the middle of the Hudson River. Early mapmakers chose the Hudson River as an easy-to-find boundary line, but that decision did not settle things. The two states kept arguing because each wanted to push the line to the other's shore. Finally, in 1834 they did the commonsense thing: they signed a treaty drawing the line down the middle of the river.

Throughout the nineteenth century, the region around the New York harbor grew and prospered. The people of the region turned a magnificent natural harbor into the economic capital of the world. New York became the country's leading port, distribution center, and immigrant gateway. It absorbed the commerce of most key trade routes and became America's marketplace. By 1860, two-thirds of all American imports and one-third of all exports traveled through the Port of New York.[2] But the development was lopsided. The wharves and piers were mostly built on the New York side, while nearly all of the railroads terminated on the New Jersey side. It was not a rational plan; it was just the way things evolved. Ships were unloaded on the New York side, but getting the cargo onto railroad cars was a problem. Similarly, railroad cars were unloaded on the Jersey side, and there was a problem getting the goods over to New York. The stuff was moved back and forth using a vast fleet of lighters, or large barges. The system worked, but it was not efficient.

From the vantage point of today, it is difficult to visualize the setup. But as late as 1900, there were no bridges or tunnels across the Hudson River. At the dawn of the twentieth century, people crossed by ferry, and goods crossed by lighter, just as they had during the days of Dutch colonization nearly three hundred years earlier. Manhattan Island was not connected to New Jersey; Staten Island was not connected to New Jersey. There was massive transportation of people by boats. "Thick as stars in the sky," wrote Walt Whitman, "all sorts and sizes of sail and steam vessels, plying ferry boats, arriving and departing coasters . . . with here and there, above all, those daring, careening things of grace and wonder, those white and shaded swift-darting fish-birds—first class New York sloop or schooner yachts."[3]

The first ferry service was founded in the 1630s, crossing the narrow East River between Manhattan and the wilderness of Brooklyn. Much later, in 1806, Cornelius Vanderbilt (1794–1877), known as "the Commodore," founded a freight and passenger ferry business between Staten Island and Manhattan. This enterprise became the basis for a vast family fortune. By the turn of the century, the double-ended steam ferry, designed so that it never had to turn around at either end of its run, was a frequent sight in New York Harbor. With their blackened smoke stacks and colorful pennants, these vessels were often portrayed in inexpensive lithographs. By 1908, there were no less than thirty-eight different ferry services traversing the waters of New York City, some of them providing twenty-four-hour service. The ferry boats were picturesque fixtures of the harbor, but hardly the most efficient way to serve the transportation needs of the region.[4]

It was clear that bridges and tunnels were the way of the future, but nobody knew how to proceed. Any long-range plan would have to have the cooperation of both New York and New Jersey. The political leaders of both states were under tremendous pressure to find answers, so in 1911 they followed the time-honored device of setting up study commissions. There were two such bodies, one from each state, and they were to come up with remedial measures. The groundwork for cooperation was laid.[5]

Later, in March 1917, there was sentiment in favor of a joint commission, the next step in the process. Governor Walter E. Edge of New Jersey said, "I want to see industrial New York and industrial New Jersey co-operating, especially as they are, with this wonderful harbor between them—and the harbor, my friends, is not New York's alone; the harbor is a national institution. . . . I would like to see a joint commission appointed representing the two states . . . with one thought that their responsibility is to develop the port of New York."[6]

The timing was crucial. In the spring of 1917, the Port of York was choked with the confusion of trying to move out war plies to the Western allies. The historic lack of cooperation between the two states was manifestly harming the war effort. A few days later, Governor Charles S. Whitman, addressing the New York legislature, declared: "All but two of the trunk lines serving the Port of New York terminate in the neighboring State of New Jersey. This makes it essential that any solution of the port problem should include a study of that portion of the port comprised within the northern part of New Jersey and, while it is beyond question that great benefits will accrue to the State of New York through a comprehensive port policy, benefits will also accrue to New Jersey. . . . It is imperative that both states should give immediate attention to this situation."[7]

With both states officially recognizing their interdependence, real plans could at last be made. Throughout the war years, no new projects could be launched, but talks continued. Many ideas for improvement of the port were discussed. With the increasing popularity of the automobile, there was more and more pressure to come up with some kind of a trans-Hudson vehicle crossing. At first the planning commission favored a bridge, because tunnels seemed to be too difficult to construct. But, as railroads developed better tunnel technology to go through the mud and silt of riverbeds, an automobile tunnel gradually emerged as a feasible undertaking.

By the end of World War I, in 1919, both states gave the go-ahead to the long-awaited project, the "Hudson River Vehicular Tunnel," as it was called. Of course, it would not have the stately majesty of a high-arching bridge reaching to the clouds, but it was a practical way to get about by automobile in an island environment. The tunnel was to cross from Jersey City over to the vicinity of Canal Street in lower Manhattan. The greatest engineering challenge was to come up with a scheme for ventilating the 1.6-mile structure. Of course, tunnels had been built before, but never one this long, and never one that had to accommodate the noxious and deadly fumes of the motorcar. The basic scheme called for powerful ventilators to bring in fresh air below the floor and take out the exhaust air above the ceiling. Work began in 1920 under the supervision of chief engineer Clifford M. Holland, who worked on the project night and day. In time the project, which is now called the Holland Tunnel in his honor, would break his health and cost him his life.[8]

While the Holland Tunnel was still being built, discussions began for bistate cooperation on a much larger scale. There was a clear need for a permanent administrative agency to develop the port with long-range planning and multiple projects. A leading agency to develop these plans was the Chamber of Commerce of the State of New York, headed by a man whose name was to become familiar to everyone in the region, Eugenius Outerbridge. Another key figure was the brilliant Julius Henry Cohen, counsel for the Chamber of Commerce.[9]

Cohen had made a study of public authorities, special organizations that functioned like private corporations while carrying out the public's business. The device was new in the United States but well established in England, where a number of authorities had been set up during the reign of Queen Elizabeth. An authority could sell bonds to finance some public improvement, then charge the public for its use in order to raise money to retire the bonds. By charging the users a fee, it was not necessary to use tax money for the improvement. The term "authority" came into use because the Acts of Parliament that set one up would begin with the words, "Authority is hereby given." By the time Cohen began his research in the early 1920s, more than a thousand such authorities were functioning in England. But the one that Cohen focused on was the Port of London Authority, which served as a model for what he wanted to do.[10]

On April 30, 1921, the Port of New York Authority was officially established. It was the first interstate agency ever created under a clause in the U.S. Constitution that permits compacts between the states, with congressional approval. The Port Authority's area of jurisdiction was called "The Port District," a seventeen-county bistate region within a twenty-five-mile radius of the Statue of Liberty. The compact between the two states gave the new agency sweeping potential power: "The port authority shall constitute a body, both corporate and politic, with full power and authority to purchase, construct, lease and/or operate any terminal or transportation facility within said district."[11]

What made this such a conceptual breakthrough was the idea that the Port Authority could take on *multiple* facilities. In the past, most boards or commissions took on a single project, such as a bridge or a road. They would issue bonds, collect revenue, and then pay off the bonds. When everything was paid for, the project would be given to the city or state and the authority would quietly go out of existence. This was a new kind of organization, a mega-organization, if you will, which would never go out of business as long as it could keep coming up with new projects.[12]

Started in 1921, the Port Authority was given a mighty charter but very little money at first. The states gave the new organization only enough funds for its administrative costs, but not enough to build anything. Eventually, the Authority would be able to raise millions of dollars through the sale of bonds, but it could not do so right away. It took time for the agency to establish its credit. The first bonds would not be issued until 1926. Meanwhile, construction continued on the Hudson River Vehicular Tunnel under the jurisdiction of an entirely different independent agency. Chief engineer Clifford M. Holland tackled many previously unsolved problems and stretched himself to the breaking point. His health broken, he passed away on October 27, 1924. At the opening ceremonies, a scant two weeks later, on November 12, 1924, the facility was officially renamed the Holland Tunnel, after its heroic builder.[13]

Financially, the Holland Tunnel was successful beyond anyone's wildest dreams. From the very beginning, it was a money-maker. As the days and months passed into years, gradually the Port Authority administration hoped to take over the Holland Tunnel as a financial cornerstone for future projects. From the Authority's point of view that was a good idea, but it would be years before it came to pass. Meanwhile, the fledgling agency continued to struggle with very limited resources.

During the 1920s, the two states gave the Port Authority a number of difficult projects that had been talked about for years, but had never been carried out. With a powerful, apolitical engineering organization in place, the two states could get together in a spirit of mutual trust to put up the money to get things done. It was the Roaring Twenties, the prosperous postwar years. Wartime restrictions on business were lifted. With prosperity came huge increases in the number of automobiles produced by Henry Ford and others. Between 1920 and 1929, the number of automobiles registered in the United States increased from 8 million to 26.7 million, a threefold rise. The increase of the 1920s was due in large part to the expansion of consumer installment credit to finance the sale of automobiles.[14] With increased traffic, there was enormous pressure to build long-deferred bridge projects. In the period between World War I and World War II, the Port Authority was to build a number of bridges of significant architectural and engineering beauty spanning the area's waterways.

The western edge of Staten Island, New York, is separated from New Jersey by the narrow Arthur Kill. ("Kill" is a Dutch word meaning channel.) The area had long been served by ferry boats, but people were clamoring for bridges. Because the Arthur Kill was an active shipping channel, used as an approach to Newark Bay, they could not just put up cheap low-level bridges built on a series of piers. Any bridge would have to have at least 135 feet of clearance so as not to interfere with navigation. Both states agreed that the time had come to deal with the problem, so they authorized the Port Authority to build not one but two bridges simultaneously. Both were to be steel-truss cantilever bridges supported by concrete piers.

One bridge was to be built at the northerly end of the Arthur Kill, crossing from Elizabeth, New Jersey, to Howland Hook, New York. With a span of 1,152 feet, this was called the Goethals Bridge, after General George Washington Goethals, who had earlier been appointed by President Theodore Roosevelt as chief engineer on the Panama Canal Commission in 1907, after two civilian engineers had successively resigned. Perhaps the last in the age of heroic engineers, Goethals carried canal construction through to completion. Historian L.T.C. Rolt, in his book *Victorian Engineering*, said that Goethals's work on the Panama Canal was "the drama of a single individual striving against the odds."[15] During World War I, Goethals went on to serve as acting quartermaster general in charge of purchase, storage, and traffic. After leaving U.S. Army service, Goethals was recruited as the Port Authority's first consulting engineer.

From the very beginning, the Port Authority was aggressive in recruiting the very best talent available. In personnel matters, they were able to compete in the free market against all employers, public and private. Hiring someone of Goethals's stature increased the prestige of the Port Authority, and naming the bridge as they did honored not only Goethals, but also themselves.

The other bridge was to be built at the south end of the Arthur Kill, crossing from Perth Amboy, New Jersey, to Tottenville, New York, with a somewhat longer span of 2,100 feet. This was called the "Outerbridge Crossing," after Eugenius H. Outerbridge, a signer of the original port compact in 1921 and the Port Authority's first chairman. The name was chosen to avoid the silliness of calling it the "Outerbridge Bridge." Construction on both bridges began in July 1926, and both were finished in June 1928.[16]

The very next month, the Port Authority awarded the first construction contract on a new bridge which was to span the Kill van Kull, a narrow channel separating Staten Island from Bayonne, New Jersey. The Bayonne Bridge, spanning 1,652 feet with 150 feet of clearance, was dedicated on November 14, 1931. At that time it was the world's longest single-arch bridge. The following year it received an award from the American Institute of Steel Construction as the most beautiful large steel bridge of the year.[17]

Unfortunately, none of the three Staten Island bridges were big moneymakers. Nonetheless, they were valuable projects for the Port Authority because they established the agency's credibility and reputation and helped it to build up its staff of engineers, lawyers, and real estate experts. If we can think of the Port of New York and New Jersey as a kind of giant Monopoly game, then owning the Staten Island bridges was a bit like owning both of the least valuable properties in the game—Baltic Avenue and Mediterranean Avenue. These properties were not impressive, but they represented a solid beginning.

Even before the Staten Island bridges were built, plans were being made for an immense new bridge of an entirely different order of magnitude. This was to be the George Washington Bridge, spanning the Hudson River by an immense main span of 3,500 feet. The total length from 179th Street in Manhattan over to Fort Lee, New Jersey, came to a mind-boggling 4,760 feet. Over the years, several schemes to cross the Hudson at the northern end of Manhattan had been advanced. The northern crossing had some distinct advantages. Because it would leap the Hudson at a high point in Manhattan, there would be plenty of clearance for passing ships. It was also much easier to accomplish politically because there were business owners in Manhattan who would have objected to the disruption caused by building access roads in midtown. The original idea had been for a railroad bridge, but all of the private railroad companies had shrunk from the enormous financial burden of the project. The project faced enormous obstacles. For one thing, engineers would have to dig very deep in order to hit the solid rock needed for foundations. For another, this very high bridge could have no piers to avoid interfering with navigation. It all added up to a very expensive project.

Despite all these obstacles, the Port Authority obtained approval to proceed with the project in 1925. It was personally supervised by the Port Authority's chief engineer, Othmar H. Ammann. Born in Switzerland in 1879, Ammann had come to the United States in his twenties. Aloof and formal, he gradually became the country's leading expert in bridge design and construction. This was an era when big projects could be pushed through quickly. There were no environmental impact statements or lengthy hearings to listen to local residents' objections. With the full backing of Governor Al Smith of New York and Governor A. Harry Moore of New Jersey, blueprints were drawn up quickly. Under Ammann's direction, groundbreaking for the George Washington Bridge took place in 1927. By all accounts, the genius of Ammann was not just in engineering but in administration. Confronted with a gigantic project like the George Washington Bridge, he was simultaneously able to visualize the big picture while breaking it down into its component parts and assigning the right people to each task.[18]

Allston Dana was design engineer, and Cass Gilbert was the architect. Of course, Gilbert was already well known for his work in New York City on both the U.S. Customs House and the Woolworth Building. As it turned out, the George Washington Bridge became, for a time, the center of national attention not just for engineering reasons but for esthetic ones as well. The avowed aims of the original design engineers were "purity of type, simplicity of structural arrangement, and ease and expediency of construction."

But there was more to it than just these functional considerations because "it was realized that more than the usual attention must be paid to the aesthetic side." There was a real concern that the bridge be not just a bridge but "a truly monumental structure, which will cast credit upon the aesthetic sense of the present generation."[19] There was a laudable recognition that, given its great size and prominent location, the bridge should be suitably monumental. But how was this to be achieved?

The issues involved bring us to the heart of the most basic conflict in American art. To most Americans, art and technology seem to be irreconcilable. A bridge is designed to be functional, not beautiful. American bridge design had nearly always focused on building structures as rapidly and cheaply as possible. Since the George Washington Bridge was supposed to be better, more "cultivated" and less "vernacular," the designers came up with a plan to embed the two 635-foot steel towers in concrete and then to face the concrete with granite, thus covering up the steel and ensuring the bridge's place in history as a suitable American monument. When the steel skeletons of the towers were finished, something completely surprising happened. Everyone liked the raw and stark structure just the way it was. John A. Kouwenhoven, in his 1948 book *Made in America*, wrote, "The 'unexpected' functional beauty of the naked steel work fascinated people, and there was a widespread popular protest against applying the masonry covering which, according to the original plan, was to be the chief element in the aesthetic appeal of the bridge."[20]

Even as the George Washington Bridge was being built, there was an important related development for the Port Authority. After years of pleading, the two states of New York and New Jersey in 1930 gave the agency control of the Holland Tunnel.[21] With this financial cornerstone in place, the Port Authority could proceed with confidence on the George Washington Bridge project, which was dedicated on October 24, 1931.[22] At that time, it was the world's longest suspension bridge. Securing control of the Holland Tunnel along with completing the George Washington Bridge was, to continue our Monopoly analogy, like getting control of the two most valuable properties in the game—Boardwalk and Park Place.

Even during the Great Depression of the 1930s, the Port Authority was able to proceed with its grand design. The next project on the drawing boards was a Midtown Hudson Tunnel, with an ambitious length of over 8,000 feet. The agency was unable to get the capital to proceed from the regular bond market, but the project was saved by the New Deal. The Federal Emergency Administration of Public Works agreed to buy the bonds, and work began on May 17, 1934. The project, now known as the Lincoln Tunnel, was to go from the vicinity of West 39th Street and 10th Avenue in Manhattan over to Weehawken, New Jersey. The first tube opened in 1937; that same year work began on the construction of a second tube.[23]

Our brief examination of the bridge and tunnel projects of the 1920s and 1930s shows that the Port Authority had the potential to build things. But with the outbreak of World War II, many projects were put on hold. When gasoline rationing was imposed, traffic declined and revenues fell. It was 1942 and American military pride was subject to many rude shocks as island after island fell in the Pacific. In these grim times, the Port Authority appointed a new leader, Austin Tobin, who was then thirty-nine. Tobin had already served a long apprenticeship of fifteen years in the law department of the Port Authority, mainly working on real estate acquisitions.[24]

Austin Tobin had gone to college at Holy Cross, where he was a serious student who wrote poetry on the side. Later, he went to Fordham Law School, famous for turning out New York politicians. At the Port Authority law department, Tobin had gained a reputation for being both brilliant and dedicated. He had an amazing knowledge of New York history, politics, and culture. Tobin was known for working long hours seven days a week and for taking paperwork home every night, yet he loved New York and found time to attend the opera. As executive director, Tobin made a practice of keeping a low profile. Unlike the publicity-seeking Robert Moses, head of the Triborough Bridge and Tunnel Authority, Tobin preferred to work behind the scenes. He tried to stay out of the public eye; he encouraged his commissioners to give speeches, cut ribbons, and get their pictures in the papers. Tobin devoted his life to the Port Authority, and he gradually built up a sincerely paternalistic organization that earned the complete loyalty of his staff. By all accounts, he was an effective leader who inspired people to give their best efforts to the agency.

While the war was being waged, the hands of the Port Authority were tied. Large sums of money and material were not available for domestic infrastructure projects. But Tobin refused to sulk and brood. Instead, he optimistically looked forward to a bright postwar future by aggressively developing ambitious regional transportation plans. The agency developed plans for all kinds of regional development including marine terminals, airports, bus stations, roads, and bridges. But Austin Tobin was not just a quiet technocrat drawing up plans; rather, he was a cheerleader for his beloved Port Authority. Whether addressing businessmen at a national convention or his own people at a staff luncheon, Tobin was fond of quoting Daniel H. Burnham, the Chicago architect who built New York's first great skyscraper, the Flatiron Building, in 1902. "Make no small plans," said Tobin, quoting Burnham. "For they have no power to stir the blood."[25]

Drawing up plans during the wartime period of enforced idleness was a clever move on Austin Tobin's part. Another equally clever move was to reconstruct the image of the Port Authority, which was constantly being hammered in the press as being too slow moving in updating the transportation infrastructure. In 1944 Austin Tobin recruited Lee K. Jaffe, an experienced reporter and government press officer, to turn the agency's image around. Tobin and Jaffe worked well with each other, and soon she was included in top-level policy meetings. Jaffe established rapport with editorial writers and reporters on the daily newspapers of New York and New Jersey. She kept coming up with positive story ideas about the Port Authority, many with a human-interest angle. One veteran reporter recalled, "She always had the facts, and if you needed more, she would get them and call you right back. . . . She was head and shoulders above everyone else in the public relations field."[26] Over the years, Jaffe became so influential in Port Authority management that she was not just explaining policy; as we shall see later on in our narrative, she helped to make policy.

When the war finally ended, there was a period of general euphoria, a broad national confidence. The returning troops and their families looked forward to the economic cornucopia of peace. Americans had jobs, and Americans had money. There was unprecedented demand for automobiles, refrigerators, and cook stoves.[27] At the same time, the Port Authority in this postwar period began to expand into airports, marine terminals, and vehicular bus traffic.

Austin Tobin's power grew as he mastered the art of mobilizing the financial community, contractors, labor unions, insurance firms, and the press to serve his agency.[28]

It was during this period of unsurpassed material well-being that the idea for a World Trade Center was born. It was apparent that the reconstruction of Europe would be accompanied by a big increase in international transatlantic trade. Not to be left out, the New York legislature in 1946 set up a World Trade Corporation to study the feasibility of a trade center in Manhattan. There was a growing realization that New York City was the home to many corporate headquarters that generated paperwork reflecting the enormous movement of goods not only within North America but throughout the world. Put simply, the proposed trade center would be a place for the exchange of paper.

Conceptual drawings were prepared that showed a $140 million complex of twenty-one buildings covering about ten blocks. The whole project called for the creation of some five million square feet, most of which would be devoted to exhibition halls. However, market research indicated that there simply was not enough demand for such space to make the project viable. To make it pay, 80 percent of the nation's 6,000 largest companies would have to participate. So the World Trade Corporation recommended that the city focus on modernizing its waterfront instead. The Port Authority at that time was all set to embark on this project, but the city resisted this encroachment on its autonomy. Thus, the agency turned to the Jersey side, focusing on developing marine terminals at Port Newark and Port Elizabeth, which today stretch over 2,100 vast acres.

The trade center idea was shelved for more than a decade. During that time, New York City grew and prospered, becoming more and more a world-class center for business and the arts. But the city's leaders were frustrated that most of the growth was centered in midtown Manhattan. Lower Manhattan, the oldest part of the city, was not sharing in the growth and new construction. Most investors stayed away from that area, but there was one exception. David Rockefeller, grandson of John D. Rockefeller, the nineteenth-century founder of the Standard Oil empire and America's first billionaire, had a vision of a bustling downtown. With a leap of faith, Rockefeller had built the sixty-story Chase Manhattan Bank Tower downtown between Pine and Liberty Streets, from William to Nassau Streets. Designed by Skidmore, Owings, and Merrill, the building was completed in 1960 with 800 feet of aluminum and glass rising from a paved plaza graced with a sunken circular courtyard. It was a suitable headquarters for one of the largest banks in the world. Having invested so much in the neighborhood, David Rockefeller went on to set up a new business organization, the Downtown–Lower Manhattan Association (DLMA). He recruited the chief executives of other key corporations with an interest in the area, including Morgan Guaranty Trust, AT&T, and Guardian Life Insurance.

In 1958 Rockefeller and the DLMA asked the blue-ribbon architectural firm of Skidmore, Owings, and Merrill (SOM) to work up a plan to revive Lower Manhattan. It was a tough challenge since the area with its banks, insurance companies, shipping offices, and investment houses was known as the dullest place in New York to visit. There were few amenities or attractions. The architectural firm presented a bold plan that called for reinvigorating the financial district. Some streets would be closed; others, widened. Some old buildings would be razed; others, renewed. The plan called for a large marina on the East River with a modern heliport nearby. And the plan called for a World Trade Center.

Rockefeller liked the idea of a World Trade Center as a catalyst for regional development, so he urged SOM to develop a more detailed plan. By January 1960, the downtown association had the specifics. A trade center, costing $250 million, could be built on a thirteen-acre site at the east end of Wall Street. There would be a seventy-story office-hotel building, an international trade exhibit hall, a securities exchange building, an enclosed retail space, and a large plaza. All this would be built upon "a two-story platform that would supersede and displace the conventional street grid."[29]

David Rockefeller sent the downtown association report to Mayor Robert F. Wagner, to his brother Nelson Rockefeller, the governor of New York, and also to Robert Meyner, governor of New Jersey. As the plan was picking up political support, the DLMA took the important step of proposing that the Port Authority "study" the plan. Rockefeller knew all along that only the Port Authority could activate it. The agency had the power of eminent domain and an enormous capacity to secure credit, not to mention its institutional pride, which could be exploited to Rockefeller's advantage.

Of course, the Port Authority wasted no time in accepting Rockefeller's suggestion that they study the SOM plans for a World Trade Center. They put together an architectural advisory board composed of three of the nation's leading architects. One was Wallace K. Harrison, the Rockefeller "family architect," who was also one of the principal architects in the construction of the United Nations Secretariat in New York, built in 1947–1950. Another was Gordon Bunshaft of SOM, designer of the first trend-setting postwar skyscraper in New York, Lever House, with its innovative glassy curtain wall, built in 1950–1952. The third was Edward Durell Stone, an architect who became famous for harmonizing buildings with their surroundings. Perhaps the best example is his U.S. Embassy building with extensive grillwork in New Delhi, India. He also designed the original 1939 Museum of Modern Art in New York City as well as the U.S. pavilion at the 1958 Brussels World's Fair. The work of these three distinguished architects was coordinated by a former Port Authority architect and planner, Richard Adler.[30]

While architectural planning was key, other kinds of planning were also needed. The engineering department prepared construction cost figures. The department of finance compiled financial data of all kinds. The law department looked into areas of interest such as urban renewal. In a large bureaucratic organization such as the Port Authority, nearly every department had some role to play. However, at this early stage it could be argued that the most important player was the port development department, then under the leadership of Roger Howe Gilman, age forty-seven. After graduating from Harvard in 1936, Gilman studied traffic engineering and administration with the Harvard Bureau for Street Traffic Research. He joined the Port Authority, worked as a statistician-economist, and earned a reputation as a problem solver. Gilman served in the U.S. Navy during World War II as a lieutenant commander on the battleship *Arkansas*. He returned to the Port Authority in 1945 and later became director of port development, reporting directly to Austin Tobin. His work and that of his associates involved analyzing the merits of various sites for the center, investigating transportation access, and establishing the size and types of firms that made up the world trade community.[31]

By March 1961 the Port Authority was ready to make public its plans for a World Trade Center. The plans were submitted in a public report to the governors of both states and the mayor of New York City. The architects called for a multiple-building project along the East River rising from a large enclosed concourse and landscaped plaza on a sixteen-acre site. The glass slab of a seventy-two-story World Trade Mart dominated the proposed complex. The stated rationale for building a World Trade Center was to provide a physical setting that would centralize the many sectors of the world trade industry in a single location. Unstated, but understood by everyone, was that such a large project was expected to trigger renewal of the downtown area, just as the Rockefeller Center did for midtown in the 1930s. At this point no one could have foreseen how many years of financial and political maneuvering would be required before actual construction could begin. It turned out to be a very long process indeed.

Initial reaction to the report was encouraging. An editorial in the *New York Herald Tribune* said: "About the proposed World Trade Center; let's pull out all the adjectival stops at once and cheer."[32] Another editorial in the *New York Journal American* called the proposal "dramatic and exciting."[33] Even the *Newark Evening News*, normally suspicious of any Port Authority proposal because it might favor New York over New Jersey, glowed: "Both in scope and cost the proposed trade center is in the Port Authority manner. It is big, imaginative, and architecturally and financially glamorous."[34] A variety of trade and civic groups in both states quickly endorsed the proposal.

Governor Robert B. Meyner of New Jersey said that "the idea seems basically sound, and we will give the proposal careful study."[35] What Meyner did not say during this euphoric period was that on the New Jersey side there was smoldering resentment against the Port Authority for an unrelated problem of long standing: the problem of the failing commuter railroads, most notably the Hudson and Manhattan Railroad, which had filed for bankruptcy. Time and time again, New Jersey commuters and politicians had asked the Port Authority to shoulder the burden of rail transportation. Austin Tobin, recognizing a money-losing proposition when he saw one, refused each time.

Of course, the commuter railroads had not always lost money. When the Hudson and Manhattan opened on February 25, 1908, no one was worried about the financial status of the line. This was long before the automobile was the usual vehicle for Americans. On that date, New York governor Charles Evans Hughes and New Jersey governor Franklin Fort officially cut the ribbon to open the line. The new Hudson Tubes, linking New York and New Jersey, were regarded as a wonderful improvement over the ferry boats. The tubes had been built at great financial and human cost. At one point during construction, a tunnel flood had drowned twenty workers. But opening day was glorious.

"We rode under the river in gleaming new cars, freshly painted, glittering and shiny," wrote William G. McAdoo, who had financed the building of the tubes. McAdoo was President Woodrow Wilson's son-in-law and former secretary of the treasury. "In the cool, under-river air there was a faint smell of varnish, of cement, of freshness of things newly finished. Inside the cars, the silk-hatted gentlemen sat in rows, leaning on their canes, and looking a little uneasy as they glanced out of the windows and saw the curving iron walls flash by. It was all very sedate, and very amiable, and very pleasant."[36]

For the first twenty years, the Hudson and Manhattan Railroad was financially successful. In the very first year, it had 49 million passengers. By 1927 the number had risen to a peak of 113 million passengers. But trouble started with the opening of the Holland Tunnel in 1927. And trouble continued with the opening of the George Washington Bridge in 1931 and the Lincoln Tunnel in 1937. Former rail passengers switched to bus lines and cars to get to work. By the early 1960s the line was in debt and carrying fewer than thirty-one million passengers a year.[37] During the prosperous late 1920s the common stock of the Hudson and Manhattan Railroad sold for as high as $73.50 a share, and the preferred stock reached a top of $93.50. But by the 1960s the stock's only value was as wallpaper.[38]

There were no easy answers. It was true that many commuters preferred the comfort and convenience of their private automobiles over the dirty and unreliable trains run by discourteous crewmen. But critics still blamed the Port Authority for siphoning off the railroad's riders, which resulted in poorer and poorer service. Regardless of who was to blame, Governor Meyner made it clear to Austin Tobin that the time had come for the Port Authority, with its reputation for effectiveness, to do something about the rail problem. It was a standoff, but then something amazing happened: Tobin blinked. Reluctantly, he agreed to assume control of the Hudson and Manhattan Railroad at a cost of about $70 million to acquire and rehabilitate the tubes. He also agreed to commit up to 10 percent of the Authority's annual surpluses, then running at about $7 million a year for operating subsidies. The railroad would be renamed Port Authority Trans Hudson (PATH). There was a significant condition: the Port Authority would only take control of this one railroad. No more, ever.

After forty years of flat refusal, what made the Port Authority change its mind? We may never have all the answers, but two things are clear. First, something had to be done for New Jersey to make up for the fact that New York was getting the $335 million World Trade Center. Second, the collapse of the Hudson and Manhattan Railroad would have dumped thirty million additional passengers a year onto the bridge and tunnel system, resulting in the strangulation of Port Authority motor vehicle services.[39]

In any event, the *Bergen Record*, in a hard-hitting editorial, spelled out for its readers what was going on: "No maneuver in statecraft is older or more useful than the deal. Verbally it has been refined into 'compromise' or 'agreement' or 'reciprocity,' and it has been called back-scratching and log-rolling and even pork-barreling, but a deal is still a deal, and as an instrument of government it is highly regarded in private if deprecated in public."[40]

In Albany, Governor Nelson Rockefeller was so pleased with the "deal" which seemed to promise something for both sides that he decided to sponsor a legislative "package" covering both the World Trade Center construction and the Hudson and Manhattan acquisition. His purpose was to make explicit New Jersey's acceptance and approval of Port Authority development of the World Trade Center as New York's price for Port Authority acquisition of the Hudson and Manhattan tubes.

The chairman of the Port Authority's gubernatorially appointed Board of Commissioners, Sloan Colt, an important New York banker, realized at once that Rockefeller's overeagerness might kill the deal. So Colt wrote Rockefeller: "We have been hard at work, as I told you, on the task of gaining public understanding and acceptance of the World Trade Center project in New Jersey and, as you know, Governor Meyner has also been working toward that end. Nevertheless, I understand that he holds the view, which our New Jersey Commissioners unanimously share, that the combination of the Hudson and Manhattan Railroad and World Trade Center projects in a single bill will court defeat of the bill in the New Jersey Legislature." The vice chairman, James C. Kellogg III, a New Jerseyan, sent Rockefeller a telegram warning that his strategy "would be certain to defeat the World Trade Center in New Jersey."[41]

Heedless of the warnings, Governor Rockefeller got the New York legislature to approve the "package" on March 25, 1961. Linking the two projects was unwise because it called attention to the fact that the railroad deal was worth only $70 million as opposed to $335 million for the World Trade Center. Almost immediately, the New Jersey legislature took offense at this apparent dictation from Albany. New Jerseyans saw it as an infringement on their sovereignty.[42] Governor Meyner told reporters that he had called the New York governor about the matter and the call was never returned. Governor Rockefeller called the whole matter "a tempest in a teapot." He added, "I did not call him back because there was no change in the status."[43]

The situation remained deadlocked until November 1961, when New Jersey elected a new governor, Richard J. Hughes. Although he was not to be inaugurated until January, Hughes set up a series of meetings with Rockefeller to discuss taxation and transportation issues. Meanwhile, the Port Authority continued to look into the specifics of taking over the Hudson and Manhattan, which involved acquiring two large decrepit office towers above its lower Manhattan terminal on Church Street. The Port Authority did not want to spend the estimated $9 million to renovate the old buildings. Instead it contemplated demolishing the buildings and selling the air rights. But who would possibly be interested in those air rights? Tobin's staff suggested that it might be a fine location for the trade center.[44] Several advantages became apparent: the new site had better subway connections than the East River site and the Tubes themselves would directly link the trade center to New Jersey.[45]

The conceptual breakthrough of moving the project from the east side to the west side of lower Manhattan was the key ingredient in the Port Authority's winning over Governor-elect Richard J. Hughes. Swiftly, the pieces of the puzzle fell into place. Some of the credit for breaking the logjam has to go to the Port Authority staff for coming up with new ideas, but we must not overlook the role played by Hughes, who succeeded Governor Meyner. Trenton insiders pointed out that the two men had very different personalities. Where Mr. Meyner was cautious, skeptical, and guarded in his dealings with reporters, Mr. Hughes was talkative, expansive, and friendly. On the one hand, Mr. Meyner had the ability to look someone right in the eye and say, "No." On the other hand, Mr. Hughes was more inclined to pursue negotiation and compromise.[46] It seems clear that Austin Tobin liked and trusted Hughes and found him easier to deal with.[47]

New Jersey had objected to the package originally presented by Governor Rockefeller and the New York legislature because it seemed to be such a one-sided deal. The new proposal made the trade center more accessible to New Jersey. In an editorial, the *Bergen Record* summed things up: "And, perhaps as important as anything else, the formula gives New Jersey legislators, who are human and vain, a chance to say they have won a victory, if only by the breadth of the tip of Manhattan Island, and thereby to drop their opposition without losing face."[48] In another editorial, the *Newark Sunday News* concluded: "The beauty of the compromise is that while substantially meeting New Jersey's objections, it gives New York all it really wanted in the first place."[49]

The prospects for the World Trade Center seemed bright in January 1962, with substantial agreement in place. Now the work shifted to teams of lawyers who would craft the necessary legislation. Their work, mostly tedious, involved some fascinating details. For example, the Port Authority could not very well take over the Hudson and Manhattan Railroad and set it up as an operating department. Such a move would have placed the entire Port Authority under the supervision of the Interstate Commerce Commission, with the prospect of endless red tape slowing everything. Instead, the lawyers set up the Hudson and Manhattan as a subsidiary of the Port Authority—a move that would limit the burdensome oversight role of the ICC.[50]

Once the bill was crafted, it was forwarded to the New Jersey state legislature. A state senate committee held a public hearing on the proposed legislation on February 9, 1962. Though passage of the bill was largely a foregone conclusion, the hearing gave opponents of the Port Authority a final opportunity to voice their opposition. According to a reporter who was there, what happened was this: "A few of the speakers discussed the bill's provisions intelligently and sincerely and suggested changes they believed were in the public interest. They were terse and to the point. But there were others who, for one reason or another, just didn't like the Port Authority and who found the hearing an ideal public forum for long-winded speeches that had nothing to do with the Hudson Tubes. They gloried in the presence of reporters, photographers and TV cameras, all focussed on them."[51]

While the long-suffering Austin Tobin listened to this public circus, Governor Hughes himself was working quietly behind the scenes to ensure passage of the legislation. Hughes met with the representatives of the utilities, the railroads, as well as Jersey City and Hoboken officials. He also had frequent meetings to keep in touch with legislative leaders. Finally, on February 13, 1962, the legislation sailed through both houses of the New Jersey legislature without any trouble.[52]

With this legislative success, Austin Tobin was ready to make some changes within the Port Authority. It is important to understand that every department in the organization, like its counterpart in the military, was classified as "line" or "staff." In the military "line" refers to combat troops, and "staff" refers to everyone else. In the Port Authority "line" referred to an operating unit such as a bridge or a tunnel or an airport, and "staff" again referred to those with a supporting function. What Tobin did in February 1962 was to create a new line organization unit, the World Trade Office. It was to be responsible for the development, planning, construction, and operation of the World Trade Center (as well as continuing its responsibility for the transportation section of the New York

World's Fair, which was just over the horizon). So the main responsibility for the World Trade Center would shift from Roger Gilman to the new manager of the new department.[53]

Austin Tobin named Guy F. Tozzoli for the job. It was a good choice since Tozzoli was loyal and hardworking and, above all, ambitious. He had received his B.S. in analytic mechanics and his M.S. in physics from Fordham University. Tozzoli served in the U.S. Navy during World War II as a lieutenant and was recalled for service during the Korean War. In 1946 he started his Port Authority career in the engineering department as a junior engineer. He later served as a civil engineer, supervising construction at Port Newark and Newark Airport.

Returning to the Port Authority in 1952, he was involved in a number of airport projects. He was later promoted to manager of the marine planning and construction division. He supervised the construction of marine terminal facilities in Brooklyn, Port Newark, and Elizabeth, including the new container handling facilities at Elizabeth.

With such an extensive background, Tozzoli was ideally positioned to take on the job of planning for the World Trade Center. From this point on, every detail in the project would be subjected to his scrutiny. Tozzoli was both a dreamer and a man of action. To carry out the planning process, he surrounded himself with other ambitious people. Austin Tobin told him, "You can pick the best the Port Authority has because this is our greatest project."[54]

Tozzoli wasted no time in selecting Malcolm P. Levy, a forty-year-old engineer, to direct a planning staff of some twenty architects and engineers. Levy had received his engineering degree from New York University in 1941. During World War II, he was an engineer in the U.S. Merchant Marine. He joined the Port Authority in 1948. Levy built a reputation as a person who got things done by helping to design hangars at the John F. Kennedy International Airport and supervising planning at the Port Authority's piers in Brooklyn.[55] "Levy was a tough guy," Tozzoli said. "If you were going to build the world's biggest project, you had to have a tough team."[56] As Levy and his staff brainstormed the project in private conferences, it became more and more grandiose. But at this stage, they did not yet reveal the colossal height they had in mind.

Publicly, attention was now focused on the New York legislature. While in New Jersey most of the debate centered on the Hudson Tubes, in New York one of the main concerns was what to do with the small businessmen in Lower Manhattan who would be displaced by the World Trade Center project. Nonetheless, the bill passed the New York senate on March 1 and the New York assembly on March 7. Finally, on March 27, 1962, Governor Rockefeller signed the legislation into law.[57]

Some of the wise observers in Trenton and Albany thought that the political battles were now concluded and that groundbreaking on the new complex might start any day. But the wisest among them might have known that the fight had only begun. Many opponents would surface to oppose the project before construction could begin. The first was Robert Wagner, mayor of New York City. Privately, Wagner must have been delighted that the Port Authority was planning to locate an ornamental and costly facility in an area *almost dead* of urban blight. Yet publicly, Wagner had to pretend to great unhappiness in order to squeeze as much as possible out of a deal already in his favor. At this stage Wagner could not afford to express even a glimmer of appreciation for the windfall that was about to be laid at his doorstep.[58] Three weeks after the governors of both states had ironed out an agreement, Mayor Wagner issued a statement that said in part: "It is astonishing to me that New York City, which is the major unit of government involved and affected by this legislation—fiscally, economically and socially—should not have been at the center of negotiations and deliberations and its interests given paramount consideration."[59]

Naturally, the issuance of such a statement got the attention of the Port Authority, which was eager to limit the damage and contain the problem. The city and the Port Authority met quietly in a number of sessions to iron out their differences. Most of the issues were routine, such as controlling the urban renewal procedures and conformance by the Port Authority to city ordinances and regulations. The most difficult negotiations were over how to arrive at an equitable formula for payment in lieu of taxes on the World Trade Center project. It was a high-stakes poker game. For all practical purposes, the city had a veto power over the World Trade Center, and both sides knew it. The necessary closing of streets and relocation of utilities were all within the city's power to grant or withhold.

After Mayor Wagner had wrung as much as possible out of the Port Authority, he agreed to the project.[60]

The next group to object to the World Trade Center was made up of the small businessmen in the area of the project. The Port Authority knew all along that within the fifteen-acre site were located 280 commercial tenants, forty-three industrial tenants, more than a thousand offices of varied sizes, and about one hundred residential tenants, most of whom lived in furnished rooms. What the Port Authority had not counted on was the shrillness and vigor of their objection. Most of the articles in the press, featuring interviews with shopkeepers and merchants, took the side of the little man battling with the ruthless agency.[61]

"It's just as though we were living in Russia or Cuba where a man doesn't have anything to say about what happens to him," said Oscar Nadel, a fifty-seven-year-old businessman with a tiny radio shop on Greenwich Street. "The Port Authority will tear down my business, and I have not yet been heard. If it were for the betterment of the city, that would be one thing. But this is simply big business running over us," he added.[62]

Day after day, these stories appeared in the newspapers about the imminent disappearance of the little delicatessens, cobblers, key shops, hardware stores, and local barbers. Many of the merchants were in the electronics retail field; so many, in fact, that the area was known as "radio row." One of the group's leaders, Leonard Levy, said that none of the big officials had paid any attention to their hardship. He explained: "Several hundred people are directly dependent on me alone. What can I tell them? Is this what they call a democracy? What do I say to the families of the men I will have to let go?"[63]

One of the most poignant stories was that of Barry Ray, a forty-six-year-old delicatessen owner. Ray had fought in World War II as an artillery spotter for four and a half years. He was out of the service for two and a half years. Then along came the Korean War and he was back in uniform again for three and a half more years, again spotting enemy fire in a small plane. By the time he got out, he was thirty-eight years old. He borrowed money and went into the delicatessen business. So at age forty-six, this quiet man, with ten decorations from his government for his service in two wars, had to start all over again. Ray told a reporter, "I'm forty-six. But it's almost a sin to be forty-six. I know nothing else. I want nothing out of this but a fair shake."[64]

It was difficult for the Port Authority to counteract this drumbeat of criticism, but they tried. They set up an office in a storefront at 136 Liberty Street to help property owners and tenants in the area prepare to move. The office tried to help by finding suitable nearby alternative sites.[65] Some merchants accepted the help, but others organized in noisy protest. On July 13, 1962, a number of merchants organized a "coffin" protest against Port Authority plans to condemn their property for the construction of the World Trade Center. The body of "Mr. Small Businessman" was paraded around the Church Street neighborhood in a mock funeral procession. Signs carried by the mourners challenged the Port Authority's right to oust them from the area.[66]

The Port Authority fought back against this public relations disaster by portraying the area as an antiquated thirteen-square-block area full of firetraps. In an official report, they wrote: "Over 60 percent of the 158 buildings within the proposed site are over 100 years old. . . . Eighty-nine percent of all the buildings are of nonfireproof construction and many of the remaining 11 percent are in poor repair."[67] Nonetheless, throughout the summer of 1962 stories kept appearing about struggling small businessmen who were being wronged. One of them was Edward W. Volk, who ran Volk's Restaurant at 51 Cortlandt Street, a quaint establishment opened by his grandfather in 1882. The restaurant featured one of the first electric cash registers and a fine old mahogany bar. Volk said: "If the trade center is built, Volk's will never reach the fourth generation of my family. My children won't have this business to go into. The Port Authority is offering up to $3,000 for moving expenses. I couldn't even move the bar for that."[68]

Of course, the real battle for the neighborhood was not being fought on the streets or in the newspapers. It was being fought in the courts. Opponents of the Trade Center began a series of court challenges. Some decisions were for the Port Authority; others were against it. Finally, the New York Court of Appeals upheld the agency, and the U.S. Supreme Court declined in December 1963 to review the matter.[69]

While the Port Authority was publicly battling the mayor and the small businessmen, it was quietly lining up tenants for the proposed World Trade Center. Though logical, it was not practical to build the structure first and then try to recruit tenants. Financing the building meant borrowing large sums of money, and repayment of the money could not start until the property was leased. Interest charges would have amounted to perhaps a million dollars a month, so the sooner rentals started coming in, the better.

One of the first prospective tenants to be approached in 1962 was the U.S. Customs Service. It was an ideal match. The Port Authority urgently needed a high-prestige tenant with unmistakable links to world trade to serve as a magnet for other tenants. Meanwhile, the nearby Customs Service was desperately unhappy with its landmark 1907 Custom House on Bowling Green designed by Cass Gilbert. To be sure, it was a grand Beaux-Arts monument with ornate statuary, marble corridors, and curving stairways. However, to the people who had to deal with Customs and to the Customs officers themselves, the building was completely inadequate, cramped, and crowded.[70]

Recruiting the Customs Service enhanced the prestige and credibility of the project at a delicate and precarious time. Austin Tobin had a vision of the World Trade Center built on the faith the Port Authority could indeed build it, if given the chance. But in 1962, success was not a foregone conclusion, even with a political consensus forged between the two states. It was important to keep lining up support. Thus, it was most welcome that President John F. Kennedy came to New York in December 1962 and put in a good word for the Trade Center. In a question session following his speech before the Economic Club of New York, Kennedy referred to and supported the World Trade Center, linking the importance of trade expansion to the national economy.[71] Over the ensuing decade, Austin Tobin never missed an opportunity to tie the Trade Center to JFK's policies of liberalizing trade and reducing tariffs.

The next important tenant to be signed up was the State of New York in January 1964. Officially the reason was to consolidate state offices scattered throughout New York City. The announcement said the move to the World Trade Center had been decided on "because of its unusual access to transportation as a convenience to the public, as a means of increasing the efficiency of state operations, and with a view to assisting in the development of New York City."[72] Of course, the announcement was mainly designed to save face. The fact of the matter was that New York State, in taking 1.9 million square feet of space, was coming to the rescue of a troubled project. There simply were not enough private-sector tenants stepping forward to carry the project.

While the legislative maneuvering was being played out in public, behind the scenes the Port Authority had been formulating and refining plans for the World Trade Center. In 1960, which was very early in the process, the public relations expert Lee K. Jaffe wrote a memorandum to the study group which said in part: "Incidentally, if you're going to build a great project, you should build the world's tallest building." Briefly then, the seed of this ambitious scheme came from neither architectural nor engineering considerations. It was a marketing device to attract tenants. Years later Guy Tozzoli recalled, "I remembered that memo. Of all the papers that I ever read over all those years, it was that memo written by Lee Jaffe which stuck in the back of my head."[73] Although Tozzoli was gracious about crediting Jaffe with the initial suggestion, it must be remembered that it was Tozzoli who became director of the World Trade Center and thus had the power to keep the idea alive.

The planners of the trade center were acutely aware that they were doing a new thing, that it was a new idea. Because of its novelty, considerable risk was involved. At stake was the Port Authority's money and the planners' careers. Surprising as it may now seem, at that time in the United States, international trade accounted for less than 3.8 percent of the gross national product. And of that sum, 80 percent was being handled by large multinational corporations, to whom a world trade center meant nothing since they already had well-established international activities. Tozzoli and his planners were worried because they were betting their careers on building this complex as an income-producing entity. This was a task complicated by the fact that they had a goal, which specified that at least 75 percent of the tenants should be either directly involved in international business or in servicing it. Tozzoli recalled, "I came to the conclusion, with Austin, that the only way to achieve that was to build the world's biggest project."[74]

Tozzoli thanked the three architects who had been on the study team and let them go. He went on to seek out a new architect—a Japanese American named Minoru Yamasaki, born in Seattle. In his initial conversations with Yamasaki, Tozzoli was unconcerned about the appearance of the complex. Tozzoli had come to the conclusion that, if the concept were correct, then it needed to be one focused, centralized, and integrated facility—in other words, a city within a city, albeit connected to existing subway lines. Tozzoli approached Yamasaki with no plan, no physical plan. Instead, he had a program—so many feet of office space with so many feet of retail stores, restaurants, parking space, and so on. Plus there was provision for a hotel and a customs house. The idea was that this would be a place not only where people worked, but also where they could enjoy themselves. After all, if this were to be a place with 50,000 workers and a place with 100,000 daily business visitors, they would have to have places for lunch and places to take breaks from their routines.

So the Port Authority gave Minoru Yamasaki the program to be accomplished, but left him free on how to render it in space. Thus the actual plan would be left up to the architect, who promised to keep Tozzoli up to date on the plans. Yamasaki, at his studio in Detroit, devised perhaps a hundred different schemes and then began to work in models. One plan called for a single big building; another called for ten smaller buildings. The architect tried out different kinds of shapes, but he kept coming back to two towers with a plaza where people could come and sit for lunch or listen to a concert on summer evenings. It would be a plaza with sculpture and benches, a place for people to gather. The plaza would flow right into the two balconies, which were in fact the mezzanines of the two towers. Down below would be the concourse level with shops and restaurants, and below that would be the subways.

About every two weeks, Tozzoli would fly out to Detroit to see how the plans were coming along. There were many such trips. Finally, Yamasaki revealed his ideas about two towers surrounded by a plaza and the other buildings. Yamasaki unveiled a drawing.

"It's great. It's a beautiful plan! Does it meet my program?" asked Tozzoli.

"No, it doesn't. It's two million feet short," said Yamasaki.

"Why is that?"

"You can't build buildings taller than eighty floors."

"Why is that?"

"They just don't do it."

"Yama, President Kennedy is going to put a man on the moon. I want you to build me the tallest buildings in the world."[75]

Working with Minoru Yamasaki on the problem of erecting the tallest buildings in the world was the well-respected and carefully chosen firm of Emery Roth and Sons, which had built more of New York's postwar office buildings than any other architectural firm. Founded in 1908 by Emery Roth, it was being carried on in the 1960s by his two sons, Julian and Richard. Julian was responsible for business; Richard, for design. Julian attended Columbia University and joined his father's firm as a specifications writer. Gradually, he became an expert on building costs, materials, and construction project budgeting. Julian's expertise enabled the firm to specialize in no-waste, economically designed buildings. Richard Roth received a bachelor's degree in architecture from the Massachusetts Institute of Technology and promptly joined the family firm. By the 1960s Richard had become chief designer. He had the last word on all plans drawn up by the firm, which was known for its work on big glass office buildings on Park Avenue and the Avenue of the Americas. During World War II, Richard Roth served in the U.S. Navy as a lieutenant commander in charge of a naval construction battalion (Seabees) in the South Pacific.[76]

If Yamasaki was the blue-ribbon expert from out of town, the Roths were the street-smart New Yorkers. They were said to build "business-like buildings for business." The Roths' prewar buildings included several landmarks such as the Ritz Tower Hotel, the St. Moritz Hotel, and the Fifth Avenue Hotel. Its postwar structures included the Sperry Rand Building and the Pfizer Building.[77]

By January 1964, with legislative approval from both states in place, the Port Authority was ready to go public with an announcement of its plans. The plans were disclosed at a press conference held at the New York Hilton. Governor Rockefeller and Governor Hughes were both there along with officials from New York City, Jersey City, and Hoboken. The stunning news, of course, was that this $350 million project with ten million square feet of space was going to take the form of two 110-story towers that would be the tallest buildings on earth.[78] As we have seen, going for the extra height was a ploy designed to get attention. It worked, but not all the attention was favorable. Setting a new record for height in Manhattan was the most controversial part of the project.

The plan was exciting and it did stimulate interest among potential tenants, but it also stimulated opposition; the Port Authority was unprepared for its ferocity. For the first time in its history, the agency was opposed by powerful members of the business community. These challengers were not the displaced store owners from the site, but major citywide real estate operators. They called upon the Port Authority to scale down its plans. They said that the proposed World Trade Center would be four times as large as necessary and would undermine the entire market for Manhattan office space.

The opponents were led by Lawrence A. Wien, who controlled the Empire State Building. He put together a Committee for a Reasonable World Trade Center, including Harold Uris of Uris Building Corporation, which had put up ten million square feet of office space in post–World War II New York, as well as the estate of Erwin A. Wolfson, builder of the Pan Am Building. Ironically, the Pan Am Building itself had aroused protest just a few years earlier because of its enormous volume of office space, 2.4 million square feet, the most in any single commercial office building at the time. Wien appointed Robert Kopple, a fifty-three-year-old lawyer known to be fond of a good legal fight, to head up the committee. Kopple promised, "We are ready to go to court to try to get this bloated project—these 'Tobin Towers'—brought down to size."[79]

In actual practice, these new opponents were too sophisticated to attack the powerful Port Authority directly. Instead they enlisted the help of city government, which, they hoped, could use its influence to reduce the size of the project. As it turned out, the city had a powerful weapon—the authority to grant or withhold street closing permits, needed for any large-scale urban project. The city approached the conflict gingerly. Milton Mollen, chairman of the Mayor's Coordinating Committee, said in late March of 1964: "We're for the Trade Center. We think all the problems can be worked out. But we are naturally worried about the economic health of the city, and the real estate business is an important part of that."[80]

Behind the scenes, Austin Tobin worked quietly to reassure

realtors that there was nothing to worry about. Publicly, he tried to portray the opposition as the pet peeve of a single man, saying, "Wien is causing all this commotion because he doesn't want his building to be the third tallest in the city."[81]

Naturally, the opposition resisted this characterization. Harold Uris spoke for the whole committee when he declared, "They say they're going to rent four million square feet to export-import firms. That's twice the space in the Pan Am Building. I just don't believe they can do it. And when they find they can't, they're going to dump the space on the open market at reduced rents. With their tax advantages and the low rates they pay for money, they could rent for far less than I can and still break even. I'm not afraid of losing the tenants I have now. I'm afraid there won't be any tenants for the buildings I put up five years from now."[82]

The Port Authority kept insisting that it could rent mainly to companies whose principal business was in the import-export trade. If that's so, the opposition countered, why does the Port Authority need to recruit the state of New York to take office space? Robert Kopple suggested that the state was taking space in the trade center because Governor Rockefeller was looking out for his brother David, one of the originators of the project. Kopple also objected to the idea that the Port Authority was moving its own offices into the trade center to use up 700,000 square feet. The normally cool Austin Tobin lost his composure and responded, "We'll have our offices anywhere we damned well please."[83]

For two full years the opposition put up argument after argument to scale down the trade center. They took out a series of full-page advertisements in New York newspapers. They arranged for public hearings. They charged that the project was a real estate venture, that it was being built for profits to cover PATH's deficits, that the agency's figures relating to rentals were wrong, that the agency paid no taxes, that the towers would cause television interference, that traffic and transit would be impossible because of the large number of people at the site, and that the project would cost more per square foot than any other office building in history. At one point, Wien even suggested that the city was risking physical disaster since such a tall experimental design might fall or collapse.[84]

As the cost of the project went up to $575 million in 1966,

even the *New York Times* began to question whether it was worthwhile. It called some of the questions raised by the opposition "legitimate and disturbing."[85] As Wien and his group pressed on, they found support for their position in the young and handsome newly elected mayor of the city, John V. Lindsay. Publicly, Lindsay had said that he thought the Port Authority should focus its efforts on transportation and port development. Privately, his bright and eager aides were negotiating for higher payments by the Port Authority to the city in lieu of taxes. Showing how important the talks were, Mr. Lindsay put at the head of his negotiating team his most aggressive bargainer, Deputy Mayor Robert Price. The Port Authority offered to pay about $4 million a year in lieu of taxes, and it offered to explore the possibility of building a luxury passenger ship terminal on the Hudson River. Price was asking for a sum closer to the $16 million a year the center would have brought in taxes if it were built by a private developer.[86]

The city's only power with regard to the project was its right to hold up the street closings that the Port Authority needed to go ahead with building the trade center, which would cover some fifteen city blocks. One of Price's committee members said, "If it weren't for the street closing he needs for the Trade Center, Tobin wouldn't be giving us the time of day. We know it, and he knows it."[87]

Negotiations dragged on for months, and by July 1966 they appeared to be deadlocked. The city was concerned about its many urgent public needs in mass transportation, schools, and hospitals. The agency was concerned about its autonomy and the viability of the trade center project. Austin Tobin wanted to start the building right away and reach an agreement with the city later. Lindsay knew that his best bargaining chip was to continue to refuse to issue the street-closing permits, though he did offer to submit the matter to arbitration, to solve the matter through an independent third party. The Port Authority refused. Lindsay told reporters, "We're not intentionally stalling on the trade center. We want to see the ground-breaking process go forward, but we must protect the interests of the people."[88] A few days later, reportedly with a trace of a smile, Mr. Lindsay said of the stymied negotiations, "Of course, if we were willing to give away Manhattan, they could start digging up the city any time."[89]

The long and frequently rocky negotiations continued for five months. Then the talks reached a complete impasse and were broken off. There seemed to be no face-saving way out of the dilemma. Finally, almost miraculously, the stalemate was broken by a civic-minded lawyer who had no official connection with either the city or the authority—George Milstein Shapiro, age forty-six, who had been counsel to Governor Thomas E. Dewey in the early 1950s and was by this time a partner in an important New York law firm. The way it happened, according to subsequent accounts, was that one weekend Shapiro and Price, as old friends, were talking on the telephone. Price said that negotiations between the city and the authority had broken down. Shapiro asked Price to describe the difficulties. When he did so, Shapiro said that they did not sound insuperable. Would Price like him to have a chat with Rosaleen Skehan, the general attorney for the authority? When Price agreed, Shapiro went to work. The key to the process was that both sides trusted Shapiro. Samuel Johnson once said, "It is difficult to negotiate where neither will trust."[90]

Thus began patient days and hours of behind-the-scenes negotiations. Shapiro said, "I wanted complete anonymity so we could work quietly and without interruption. There were able and dedicated people on both sides, and I soon saw that my job was to try to develop an understanding on each side of the practical problems that the other faced." The dispute, of course, turned on the question of how much money the authority would have to pay the city in lieu of taxes. Shapiro got both sides to come back to the bargaining table after they had walked out in anger. Shapiro got both sides to agree that the authority would make an annual payment equivalent to the taxes that would be paid by a private developer *on the portion of the project to be leased to private tenants*. For the first year, the payment was to be $6,175,737. The city would have to accept less than it wanted; the authority would have to pay more than had been expected. About 40 percent of the project was to be occupied by private tenants at the start; the rest would be occupied by federal and state offices and would not be taxed, a provision that favored the authority. Another breakthrough was that Shapiro got both sides to agree to the concept that the size of the payment would be subject to annual review and would be increased or decreased as the official valuation of comparable property rose or fell. Clearly this last provision favored the city.

In addition to the annual payment, the city won the authority's agreement to proceed with the construction of a $100 million passenger ship terminal for Manhattan's west side. The authority also agreed to develop a $16 million containership operation in South Brooklyn. Finally, the authority agreed to use landfill from the excavation of the site to create twenty-eight acres of new land along the edge of Manhattan. The land, valued at $30 million, would be turned over to the city, which hoped to lease it to private developers.[91] This final provision was presented by the authority as a gift to the city; but, as Guy Tozzoli wisely pointed out later, it actually solved a problem for the builders: where to put the excavated dirt. To have taken it anywhere else would have been very expensive for the authority.[92]

From the time the Port Authority had first issued its initial proposal for a trade center in March 1961 to the point when the city removed the final roadblock in August 1966, more than five years had passed—five years of negotiation, of compromise, of frustration. But now Austin Tobin, the dreamer of big plans, was unshackled. He could direct his staff to begin the next phase, the phase of construction. The project would no longer belong to lawyers with briefcases. It would now belong to engineers with blueprints.

2

It Can't
Be Done

Overcoming Obstacles
in Building Tall Towers

Once I'm started, what are you going to do to me?

Stop the building in the middle? We're now rolling!

—RAY M. MONTI, CONSTRUCTION MANAGER,
WORLD TRADE CENTER PROJECT
(INTERVIEW, 1994)

I T W A S in 1956 that a young U.S. Navy lieutenant from the civil engineering corps left the service and came to work for the Port Authority. He was made a staff assistant to the engineer of construction. After a few days, his supervisor called him in and said, "You're part of this elite force. Here's a credit card made out with your name on it. When you go out to meet contractors and consultants there will be situations when you're in a meeting and it comes to be lunchtime. You go right ahead and pick up the tab."

The young engineer was amazed at the policy. Nothing like that had ever happened in the navy. Later, he was sent over to Pennsylvania to inspect some storage tanks in a rural area. The engineer, only twenty-seven years old, carried out his assignment and met the people from the tank company. It came time for lunch, and they all went out to a restaurant. At the end of the meal, the young engineer whipped out his wallet and said, "I'm paying."

The president of the company said, "You can't."

The young engineer said, "Why not?"

The president answered, "Nobody will ever believe you're paying. They won't believe me. They know I took you out."

The young engineer said, "Well, that's the way it is." He charged it to the Port Authority. After all, it wasn't coming out of his pocket.

That young engineer was Ray Monti, who fifteen years later became construction manager of the World Trade Center. The credit card story, though trivial on the surface, is quite revealing. Being able to pay for the lunch put Monti on the same level as the president of the company. The credit card itself was a small thing, but it represented the trust that the Port Authority placed even in its most junior engineers. The engineering department was the training ground for future executives, and the organization wanted its executives to have a high level of self-confidence.

Recalling the credit card business nearly forty years later, Ray Monti said that it gave him the assurance of success. "We were the elite," he said. "There was nothing we couldn't do. There was no challenge that we couldn't tackle. There were no rules we couldn't find a way around—without being illegal—to get the thing done."[1]

The Port Authority administration carefully fostered the idea that the agency was giving its young professionals a career path, not just a job. The agency nurtured its employees with privileges and perquisites, and it paid them better than their civil service counterparts. The result was an agency with tremendous esprit de corps. So when it came time to build the tallest building on earth, they were ready for the challenge.

Monti graduated in 1952 from Manhattan College, which is now in Riverdale in the Bronx, with a bachelor's degree in civil engineering with a structural major. While he was in college, the Port Authority came on campus to recruit trainees. But Monti had already enlisted in the navy reserve when he was eighteen, and he had gone to officers' school in the summers. So he was prepared to take a commission upon graduation. Just for fun, Monti took the Port Authority examination for junior professional trainees.

"The Port Authority has an insidious way of doing things," said Monti. "First they told me I was one of 2,200 under consideration. Then they wrote to say I was one of 200, and they wanted me to take more tests. I did and I came out one of 25. By that time it became a challenge. Finally, I was one of nine accepted for the program."[2]

Though Monti was supposed to begin a two-year tour in the navy, the Port Authority got the navy to postpone the service. Monti spent a year in the Port Authority junior executive training program serving in each major department for a short rotation.

Monti reported for duty with the navy civil engineering corps in 1953, and was told that he would have to leave within three days for North Africa. When he arrived in Port Lyautey in what was then

French Morocco, it was quite a surprise to his commanding officer who was expecting a lieutenant commander, not just an ensign, to supervise construction of 800-foot-high radio antennas.

Things went well in the navy, and Monti was planning to stay with it. But the chief engineer of the Port Authority, John Kyle, would write to Monti every few months describing current projects and encouraging him to return when his service was complete. Without the prodding of Kyle, Monti might not have returned to the Port Authority.

It was a good career move for Monti, since the 1950s was a period of tremendous growth in large-scale public works projects throughout the United States. Nowhere were there more projects than in the New York and New Jersey region. Monti worked at the Kennedy and Newark airports as well as on the third tube of the Lincoln Tunnel. By 1959 Monti was promoted to assistant resident engineer on the $30 million expansion of the Port Authority's mid-Manhattan bus terminal.

At the terminal job, the resident engineer was Frank Corey, "a real old-line construction man, a tobacco-chewing type," said Monti. "I learned a lot from him and through him. After the foundation phase was done, Corey called me into his office and said I was relieved of all other duties and from that time on I'd handle only the electrical and mechanical work. I pouted a bit; thought he didn't like my work on the structural part of the job. But that was the best lesson I ever had. That background in electrical-mechanical has been invaluable to me."[3]

As the bus terminal project was winding down, Monti and another engineer were sent to a three-day course at Saranac Lake, New York, in critical path method. The method, called CPM, is a kind of highly detailed master plan for any project which schedules every component to arrive in time so that the next step can proceed without delay. At the time, Monti had no idea how important this course was to be to his later career. "Sometimes things happen in strange ways," said Monti. "We considered it a junket. At that time CPM was just breaking out. We came back and kind of forgot about it."[4]

Because of his success with the bus terminal, Monti next was promoted to resident engineer in charge of the $5 million Port Authority exhibit at the New York World's Fair, which was to be the largest and most lavish fair ever held. The Port Authority's contribution was to be a 120-foot-high heliport, which resembled a card table with the legs at the midpoints of the sides instead of at the corners. Monti decided to try out the new critical path method in the construction of the building. The technique enabled him to anticipate problems before they held up the work, and so the job was finished on schedule, a rare accomplishment for a major experimental construction job.

It was Monti's success at the World's Fair job that drew him to the attention of Guy Tozzoli, head of the World Trade Department. Tozzoli, along with his deputy Malcolm Levy, tapped Monti to become construction manager of the World Trade Center project.

Part of the excitement of a big project like the World Trade Center was the sure knowledge by everyone that its construction would be a stimulus to the economy of the region. Based on the original cost estimate of $350 million, the Port Authority was expected to spend some $200 million in wages to labor. It was known that the job would require up to eight thousand men working at the site during peak periods of building. Material requirements for the project called for 200,000 tons of structural steel. Some 1.25 million man-hours of work would be needed to excavate 1.2 million cubic yards of earth and boulders, not to mention about 45,000 yards of bedrock prior to laying the foundations. The World Trade Center would require six million square feet of masonry walls and five million square feet of painted surfaces. Also needed would be 1,520 miles of wire, 400 miles of conduit, and 200,000 lighting fixtures. Toward the end of the project, ceiling workers would install seven million square feet of acoustical tile. Similarly, floor installers would lay seven million square feet of floors.[5]

With this kind of money at stake, there was keen interest in the construction industry in just how the work would be allocated. In March 1967 the Port Authority chose Tishman Realty and Construction Company as general contractor for the World Trade Center. The patriarch of the firm was David Tishman, described by *The Encyclopedia of New York City* as "the city's most prominent and successful developer." In 1947 he built the first postwar office tower in Manhattan at 445 Park Avenue. His headquarters was in the Tishman Building, a skyscraper he built in 1957 at 666 Fifth Avenue.[6] Tishman's estimate for its fee and its field costs came to

$19.25 million, of which $3.25 million was its fee. Tishman's competitors were the George A. Fuller Company and Turner Construction Company. Their bids for field costs were almost the same as Tishman's. Tishman had the lowest bid for the fee component.

Tishman had already served for about a year as a consultant contractor, aiding in design and planning. The company had provided expertise and knowledge on a variety of matters, including negotiations with steel fabricators. Tishman was well established in this kind of work, serving as general contractor on the one-hundred-story John Hancock Building in Chicago as well as general contractor for the twenty-nine-story office building part of the Madison Square Garden complex built over Pennsylvania Station in New York.

Tishman was to be responsible for all subcontracts: receiving bids, negotiating, awarding, and signing them. But all of this was to be subject to Port Authority approval. Tishman was to provide staff to coordinate and supervise construction, hoist men and materials, secure the site, protect finished construction, and provide barricades and temporary power.[7]

Officially, then, Tishman was in charge of negotiating contracts. But in actual fact, contracts that really mattered were handled by the Port Authority. Guy Tozzoli, with his staff, personally conducted the contracts. His principal assistants were Malcolm Levy and Ray Monti. Take, for example, the matter of concrete contracts. Tozzoli sat in a room with the concrete suppliers of Manhattan and negotiated the price. It was done competitively, one after another. They took prices and proposals, but they also had the right to negotiate with a contractor. An auditor and an attorney were present to keep everything aboveboard, but there was latitude to negotiate. The most suitable bid came from Fortune Pope, the neatly dressed head of Colonial Concrete. Guy Tozzoli called him in to get the best possible price. Fortune Pope tugged at his beautiful cuff links as he listened to Tozzoli's arguments. The negotiations wore on. At one point, Pope tugged once again on his cuff links and said in a low, soft voice, "Mr. Tozzoli, I think you better go into the concrete business yourself because I'm finished with reducing my price. Thank you very much." He shut his briefcase and calmly said, "I'm leaving."

Tozzoli said, "Sit down! You got the job." Tozzoli knew there was no more to give.[8]

Of course, before anything new could be constructed, old buildings had to be demolished and the land cleared. The process started on March 21, 1966, when the Ajax Wrecking and Lumber Corporation began demolishing the first of the twenty-six structures on the site which were then vacant. The contract with Ajax covered the first seven of those buildings. It was a humble beginning for a multimillion-dollar project, which would take years to complete. Nine men with sledges and crowbars walked into the old building at 78 Dey Street and began to smash it up. The five-story, red-brick structure, last occupied by a dealer for goods and equipment for ships, fell into tiny pieces easily as the crew demolished the interior. The building was at least a hundred years old, but even the Buildings Department had no record of exactly when it had been built.[9]

After demolition, hundreds of pipes, utilities, and water lines that ran under the site had to be relocated. It was a nightmarish job because one blunder might cause telephone service and lights to go out in hundreds of busy offices. Beneath the site was a maze of only partly mapped pipes and cables, forgotten foundations and tunnels, underground streams and old graves. When the specific agency that had put a particular pipe down fifty years earlier was contacted, they might not even be able to acknowledge that it was theirs. Two or three weeks could easily pass while the problem was being solved, an expensive delay in the work.[10]

The building site (fig. 2.1) presented a tremendous obstacle. It must be remembered that Manhattan is an island situated at the confluence of a major river and the ocean. When the English explorer Henry Hudson, sailing for the Dutch East India Company in 1609, explored the Hudson River, the waterfront was at what is now Greenwich Street. Over hundreds of years since then, it has been extended by landfill operations and filled with dirt, rubble, construction debris, old piers and wharves. This process had extended the bulkhead line 700 feet west over the centuries. To reach bedrock, engineers would have to dig down sixty-five feet.[11]

When Port Authority engineers started to plan the World

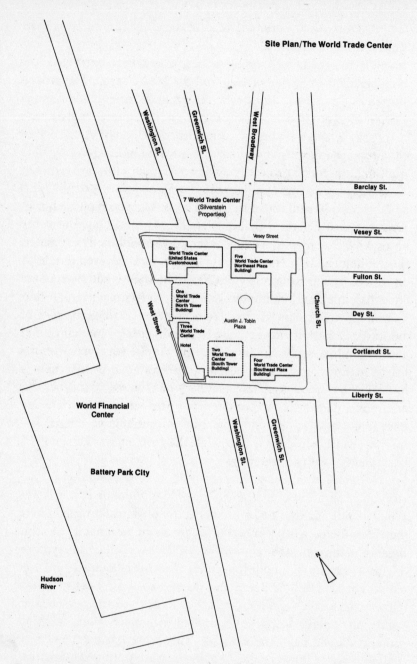

Figure 2.1. Site Plan of the World Trade Center

Trade Center, they knew that half the site would be where the Hudson River used to be. To be sure, it had been filled in. But excavate only three feet, and they would hit water. Since they were planning to build two towers of 1,350 feet each, they wanted to be sure that they placed them on bedrock. So the first challenge was how to remove the water to build the foundation.

Ray Monti explained, "The entire area was thus subject to tidal flow. To excavate a foundation box 800 feet long and 400 feet wide, and to go down as far as needed would literally have required pumping out the Hudson River in order to keep the site dry—a formidable task. Even if the excavations could have been pumped out, there was another complication. Doing so would draw down the natural water level within considerable distance of the Trade center, threatening the stability of nearby buildings which were not built on rock. Sagging streets and collapsing buildings would hardly have endeared an already controversial project to anyone."[12]

All conventional methods for building the basement wall had substantial drawbacks. The old pneumatic caisson method was too slow. The open cut method was too expensive. They went down the list, considering more than ten different textbook possibilities. It looked as if nothing would work. Then John M. Kyle, Jr., the chief engineer of the Port Authority, came up with a solution: the slurry trench method (fig. 2.2). Although it had been used in Europe and in Canada for subway construction, the method was practically brand new in the United States. True, it had been used in Allegheny, Pennsylvania, for the installation of a cutoff wall under a dam to stop the infiltration of water, but never in foundation work. It was a big gamble because no one knew if it would really work. There were no American firms available for the work, so it had to be done by an Italian company.

The principle, familiar to drillers of oil and gas wells, was simple enough. How did it work? First, excavating machines with clamshell buckets would dig out a three-foot-wide trench, the same width as the basement wall planned for that space. The excavation proceeded in twenty-two-foot segments. As the dirt and rock were removed, it was constantly replaced by a "slurry, " a mixture of water and bentonite. Geologists tell us that bentonite is a type of fluffy, expansive gray clay that comes from Wyoming. It was mined and

The Excavation Job

This was the "bathtub," inside the 3,100-foot rectangular concrete
basement perimeter wall. Here more than a million cubic yards was
excavated for the 110-story twin towers to soar from bedrock. The
exposed tubes enclose the PATH railroad, which operated as usual during

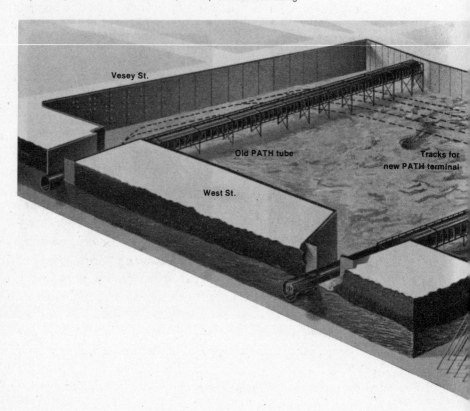

Figure 2.2. The Excavation Job

bagged in Greybull, Wyoming, and then shipped to New York. The
slurry had a texture which some compared to pea soup and others
compared to buttermilk. It had a swelling tendency and would plug
any holes along the sides as excavators dug deeper. It was constantly being stirred up as the excavation machinery went deeper
and deeper. The wonderful property of this mixture was that it was
strong enough to hold back the groundwater and maintain the sides
of the trench without any bracing. They were able to continue this
process right down to the bedrock.

construction. Dotted lines indicate tracks for new PATH terminal.
Diagonals in cut-out at lower right show a number of the steel tendons
used to anchor wall to the outlying rock. At upper right is IRT
South Ferry subway.

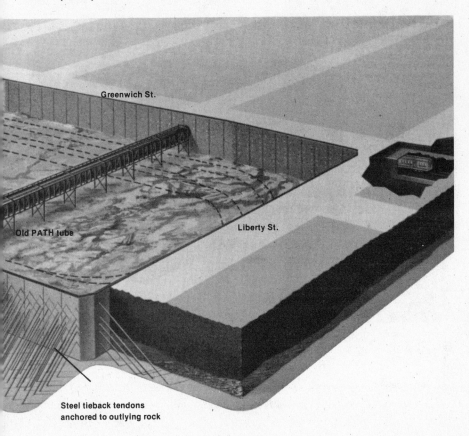

Greenwich St.

Old PATH tube

Liberty St.

Steel tieback tendons
anchored to outlying rock

When the trench segment was finally dug out, the workers lowered a preassembled seven-story-high steel cage of reinforcing rods
weighing twenty-five tons into the slurry (fig. 2.3). The cage provided a framework for the concrete wall that was to come. Then the
concrete would be poured in at the bottom of the trench through a
big pipe that sort of resembled an elephant's trunk. As the concrete
wall rose up to ground level, the slurry (which had served its temporary stabilizing purpose) would be forced out and piped over to
other trench segments or removed. All in all, they had to make 152

**Building the
Basement Wall**

(Three cut-away views
looking into the site)

1
The perimeter wall was built in
22-foot segments like this
one—152 in all. Excavation
proceeded 70 feet down to
bedrock. As material was
scooped out, bentonite slurry
was piped in to fill the
deepening trench.

2
When the trench segment was
finally dug out, a seven-story
25-ton steel cage was lowered
into slurry. This formed the
skeleton for the concrete wall
to come. Dark protuberances
are "guides" for system of
rock anchors.

3
Now the concrete is poured
through a big hopper down the
pipe to bottom of trench.
The slurry has served its
interim stabilizing purpose,
and is forced out as the
permanent wall rises to
ground level.

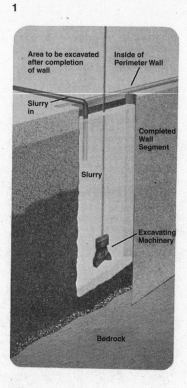

1

Area to be excavated
after completion
of wall

Inside of
Perimeter Wall

Slurry
in

Completed
Wall
Segment

Slurry

Excavating
Machinery

Bedrock

Figure 2.3. Building the Basement Wall

of these twenty-two-foot trench segments to enclose an area two
blocks wide and four blocks long. The final result was a waterproof
"bathtub," or perhaps "reverse bathtub," since it kept water *out* of
the excavation site and preserved the integrity of the surrounding
streets and buildings.[13]

Credit for the slurry wall breakthrough went to John M. Kyle,
Jr. (1904–1970), who as chief engineer had participated in the design and construction of every major Port Authority project for
almost a quarter of a century. Jack Kyle was the latest in a line of
engineering greats—General George Goethals, Othmar Ammann,
and John C. Evans—in the agency's highest engineering post. Jack
Kyle was known as a creative engineer, always looking for new
concepts in construction methods. The slurry wall idea was the first

2

3

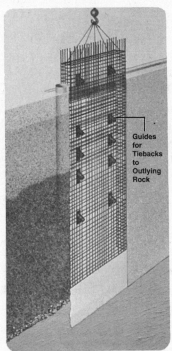

Guides
for
Tiebacks
to
Outlying
Rock

Slurry
out

Concrete
in

Concrete

of three important technological innovations that made the World Trade Center possible. (The other two, elevatoring and load-bearing exterior walls, we shall come to later.)

Kyle, who was born in New York, was graduated from Stevens Institute of Technology and did graduate work in architecture at Columbia University and in airport design at New York University. He served as a major in the Army Corps of Engineers during World War II, taking part in the training of airborne aviation engineer units and serving as a staff officer at Army Air Force headquarters. Later he did survey and field evaluation of major air force facilities throughout the world. For his service he received the Army Commendation medal.[14]

Kyle was not just an engineering practitioner; he was also a researcher. He was the author of more than forty papers on soil consolidation, prestressed concrete, foundation design, and construction of complex structures. So when the World Trade Center foundation problem came along, he was well prepared to deal with it. In this work, Kyle was assisted by another distinguished engineer, Martin S. Kapp. A graduate of Swarthmore and Harvard, with B.S. and M.S. degrees in soil mechanics and foundation engineering, Kapp served with the U.S. Navy during World War II. He lectured at many universities and wrote numerous technical articles on soil mechanics and foundation engineering.[15]

It was one thing to come up with the slurry wall concept, and another to come up with a company that could do the work. The contract for the perimeter wall went to Icanda, Limited, of Montreal, Canada, in November of 1966.[16] Icanda was the Canadian offshoot of an Italian company based in Milan, Impresa Costruzioni Opere Specializzate (I.C.O.S.), which means "company for special jobs." The firm had extensive experience in constructing foundations in marshy areas. Kyle was impressed with Icanda's work while he had traveled in Italy, and he managed to interest the company in bidding for the World Trade Center job.[17]

When Icanda first began work during the winter of 1966–1967, there were plenty of problems since the ground was full of obstructions, including crisscrossed heavy timbers spiked together from old wharves and piers, not to mention abandoned sewers and utility ducts. Ray Monti went down to the construction site one Sunday morning while no work was being done, and he saw a man with a woollen cap pulled over his head. It was freezing cold. The man was staring forlornly into the hole for the first panel, which was not going well. Monti called to one of the security guards and said, "Go throw that bum off the site. He doesn't belong there." It turned out to be Arturo Ressi di Cervia, a twenty-six-year-old engineer from Icanda who was in charge of that aspect of the project. The rosy-cheeked, husky Italian took the error in stride.[18]

Construction of the perimeter wall took fourteen months, often requiring around-the-clock operation. When it was finally finished, it was possible to begin excavating the interior materials. More than a million yards of debris, earth, and rock were inside the bathtub. As the excavation proceeded, it was necessary to support the wall. They could not use internal braces because they would have interfered with the work and with future steel erection, so they used external tension ties to hold back the wall panels. Although this sounds simple, it was difficult to route the tie-rods away from sewers and wires. There were also legal complications because many of the tie-rods had to be anchored into rock on property belonging to other people.[19]

At about this time a young engineering student from Manhattan College started working as a provisional employee of the Port Authority. He had classes that started at 8 A.M. and ended by 11 A.M., so he was able to work from 1 o'clock in the afternoon until 9 at night. One of his jobs was to stress-test the temporary tie-back tendons. Later the young engineer worked on sounding the rock for the foundations. In a process that is part art and part science, they would hit the rock with an iron bar hoping to hear a certain "ding" rather than a "thud," in the effort to put the towers on solid rock. That young engineer was Charles Maikish, who by the time this book was being written had come up the ranks to be director of the World Trade Center.[20]

A major embarrassment for the Port Authority occurred in December 1966, when Austin Tobin was forced to announce publicly that the cost of the World Trade Center had increased to $575 million, up from the original estimate of $350 million. Much of the increase was attributed to the delay suffered by the project as a result of the negotiations with the city. Additional increases were caused by revisions in the design of the plaza buildings and incorporating the landfill project agreed to with the city. Tobin also explained the original figure had been a *construction* cost estimate, while the new figure was an overall *project* cost estimate, including not only construction costs but also allowances for site acquisition, engineering and design, and all other costs.[21]

Critics of the project immediately complained that the new figure was unrealistically low. They hinted that the agency was "notching up" the total little by little rather than face the embarrassing truth of the staggering cost of the project, described as "grandiose" in conception. A spokesperson for the Committee for a Reasonable World Trade Center, a group of private real estate operators, said: "They couldn't build it for $525 million; they can't build it for

$575 million, and they won't be able to build it for $625 million. On that basis, they'll never be able to make it run at a profit, and it will be a drain on their resources."[22]

The chairman of the committee was Lawrence A. Wien, head of the organization that operated the Empire State Building, which at 102 stories would obviously have to give up its long reign as the world's tallest building upon completion of the center.

"Our minimum estimate is $750 million," Mr. Wien said, "and some think it will go beyond $1 billion. I think they owe it to the public to make a full statement of how they arrive at such a figure. This is not the way to present cost estimates—by an off-hand statement over the telephone from some spokesman. They should make public the figures on which they compute such a cost. They're inching up. If they keep going, they'll hit the $1 billion, I'll tell you."[23]

Clearly, Mr. Wien had his own selfish reasons for opposition, but the concerns he voiced were taken seriously. Even the *New York Times*, which had initially supported the project, editorialized: "While the committee members may be motivated mainly by fears that the Port Authority's addition of over ten million square feet of office space will damage the values of their own properties, some of the questions the group has raised concerning the feasibility of the World Trade Center are legitimate and disturbing."[24]

Viewing the dispute with the objectivity of hindsight, one can clearly see that there are basically three kinds of cost estimate—the optimistic, the realistic, and the pessimistic. There is no question that the original figure of $350 million was optimistic. That figure was published by the Port Authority in the first phase of conception when its executives were euphoric, upbeat, and enthusiastic about the project. The number came about in a simple way: they figured on ten million square feet of space to be built at a cost of $35 per square foot. At the time, ordinary speculative structures of forty stories were being built in midtown Manhattan for $35 per square foot. But after Minoru Yamasaki and all the other architects and consultants got through with it, the project was no longer an ordinary building; it became a monument. So the price kept creeping up.

Nearly thirty years after the original dispute, I asked Ray Monti about the problem of cost increases. He explained quite can-

didly, "There's a natural tendency in all government projects to want
to convince others to authorize you to proceed. One puts a favorable interpretation on the facts. If you reveal all the problems, you
are never going to get the thing going. Besides, there's another basic
principle here. Once I'm started, what are you going to do to me?
Stop the building in the middle? We're now rolling!"[25]

As discussed in the previous chapter, the Port Authority and the
city had agreed that excavated landfill from the project would be
used to create new land on the west side of West Street. It was an
idea that had occurred one morning to Guy Tozzoli as he was shav-
ing, and it was the idea that finally brought the city and agency together to an agreement that had taken months to negotiate. It was
clearly a win-win situation. Normally, the builder would have to
take the excavated material away to landfills in New Jersey or dump
it way out at sea. By anyone's calculations, that would have been
terribly expensive. To move 1.2 million cubic yards would have
required 100,000 truckloads.[26]

Creating the landfill was no small task. They had to build a
three-sided box of cellular cofferdams to hold the material excavated from the building site. The fill projected about 700 feet into
the Hudson from the existing shoreline and was 1,484 feet long,
about six city blocks. Enclosing the reclaimed area were cellular
cofferdams made up of some 8,500 tons of steel. But before the cofferdams could be constructed, the old piers and ferry slips had to
be removed. Some were pulled, others were broken off at the mud-
line. Disposing of the old wooden timbers was a big problem. At
first they tried burning them in lower New York Bay, but complaints
about air pollution caused them to be loaded on barges and towed
twelve miles out to sea, where they were finally burned.

Each cellular cofferdam was about sixty-three feet in diameter. As each cell was finished, the contractors filled it with 6,000 cubic yards of sand—seven barge loads brought from Long Island.
With the cofferdams in place to contain the excavated material, the
contractors started bringing it in. They created twenty-three acres
of the most valuable land in the country. In effect, New York City
got $90 million worth of land, the present site of Battery Park City

and the World Financial Center, in exchange for its agreement to allow the project to go forward.[27]

In the process of removing more than a million cubic yards of fill, many interesting relics were unearthed, creating some fascinating conflicts. Archaeologists, interested in the material evidence from American culture in the preceding three centuries, would have liked to have sifted slowly through the site with small picks and trowels—or as Ray Monti said, "with spoons."[28] Naturally, the Port Authority preferred to do the job quickly with power shovels. What happened in practice was a salvage operation: most large and durable artifacts of intrinsic interest were indeed rescued from oblivion. Saving all small and fragile objects was hopeless given the time constraints of the job. New York newspapers of the late 1960s record many interesting finds. For example, Herb Goldstein reported in the *New York Post*: "Old Charlie Schmidt who got docked a day's pay for losing the company's tools back in 1904—when the original Hudson Tubes were dug—can rest easy. The tools have been found."[29]

The most prized artifact believed to be at the site was not located. That would have been Captain Adriaen Block's ship, the *Tiger*, which supposedly burned in the Hudson in 1613. Captain Block sailed under the sponsorship of a group of Dutch merchants seeking to expand the fur trade. Block sailed up and down the Hudson River trading with the Indians until the fall of 1613, when the *Tiger*, at anchor off Manhattan, caught fire and burned to the waterline. The story might have ended there, but it was not so simple. In 1916, in the process of excavating for the Seventh Avenue subway, a few ship timbers were found that may have been relics of the *Tiger*. But money was not available for a complete excavation. In 1967 the Port Authority dug a test pit in the exact area of the 1916 find, but no additional relics were found.[30]

A more satisfying find was the discovery of a time capsule buried at the time of the 1884 construction of the Washington Market, on the east side of Washington Street between Fulton and Vesey Streets. The building was an arenalike structure occupying a full square block, two stories high with a mezzanine encircling the market floor. As many as 175 merchants of meat, poultry, cheese, butter, and garden produce did business there. Inside the time capsule were a number of items, including fourteen business cards from merchants of the area, an opera playbill, and a lithograph of Grover Cleveland (who had just won a close election over James G. Blaine). Significantly, there was a note which read: "This is written in remembrance of the erection of the new Washington Market and we the undersigned men do wish to be remembered that we were doing business in it and hope that it may long remain as it is . . . built for and not be changed into any other thing but a market." Thirty-two merchants signed it.

Although not in the sense that the signers intended, the site was to become a market once again. But it would have to be considered a restoration rather than a continuance. When the Port Authority took over the site, the old Washington Market had been torn down and was replaced with a parking lot; thus all surface evidence of its historic past was lost.[31]

The area of the excavation had been a natural harbor in the New Amsterdam of the 1600s. European fur traders had anchored there while trading with the Indians. So it was not surprising that among the finds were a couple of anchors. Henry A. Druding, a senior resident engineer on the Port Authority staff, was in charge of any objects of archaeological interest. Druding had accumulated a variety of objects, including clay pipes and hand-blown drinking glasses. There were three cannonballs (the largest of which weighed forty-four pounds and measured seven and a half inches in diameter). There were various coins, including an almost perfect 1749 British halfpenny. Bottles were the most common find, and many had London markings. In the hall of his temporary office on Dey Street were two anchors. One was intact but corroded, with a massive ten-foot shank; the anchor's date was determined as 1785.[32] The other was a smaller anchor with a missing fluke and a broken shank. In both cases, the hawsers probably broke and that is how the ships most likely lost their anchors.

Walking through the excavation area with a reporter, Mr. Druding pulled part of an old shoe from the heavy mud. "I've picked up a lot of nuggets of useless information on this project," he said. "This shoe, for example, was made for either foot. Archaeologists have told me they made them this way prior to 1865. So you can roughly date it."[33]

During the excavation, the PATH trains had to operate as usual, even though the old tubes under Fulton Street and Cortlandt Street became exposed as a result of the digging. Inside the tunnel things were about the same as they had always been since 1908. As trains neared the Hudson Terminal, the wheels would screech and the riders would gather up their belongings and crowd toward the doors. But outside, a strange sight greeted sidewalk superintendents: an elevated tunnel. As the digging proceeded, contractors had to place the tubes in protective metal and wood cradles so they would not collapse. The tunnels were propped up eighteen feet above the mud floor of the excavation site.[34]

Since the tunnel had been underground for so long, there was the risk that exposure to air and sunlight might subject it to sudden changes in temperature that could lead to expansion and buckling of the tubes. To cope with this situation, saw cuts were made in the tube to serve as crude expansion joints. The result was described by Ray Monti: "One of the first cuts gave an experienced PATH engineer a shock. As he brought his train into Manhattan, he saw a swath of sunlight bathing the track—something he hadn't seen in all his 20 years of driving. He slammed on the brakes, fearing the tunnel had cracked, but no one was hurt."[35]

Shortly thereafter, a metal strip was placed around the joints to allow the trains to roll along through the same gloom along the elevated stretch that prevails elsewhere. Eventually, new tracks were laid into a new and bigger PATH terminal west of Greenwich Street. Many passengers were unaware of all the work going on around them until the new station was opened on July 4, 1970.[36]

Not to belittle the importance of preparing the foundations for the World Trade Center, there were, as mentioned earlier, two other important technological innovations. Each was a response to a particular problem: the elevators and the structural system. Let us first turn to elevators (fig. 2.4). It was the development of elevators in the first place that led to the construction of skyscrapers. Elevators enabled architects to design taller and taller buildings because no one had to climb stairs to get to upper floors. But there was a big problem. The higher you go, the more people in the building. The more people in the building, the more elevators you need. The more

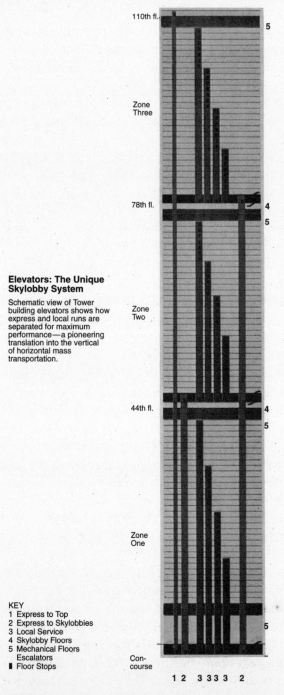

Elevators: The Unique Skylobby System

Schematic view of Tower building elevators shows how express and local runs are separated for maximum performance—a pioneering translation into the vertical of horizontal mass transportation.

110th fl.

Zone Three

78th fl.

Zone Two

44th fl.

Zone One

KEY
1 Express to Top
2 Express to Skylobbies
3 Local Service
4 Skylobby Floors
5 Mechanical Floors
  Escalators
▮ Floor Stops

Con-
course

1 2   3 3 3 3   2

Figure 2.4. Elevators: The Unique Skylobby System

elevators you have, the less floor space you have to rent. The problem was so serious that it was seen as the limiting factor, the real reason why skyscrapers seldom exceeded eighty stories.

During the planning stage, Herb Tessler, one of the staff architects, assigned Jerry Ford, a bright young architect, to search for alternate solutions. Ford spent many weeks researching and designing and reviewing with Carl Kort, an elevator consultant from the office of Jaros Baum & Bolles, and with Otis and Westinghouse. They finally came up with an idea that solved the elevator problem. Tessler discussed the idea with Malcolm Levy, who was in charge of overall planning. Levy liked the idea and told Tessler to take it to Guy Tozzoli's office.

Tessler said, "Listen, we have an idea."

Tozzoli said, "What's the idea?"

"We could design an elevator system like a subway system."

"What does that mean?"

"Well, when you take the Eighth Avenue you go from 125th Street down to 59th Street. Then you get off, cross the platform, and go to 50th Street."

"Yeah, so what's that mean?"

"We could divide each tower building into three parts, or zones. For express elevators from the lobby, we will construct the biggest elevators in the world each carrying fifty-five passengers. Then we will stick the three local parts on top of one another. Each zone will have its own lobby. People will transfer from express to local in the second and third zones by crossing the lobby. Therefore, all the locals will sit on top of one another within a single shaft, and it will solve the problem of usable space."

"You might have a good idea, I don't know. But the first thing I want you to do is to go to Otis and Westinghouse and put it on a computer."

Sometime later, Herb Tessler came back and said that Otis could build elevators where the first person in was the first one out. Elevators, with the largest and fastest cars ever built, could be designed with doors on both the front and back of the car. People could get on through the front door at the lobby level, and get off through the rear door when they reached the desired floor. It was an attractive idea, a new thing. The good news was that the computers said the building would be over-elevatored. When Tessler delivered his report to the boss, Tozzoli said, "There's nothing better for a building than to have more elevators than you need because people hate to wait."

About that same time, Austin Tobin became concerned about all the tricky design problems that were being encountered. Tobin called Tozzoli into his office and said, "Look, Guy, I have great faith in you, but you never built a high-rise building before. I'm going to give you an advisory committee of seven real estate people and bankers. You will meet with them once a month and bring them up to date. They'll give advice to me and to you."

When the idea for the elevatoring system came in, Tozzoli called a meeting of the advisory committee. The seven advisers listened patiently to the architect's explanation of the proposed elevatoring system, but they were not convinced. They voted seven to nothing that no one would rent space in the two zones above because people would have to transfer at either the forty-fourth floor for zone two or the seventy-eighth floor for zone three. Tozzoli's staff was horrified. What was Tozzoli going to tell Austin Tobin?

Tozzoli said, "They're wrong."

Levy said, "What if they're right?"

Tozzoli said, "We'll have an empty tower."

Going up to see Austin Tobin was not a pleasant prospect, but it had to be done. Tozzoli said, "Austin, I have to tell you, your committee voted seven to nothing against our elevatoring concept. But the computer says we're over-elevatored. It's a good system because people won't have to wait. It's actually much faster than the regular arrangement. People can get out in less than two minutes. Austin, we have to take the chance."

Tobin thought a minute and said, "Guy, if the computer says so and you say so, that's what we will do."[37]

With Tobin's agreement, plans could proceed and the details could be worked out. Plans were developed for huge express cars with a 10,000-pound capacity capable of carrying fifty-five people at one time at a climbing speed of 1,600 feet a minute. Passengers were to enter one side of the car and leave through the opposite side—first on, first off. To achieve the maximum service for passengers and tenants, each tower was given twenty-three express elevators, seventy-two locals, and nine freight cars. The freight elevators serve 116 floors—including six basement floors—making them by far the highest-rise elevators ever installed up to that point. Since passengers do not feel speed, but rather change, acceleration of the cars was designed so that riders would not notice sensations greater than those in a normal elevator. Local elevators would operate at conventional speeds of 800 to 1,200 feet per minute, or nine to fourteen miles per hour. So for example, a passenger could go from the ground-floor lobby on a local to the fortieth floor in about twenty-five seconds. The new concept in vertical transportation, called the skylobby system, meant that the Center's twin towers would have 75 percent of usable space per floor rather than just 62 percent, the best yielded in previous tall skyscraper designs.[38]

The elevator contract went to the Otis Elevator Company, which was to install all the elevators discussed above plus forty-nine heavy-duty, high-speed escalators for $35 million. The fabricating work for the elevators was done in Harrison, New Jersey, and Yonkers, New York. To prevent passengers from being trapped because of power failures, an emergency generator system was installed in the basement. (This system worked quite well until terrorists placed a bomb in the basement in February 1993.) Besides installing the elevators, Otis was given a five-year maintenance contract for $665,000 a year after the first year, during which Otis was required to maintain the elevator system without cost.[39]

The third important technological innovation employed in the construction of the World Trade Center was the structural system (fig. 2.5). The system was entirely new and different from other conventional high-rise buildings. Ever since the nineteenth century, the usual skyscraper had been built with a network of interior supporting columns. This was the skeleton that supported the structure. The exterior walls were just "curtain walls" that admitted light and kept out the rain. But in the World Trade Center buildings, the exterior walls carry the vertical loads as well as resisting all lateral winds. Structurally, the two towers could be said to resemble two stalks of celery rather than something one might make from a child's erector set. This neat trick was accomplished by the use of

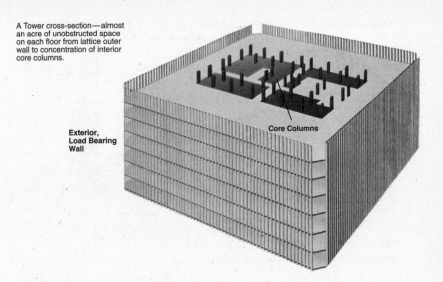

A Tower cross-section—almost an acre of unobstructed space on each floor from lattice outer wall to concentration of interior core columns.

Exterior, Load Bearing Wall

Core Columns

Figure 2.5. The Wall and the Core

high-strength steels, which had not been available before. It cost a little more, but Guy Tozzoli felt that it was worth the cost. High-strength steels were more expensive, but the additional cost was infinitesimal when spread out over the long life of the towers. Credit for this innovation went to consulting engineers John Skilling and Leslie Robertson of Seattle.[40]

Of course, Skilling and Robertson had to be absolutely sure that their innovative design would work. Structural stability for the towers was not a goal, it was a *requirement*. In 1984, novelist Robert Byrne wrote a book that told the story of a New York skyscraper toppled by a high wind. In the novel, the building was 700 feet high, crowned with a yellow metallic pyramid. It was built on the site of the old Madison Square Garden. One night, a rare but plausible storm hit New York. In the tremendous winds which ensued, the building was blown over. Of course, that was just a work of fiction, but it does underscore everyone's concern about skyscraper stability.[41]

Most of the steel was placed on the outside of the box instead of inside. These tough exterior walls (fig. 2.6) had the strength to resist the enormous force of lateral winds. The only interior columns were in the core that housed the elevators. The beauty of this

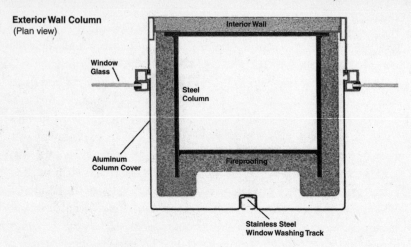

Figure 2.6. Exterior Wall Column

arrangement was that it yielded a maximum of open, usable, and rentable column-free floor space. The trick in getting the outer wall to carry vertical loads came in closely spacing the vertical columns. The columns were placed three feet, nine inches apart. They serve as dramatic frames for the floor-to-ceiling windows which are only twenty-two inches wide. Such narrow windows give a feeling of complete security, even for most people with a fear of heights. In addition, the narrow windows partially shielded by the outer ribs reduce the heating and cooling loads.[42]

One of the fascinating aspects of designing the structure of the twin towers was to conduct tests on human subjects to see just how much sway they would accept. Engineers were confident that their towers were strong and flexible. But what about people? It is possible to obtain almost any desired degree of stiffness for a building at the design stage, but very difficult to change the movement of a building after it has been completed. It was known, for example, that in a 100 mph wind, the Empire State Building, at 1,432 feet high, would sway three inches. What the structural engineers for the World Trade Center wanted to find out was just how much movement would be tolerated.[43]

The Seattle firm of consulting engineers actually built two swaying rooms to test people's reactions. It was found that many people were reluctant to believe that a room could move at all. One man had to brace himself in a corner to avoid falling down, yet he still refused to accept the idea that the room was moving. The consultants lured unsuspecting subjects in Eugene, Oregon, to an optometrist's office for "free eye exams" in a building that had once housed a car dealership. Once there, the subjects walked through the dealership into a trailer out back which was set up on springs to sway at various rates of acceleration. A similar experiment was conducted back in New York. An office, dangling from a cable, was set up inside an airshaft of the Lincoln Tunnel. It was then pushed back and forth to see how people would react.[44] From the results of both tests, it was determined that people at the trade center would accept up to eleven inches of slow or "damped" sway. In other words, they could keep working even if the outside winds reached 140 miles per hour.[45] Psychologists asked to estimate how much sway office workers in skyscrapers could get used to said, "People will get used to almost anything."[46]

Wind was not only a consideration in allowing for sway, it was an important factor in selecting the glass for the twin towers. Powerful gusts can shatter windows, so for the sake of safety tempered glass eight times stronger than needed was specified. Planners designed the towers to withstand prolonged winds of 150 miles per hour, a severe condition that New York has never experienced. That kind of wind would give each tower a thirteen-million-pound push—the equivalent of being smashed by a large ocean freighter. Planners spent hours doing mathematical stress calculations of all kinds, but they confirmed their work by constructing an exact model which was subjected to costly, but necessary, wind tunnel tests.[47]

In addition to worrying about the effects of the wind on the structural integrity of the towers, architects and engineers also took some pity on the hapless pedestrian buffeted by the wind. Critics say they could have done more about the problem, but at least they took it into account. It is a fact that winds deflected by buildings can reach speeds of two or three times what they would achieve in an open space. Wind speeds of thirty-five miles per hour or more at ground level are often found in urban areas. Not only are they unpleasant, they are dangerous as well. Such winds create an environment where it is difficult to get about.

The World Trade Center was placed on a site that ranks among the windiest in New York City. It was one of the first large-scale projects where the impact of the wind on pedestrian comfort was taken into account through aerodynamic analysis. The fundamental question: How close could the two towers be placed to each other? The answer is that they could not have been placed any closer than they are without creating an intolerable "slot" effect that would have created a major acceleration of wind speed, and possibly a catastrophic "tuning fork" effect, that is, sympathetic vibration between the towers.[48]

Before construction could begin, the Port Authority had to find contractors to supply the hundreds of thousands of tons of steel needed for the job. It was a big problem because of the sheer size of the order. Such a large amount could not be supplied by any single steel manufacturer. The contract *drawings* for the steel weighed a staggering 650 pounds. Even fulfilling a portion of such a large order might tie up a given fabricator's entire annual output. Initial negotiations had begun back in 1962. From the beginning, Austin Tobin and Guy Tozzoli had focused their discussions with the two largest domestic companies, U.S. Steel and Bethlehem Steel. Tobin authorized his staff to work with the two prospective contractors to share with them full design details and erection techniques. It made sense at the time to take a large contract to a couple of giant companies who seemed to have all the answers. Besides, it was more comfortable and convenient to deal with the big boys. Along the way, the two big companies supplied "estimates for budget purposes" that seemed reasonable. Although these quotes were merely estimates, the two companies seemed ready to make a deal based on them.

As Tobin explained to his board of commissioners, "The usual bidding procedure would be inappropriate for this work because of the work's complexity and the necessity of continuing interchange of information between the prospective contractors and the Port Authority."[49] It turned out that Tobin was dead wrong. His trust in forming a close liaison with the two big steel companies was misplaced. This crucial error, at an early stage, placed the entire project into serious financial jeopardy.

It was Wednesday, August 17, 1966, that the final proposals

for the manufacture and erection of structural steel for the World Trade Center's towers were to be received from Bethlehem Steel and U.S. Steel. When he opened the envelopes, Austin Tobin got the shock of his life: he had been betrayed. Despite working closely with the two giant companies throughout the entire design process to find ways for the buyer to help the sellers keep the cost low, *the bids came in at a full 50 percent higher than expected.*[50]

In a cold fury, Austin Tobin decided to cut out the greedy big boys from the process entirely. His staff, together with their consultant, Tishman Realty and Construction Company, developed a plan to divide the job into several "packages," each of which was an appropriate division of steel required for the job. In other words, instead of trying to buy 185,000 tons of steel from a single fabricator, they set out to buy it in fifteen smaller packages from fifteen different companies.[51] Administratively, of course, this required more work on the part of the Port Authority, but for Austin Tobin it was worth it so he could show his scorn and contempt for big steel.

The project team, fired with the feeling that the Port Authority was invincible, took up this new challenge with alacrity. With a zealous loyalty to Tobin, they flew around the country meeting with dozens of potential suppliers to figure out how to get the steel within budget and on time. They were racing the clock. They took steel where they could get it—exterior columns came from Seattle, Washington; beams, from Alabama; trusses, from Texas; columns, from Pittsburgh; floor assemblies, from Carteret, New Jersey; and so on. Steel came to the staging area by truck and by barge.[52]

The payoff for backing away from the burdensome deal offered by the two steel giants came to well over $30 million. The savings lent fresh meaning to the old saying, "Sometimes the best deal is the one that doesn't come off." U.S. Steel had submitted a bid for $122.2 million, and Bethlehem asked for $118.1 million. After the deal was broken up into fifteen smaller packages, the total under separate contracts came to $85.4 million. That was a stunning $36.8 million less than U.S. Steel's bid and $32.7 million under Bethlehem's. One result was that the Justice Department's Antitrust Division conducted an investigation, though no conclusive evidence of wrongdoing was ever found. Another result was that the tactic of breaking a huge job down into small segments began to gain acceptance as a way of doing business in heavy construction. "This knocks out the tradition of giving all the big jobs to U.S. Steel or Bethlehem," said one contractor with glee.[53]

With the assurance that enough steel would be available, the contractors could turn their attention to putting in the foundations at the bottom of the bathtub. They had to start blasting a series of pits into the rock. The rock was cut away. Later these pits would be filled with concrete to form "footings" to support the steel for the towers. The concrete was reinforced with steel bars and capped with grillages, thick steel frameworks, on which the core columns rest.[54]

Of all the stages in construction, blasting the rock for the foundations was the most irritating to the trade center's neighbors. Among them was a nearby church. One day the priest came in to see Ray Monti and said that it was impossible for him to prepare his homilies or to conduct services because of the constant noise. The priest asked if anything could be done about the noise.

Monti said, "We can't do anything about it, Father. What is it you want?"

The priest said, "Well, it would be nice if you were able to air-condition my church. Then I could conduct services and not have to hear the noise." Monti knew that the project already had plenty of opponents. There was no point in drawing down the wrath of the church. Monti agreed to air-condition the church.

The priest continued, "But I have to prepare my homilies in the rectory, so why don't you air-condition the rectory, too?" Monti agreed to that also.

Before the negotiations were completed, Monti had a favor to ask of the priest. Monti said, "There's nothing in life that's free, you know, Father. I would like something in return. I want you to become the chaplain of our safety program." The priest agreed, and construction of the World Trade Center continued with the blessing of the church.[55]

It should be mentioned in passing that despite an aggressive safety program, eight men died building the World Trade Center. None were iron workers. Officially, the Port Authority says that the toll was low, which makes sense in view of the fact that there were as many as 3,600 workers on the site during peak periods of construction.[56] Unofficially, people in the construction business say that a contributing factor in many building site accidents is alcohol. It is not unusual for someone in a group of workers to go out for beer during the break for lunch. It's easy to see that someone who has had a few beers is more prone to drop a wrench, miss a step on a ladder, or fail to notice a hole in the floor. In fact, most fatal accidents involve falling down elevator shafts. Before the core of a building is walled up, elevator shafts are just big holes that go all the way to the bottom.[57]

3
Erecting the Towers

It's One Story after Another

Today, you are looking down on construction activity.

Tomorrow millions will look up to a new landmark.

—JAMES C. KELLOGG III, CHAIRMAN OF THE PORT AUTHORITY, 1968

ONCE THE foundations were in place, the next task was getting the steel that needed to be erected to the site. The steel could not be delivered in lower Manhattan as it was produced. There was no place to put it. From the various manufacturing sites, steel was delivered to a yard in New Jersey where it could be tagged and held. At the precise time it was needed, it could be delivered to the site itself. Doing this required the synchronization of people, trains, trucks, barges, and cranes.

When pressed to describe the process of "just in time" steel delivery, construction manager Ray Monti resorted to the imagery of naval warfare. Monti said, "The outside columns come from Seattle, inside ones from Los Angeles and the connecting trusses from St. Louis. Now they've all got to be brought here and they've got to fit together. The way we've taken care of the problem is pretty much the way you would establish a marshaling area for an invasion."[1]

Monti went on to explain that the steel pieces, some weighing as much as fifty-two tons, were sent from the foundries to a Penn Central yard just across the Hudson River in Jersey City. The materials were logged in and kept ready, neatly placed in rows covering more than ten city blocks. In general the pieces, unlike those in a child's erector set, were not interchangeable. When a particular piece was called for, it would be located by code number. Smaller pieces could be trucked over to the site in flatbeds through the Holland Tunnel in the predawn, traffic-free hours. But the larger pieces had to be shipped across the river in large barges pulled by tugboats.[2]

The person, under Ray Monti's direction, responsible for the shipment of materials to the site was William C. Borland. "The worst problem is trying to put up a building complex this size in one of the most congested parts of the city. If you were doing this in the Sahara Desert, you could set up 500 acres nearby for an assembly and storage area," said Borland.

Instead of the Sahara Desert, Borland had one hundred acres of railroad yard in Greenville, New Jersey, ten miles from the construction site. In the yard were columns of steel stacked up like firewood along tracks and on flat cars in parallel rows. Each piece of steel was stenciled in white or yellow with information telling where it came from and where it was going. For example, a given piece might be marked, "PONYA WTC 213.00 236B 4-9 558 35 TONS." Translated, this meant the column was destined for the Port of New York Authority's World Trade Center as part of contract number 213.00. Its actual number was 236B, and it was to be used between floors four and nine. The derrick division number was 558, which determined which crane would lift it onto the building and the order in which it was to be erected.

"Up to thirty truckloads of steel a day go from here to the site," said Borland, "and we're planning to work that up to fifty truckloads, with an average of eighteen tons a truck. We're also trying to hold deliveries at the site to within a half-hour of their scheduled time. Traffic delays, flat tires, and things like that naturally hurt us, but with it all, we're putting up an average of six-hundred tons a day and that will jump to eight-hundred."[3]

The process went smoothly until the "steel pipeline" was interrupted by a tugboat strike. Some of the critical pieces were huge. For example, the floor elements came in sections that were sixty feet long and twenty feet wide. Without tugboats there was no apparent way to get such elements across the river. Before long, work on the Twin Towers ground down to a halt. Ray Monti was annoyed with the strikers, frustrated with the lack of progress, and angry at the world. In any large job that involves working with other people, frictions are inevitable. The relationship between Monti, the former U.S. Navy man, and his boss, Malcolm Levy, the old "get-it-done" merchant mariner, was a stormy one even when things were going well. And now, with the tugboat strike in its sixth week, things were not going well.

Malcolm Levy in the main office called Ray Monti at the site and said, "Hey, Ray, what are you doing? The whole construction is stopped. You've got everything screwed up!"

As the man on the spot, Monti was responsible for the smooth running of the operation. He replied, "Yeah, Malcolm, what the hell do you want me to do? I've got no steel!"

Levy said, "I don't care what you do, Ray. You're in charge of construction, so why don't you do something?"

Monti said in consternation, "Malcolm, what do you want me to do? Fly it?"

Levy coldly said, "I don't care what you do, you'd better get the job going."

Ray Monti put the phone down in disgust. The steel was of such size that there was no legal route that anyone knew of over the bridges. Truckers simply could not get through with those widths. The only way was by barge. Monti was stuck, but his whole Port Authority training had taught him that every problem has a solution. A few minutes later, he knew what to do. He picked up the phone and called the manager of the Sikorsky division of United Aircraft in Stratford, Connecticut.

Monti asked, "You got a skycrane?"

The manager said, "Yeah, sure."

Monti said, "What can it lift?"

"Ten tons."

"Where is it?"

"St. Louis. I'll ship it for you."

"Wait a minute. I'm going to put you on hold." Ray Monti picked up the other phone on his desk and called Malcolm Levy back.

Monti said, "You told me to do something, right? So I'm going to fly the steel by skycrane."

Levy screamed, "You're crazy! We don't have authority to do that."

Monti calmly replied, "Too bad, Malcolm. You told me to get the job going, so I dispatched the skycrane." Monti got back to Sikorsky and told them to ship the S-64 skycrane helicopter, the largest crane-type copter in the West.

A few days later, the skycrane arrived. It looked like a monster down on the pier at the World Trade Center site. Nothing quite like this had been attempted before. They agreed to try the skycrane on a Saturday morning when there would not be too much traffic. Monti was at the site in radio contact with the helicopter pilots over in Carteret, New Jersey, where the Karl Koch Erecting Company's assembly yard was located. So the helicopter took off with its load of a single undecked floor panel, flying over the Kill van Kull. Time went by. Finally, Ray Monti on the ground with his radio saw the giant helicopter coming over the water by the Statue of Liberty, but he could not see any steel. Over the radio, Monti asked, "What happened? Where's the steel?"

The senior pilot, Lee Ramage, crackled back, "I'll talk to you when we land. We pickled it."

Once the helicopter landed at the pier, Monti again asked, "What happened, fellas?"

Ramage explained, "The load started to swing on us. We couldn't control it. We had to let it go, but don't worry. Nobody saw us."

Within ten minutes, there were launches and police cars swarming all over the site. Telephones were ringing off the hook with reports from people who had seen the thing fall. The senior police lieutenant came up to Ray Monti and asked, "Do you know what's going on?"

Monti said, "Not me."

The lieutenant said, "Who's in charge of this job?"

Monti said, "Not me. It's Malcolm Levy."

Over the next few days several more attempts were made, but the Port Authority was never successful at flying the steel. The newspapers reported the failed attempts. On Tuesday morning Monti received a call from an obscure trucking company which offered to truck the steel. Monti told the trucker on the phone that the biggest trucking companies in the region had all declared the task impossible. They simply could not find a suitable route.

The trucker said, "Look, my friend. You want to try me out? You pay me so much a load. Don't ask any questions about what I do or where I go. I'll deliver the steel, okay?"

At a moment like this, a knowledge of textbook management procedures was worthless. What was needed was street smarts coupled with iron nerves. Monti said, "You've got it—on a trial."[4]

The trucker was paid in a lump sum for each load. Monti

never asked what he did, but steel did start to arrive at the site. In my subsequent research I learned that the trucker had transported the panels by convoy from Carteret to the Goethals Bridge, across Staten Island and over the Verrazano Narrows Bridge, north along the Brooklyn-Queens Expressway, across Manhattan Bridge and through a maze of lower Manhattan streets. This, of course, was done at night and with the "cooperation" of all involved police departments. Ten panels were brought over each night in five trucks— enough to keep the construction schedule on target.[5]

In a short time, the tugboat strike was over and everyone went back to work, forgetting about the seven-ton floor panel, dropped by the helicopter, which still lies at the bottom of the Kill van Kull between the Bayonne shoreline and the foot of Clove Road to this very day. Port Authority police say that it presents no obstruction to navigation.[6]

With regard to the whole problem of delivering steel to the project, one more key point must be discussed. The steel was not really "delivered" until it reached the floor of the skyscraper where it was needed. Contractors erecting tall buildings usually used derricks, mounted to the building itself, to lift steel and other heavy pieces to high places with ease. But with very high buildings, problems arose because the derrick had to be constantly lifted to a higher position, one floor at a time. Not to mention the problem of providing the derrick with a strong base from which to work. Each attempt to move a derrick up one floor normally took a day and a half or more. Then there was another problem. Power for these derricks was normally supplied from the ground and supplied aloft by long cables running down through the floors already built.

Contractors could also use towering, crawling cranes located out on the street, but these had their own problems. First, there was the safety problem. From time to time, crawling cranes had toppled over, causing property damage and injury. Second, there were regulatory problems. The city, concerned about safety, had all kinds of inspections, regulations, and red tape pertaining to the use of street cranes. Third, street cranes were normally limited to working on buildings less than their own height.

What was needed was a crane that could carry its own power aloft and could be equipped with hydraulics to raise itself atop the building as it went along. It would also have to be irrefutably safe. Such an ideal crane was found in Australia, manufactured by Favelle Mort, Limited, of New South Wales. It was officially called a Favco Standard 2700 Crane, but because of its Australian origins it was quickly nicknamed the "kangaroo crane" (fig. 3.1). At first glance, it looked rather ordinary. It had a 110-foot boom painted red and white for aircraft safety, a red cab, and a counterweight at the rear. Less ordinary was its mounting. It sat atop a thin steel structure, 12 feet by 12 feet, which was 120 feet high. The lower 80 feet of this tower fitted into the elevator core "like a sword in a sheath," according to Austin Tobin. There were four of these kangaroo cranes, one at each corner of the elevator core.

The cranes were able to lift the structural steel and the exterior wall sections. When the steel for three floors was lifted and placed, the cranes could lift *themselves* for the next three floors. The crane's diesel motors supplied the power, driving a series of hydraulic lifts installed at the base of each crane which lifted the entire crane "like a grease rack in a gas station." Moving in twelve-foot heaves or "jumps," the cranes literally lifted themselves to the next position upward in about two hours.

The lifting capacity of each crane varied, of course, with the reach of the boom. The crane could lift as much as fifty tons when extended to sixty feet. For lifts outward to 100 feet, capacity would be reduced to twenty-five tons. Fortunately, as the steel went upward, the sections, though the same dimension, became thinner and lighter. The lightest steel was at the very top of the tower. At such heights, steel lifted into place had a long way to travel. Guy wires held sections as they rose so that there was no sway in the wind. The very light floor sections, without guy wires, would have been very susceptible to being blown about by the wind. Because of the great heights, regular hand signals to the operator were impossible. Instead, telephones were used to connect the crane operator with the ground supervisor and with the workers on the floor under construction.[7]

The crane operator in the cab had five controls to operate. They were to slew the crane (rotate it on its tower one way or the other), luff (raise or lower the boom), or lift. Meanwhile, the four eleven-ton counterweights at the rear were automatically in perfect

Figure 3.1. The Kangaroo Cranes

coordination with the boom's movements. The h₂
frightening part for the crew each day was getting t
on the ladders and catwalks inside the crane stru₍

"I'm a little embarrassed by these kangaro
rassed for the American construction industry,' ₃₂₋₋
"You'd think that with all our know-how, we could have designᵤ
a piece of equipment as ingenious as they are. But no. The Aussies
were the ones."[9]

Most people have heard stories that many of the ironworkers
on skyscrapers are Native Americans. Such stories are plausible,
but are they true accounts or just contemporary folklore? In this
case the stories are not only engrossing, they also happen to be true.
Some of the earliest newspaper accounts of the construction of
the World Trade Center confirm that Mohawks were among these
skilled ironworkers. In October 1968, reporter John Metcalfe, using language that would make an anthropologist cringe, wrote: "A
force of 45 of these sure-footed, cool-headed specialists is now employed. Among them are 12 Mohawk Indians, members of that tribe
which jet-propelled itself from the stone age into the skyscraper era
by learning to handle hot rivets and cold steel. 'This gang spends
the week in Brooklyn,' said Monti, somewhat awed by the inscrut-
able ways of the Red Men, 'and every weekend they commute all
the way up to their homes in Canada.' "[10]

Perhaps Metcalfe can be forgiven for falling back on clichés in
his attempts to describe the Mohawks. In the first place, the Indians were known to be not very talkative with outsiders. In addition,
there was very little published research on this group, with the notable exception of Joseph Mitchell's splendid 1949 essay, "The Mohawks in High Steel." There Mitchell described them: "They have
high cheekbones and jut noses, their eyes are sad, shrewd and dark
brown, their hair is straight and coal black, their skin is smooth and
coppery, and they have the same beautiful, chin-lifted, haughty walk
that gypsies have."[11]

According to Mitchell, the Indians got involved with high steel
back in 1886 when they were hired as day laborers on a bridge being built across the Saint Lawrence River near their home, the Kah-
nawake reservation (also known as the Caughanwaga reservation).
In obtaining the right to use reservation land in building the bridge,

the Dominion Bridge Company had promised the Indians to use them on the job wherever possible. The company had intended to employ them as ordinary workers unloading materials, but the Indians were unhappy with that arrangement. They kept coming out on the bridge at every opportunity. In a letter to Mitchell, a company official explained:

> As the work progressed, it became apparent to all concerned that the Indians were very odd in that they did not have any fear of heights. If not watched, they would climb up into the spans and walk around up there as cool and collected as the toughest of our riveters, most of whom were at that period were old sailing ship men especially picked for their experience in working aloft. These Indians were as agile as goats. They would walk a narrow beam up in the air with nothing below them but the river. . . . They were inquisitive about the riveting and were continually bothering our foremen by requesting that they be allowed to take a crack at it. This happens to be the most dangerous work in all construction, and the highest paid. Men who want to do it are rare and men who can do it even rarer, and in good construction years there are sometimes not enough of them to go around. We decided that it would be mutually advantageous to see what these Indians could do, so we picked out some and gave them a little training, and it turned out that putting riveting tools in their hands was like putting ham with eggs.[12]

It's an amazing story because we are left to wonder what in the Mohawks' background would give them this extraordinary ability. In any event, they were soon working every high steel bridge and skyscraper job in Canada. Later, they started going all over North America, including, of course, New York and New Jersey.

While the problems connected with steel delivery were exciting moments in the construction of the World Trade Center, other problems were more mundane. During the period of construction, the various street and sidewalk closings contributed to the problem of overcrowding in the lower Manhattan area. There were days when motionless, bumper-to-bumper traffic clogged the narrow streets. Workers in the financial district were already used to congestion, but conditions during the construction became even worse.

On their way to work people had to breathe exhaust fumes from trucks and taxis and suffer the noise of heavy machinery. Just to pick up a cup of coffee required a wait in line. At lunchtime, people could hardly budge on the jammed sidewalks. Those who made their way to restaurants had to wait as long as half an hour to be seated. Even at expensive places, the patrons found themselves rushed by harried waiters. A reporter from the *Wall Street Journal* documented numerous anecdotes from various businesspeople illustrating the problem. For example, H. DuBois Plummer, a paperback bookstore on Broad Street, displayed a sign reading: "Please—no browsing from 12 to 2." The reporter asked why. "This ain't no public library," snapped the gray-haired saleswoman. And a gruff waiter at Eberlin's Restaurant not far from the New York Stock Exchange said, "I'll give you a martini and lunch and have you out of here in twelve minutes flat."[13]

For the people already working in the financial district, the construction of the World Trade Center was mostly an additional irritant. But for others, the construction was a magnet, attracting the curious. How could the Port Authority accommodate visiting dignitaries, engineers, and reporters who wanted to see what was going on? In small numbers, they could be taken directly to the site, but this procedure was not ideal. Looking at a sixteen-acre construction site from the ground was a bit like watching a Broadway play from the center of the stage. It was difficult for the viewer to see how the apparently random variety of activities contributed to the whole project.

So the Port Authority acquired the seventeenth floor of 117 Liberty Street, which provided an overview of the 7,500 workers, representing dozens of contractors, performing numerous separate tasks. Dubbed the "Visitors' Reception Area," the largest part was equipped with seventy-five folding chairs for presentations to engineering students and other groups. The room had a model of the World Trade Center, pictures of construction progress, and a rack for informational literature. Other rooms were equipped with typewriters and telephones for the public affairs department and visiting journalists. A viewing room with big windows was useful for newspaper photographers and television camera crews.[14]

From this vantage point, visitors could see yellow bulldozers, red cranes, green trucks, and pale blue drilling and excavation rigs. It was possible to watch steel lowered by crane off a barge in the Hudson River. It was possible to see the landfill project take shape. Visitors could watch demolition of old buildings and preparations for the construction of the towers. Ray Monti could give television interviews with a dramatic backdrop for the evening news.[15]

While the Port Authority provided the Visitors' Reception Area for important visitors and the press, they also operated two large information booths for the public at either end of the construction site in the summer months. From a ten-foot-high platform, visitors could view construction activity "safely and conveniently." Photogenic young women were appointed as construction guides. Outfitted in stylish uniforms, they were able to answer questions on the center's purposes and functions as well as its unique architectural and construction techniques.

The guides mastered the routine talk of construction workers. They spoke knowledgeably about bull's liver, goosenecks, clam shells, and orange peels. When they spoke of bull's liver, they referred to the red sand common to the financial district's substrate. A gooseneck referred to the gangling boom and arm arrangement of a hoisting crane. A clam shell is an excavator's tool that resembles a shell fisherman's hinged rake; it is used for tight digging jobs. Another bucketlike excavating machine used for digging rocks has four interlocking prongs on its edges; a long time ago, it reminded someone of orange peels, so the name stuck.[16]

Of course, some visitors were so important that they could be served by neither the information booths nor the reception area. Ray Monti recalled organizing a number of V.I.P. tours for visiting dignitaries while serving as construction manager. None was more memorable than one organized for Austin Tobin and Robert Moses. Their party arrived in a caravan of three Cadillac limousines. As they pulled up to the gate, they saw a big sign that warned, "TRUCKS ONLY." A uniformed security guard was at the gate. Monti, riding in the front passenger seat of the first Cadillac, got out to explain things to the security guard.

"Hello. Good morning. I'm Ray Monti and I'm the construction manager. Could you please let us in?"

"I'm sorry, sir, but cars are not allowed in. Only trucks."

"But I'm the one that made the rule."

"That may be, but how am I supposed to know?"

"My God, I've got a number of really important people here. There's Austin Tobin, director of the Port Authority, and Robert Moses, director of the Triborough Bridge and Tunnel Authority. I can't keep them waiting."

"Look, mister, I'm a security guard. I make two dollars and twenty cents an hour. I never heard of Austin Tobin, and the only Moses I know of is dead. Besides, you're not a fucking truck and you're not getting in here."

Quite embarrassed, Monti returned to explain that they would have to go around, on foot, to another entrance. Robert Moses laughed the whole thing off, saying that Monti should give the guard a letter of commendation.[17]

Bad as the Moses visit was, it was not the most embarrassing incident that befell the project. Perhaps the worst thing that happened was the collapse of nearby Liberty Street in April 1968. On a stretch between Washington and Greenwich Streets, it just caved in after too much drilling and jabbing at its underpinnings. Some of the owners of small businesses were just resigned to the problem, but others were furious.

Henry Trefflich, owner of a pet shop at 144 Liberty Street, told a reporter, "I've lost some 300 birds, snakes, monkeys, and puppies worth $22,000 because of all the drilling they've been doing out there. The noise goes to the animals' heads, they fall into convulsions and knock their heads against the cages. Ten of my pregnant rhesus monkeys aborted and died this weekend—I've got them in the freezer to prove it. And what's the Port Authority going to do about it? Nothing! I'm going to commit hara-kiri!" Actually, Trefflich did not kill himself, Japanese style. Instead, he came up with an American remedy: he filed suit for damages against the Port Authority.[18]

We have already discussed the problems that the Port Authority had in acquiring steel. Originally, U.S. Steel and Bethlehem Steel had been asked to supply bids, but their prices were so excessive that the Port Authority refused to consider them. In time, steel was acquired from smaller suppliers. But, once acquired, the steel had to be assembled. For erecting all of the 192,000 tons of steel that was required, a competent contractor had to be recruited. From the point of view of the Port Authority, it was desirable to have a single, reputable contractor do the whole job. After long negotiations, Karl Koch Erecting Company, Incorporated, of the Bronx, was awarded the contract for $20 million in January 1967. The company also received a $2.5 million contract for assembly and delivery of floor panels. From the point of view of Karl Koch, this was a good contract because it brought in an enormous amount of work and a substantial amount of money. But there was a downside to this lump-sum deal in that financial success depended on accurate estimation of costs, always tricky in construction work. Nonetheless, Karl Koch signed on the dotted line.[19]

Twenty months later, the Karl Koch Erecting Company began its actual work by placing the first steel grillage (fig. 3.2) on the southwest corner of the North Tower at 10 A.M. on Wednesday, August 6, 1968. It was a significant step. A grillage is a framework of crossing steel beams that is used to spread heavy loads over large areas. A gang of workers guided the grillage, a key component in skyscraper construction, gently and precisely onto the concrete slab or footing seventy feet below street level. Thus, this step represented the transition from foundation work to erection work, which Ray Monti has called "the most exciting and visually rewarding phase." The thirty-four-ton steel grillage was a bulky fifteen feet long, eleven feet wide, and seven feet high. It was the first of twenty-eight grillages that supported the columns of the elevator core of the North Tower.

In addition to the grillages, the contractor began to place steel base plates along the exterior walls of the tower. The base plates, less massive than the grillages, ranging from seven to nine square feet, sat on concrete footings and were used to distribute the weight of the exterior wall columns. They ranged in weight from four to twelve tons and varied in thickness from six to ten inches.[20]

Steel work continued through the fall of 1968 and through the winter. By spring 1969, steel had been erected in the North Tower in the core to the ninth floor and in the perimeter to the fifth floor. The stage was set for another important step. The architect's design

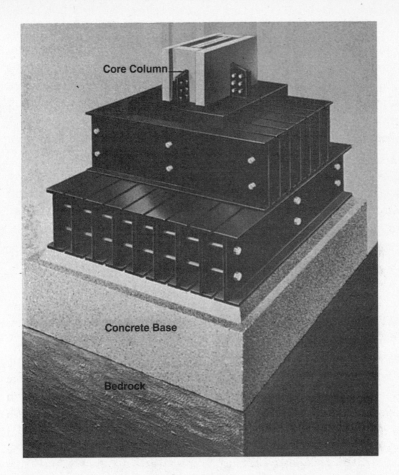

Figure 3.2. Down at the foundation, each core column rises from a grillage, a massive framework of steel beams resting on a concrete base.

had called for widely spaced columns at the plaza level to create a spacious and uplifting interior area for the lobby and mezzanine. But above that space in the office tower, the columns were to be much closer together. The closely spaced columns would provide a look of verticality from the outside and a feeling of greater security from inside. To accomplish this transition from wide columns to narrow columns required special pieces of steel at the junction between the lobby and the tower.

On March 6, 1969, the first of the perimeter column "trees" was put in place. These special columns, fifty-one feet long and weighing fifty tons, were in the shape of a three-pronged tuning fork or "tree." The function of the "trees" was to bring the ten-foot column spacing at the plaza level to a three-foot, four-inch spacing for the remaining portion of the tower. After the trees were bolted up and welded, Koch could continue steel erection for the tower.[21]

As the work continued, costs spiraled upward and Karl Koch began to have financial difficulties. One morning Koch came into Ray Monti's office at the construction site and threw his keys and his wallet onto Monti's desk.

Koch said, "You've got everything else. Now you can have my Cadillac, my twelve kids, my wife, and my house because I have nothing else left, and besides I'm going to kill myself so it really doesn't matter."

Monti replied, "Karl, why don't you let me take you to lunch? Then you can kill yourself this afternoon."

Over lunch they were able to work out the framework of an agreement that the Port Authority would bankroll the firm so that Karl Koch could finish the job. There was no point in sticking to the letter of the contract if the contractor was just going to walk away in despair.[22]

It was just as well that Ray Monti and Karl Koch were able to work out a way of getting along since the contractor had been chosen not only for his price but also for his capacity and integrity, which were known to the Port Authority. By its very nature, steel construction is costly, requiring specialized manpower and dangerous work at great heights. After all, Monti was depending on Koch's assurances that every connection in the framework would carry the load it would receive when the building was up. It is difficult to put a dollar value on that kind of trust.[23]

The history of engineering is full of stories of disasters caused by inattention to the impact of loads and forces on steel connections. One of the most memorable disasters of modern times was the collapse of two walkways in the lobby of the Hyatt Regency Hotel in Kansas City, Missouri, in July 1981, killing 113 people and injuring more than 180, some of them badly maimed for life. After the collapse, several detailed investigations were carried out. But it was difficult to fix the blame since the process of design and construction of the walkways involved the architect, the steel fabricator, the structural engineer, the contractor, and the construction manager. Suffice it to say that the disaster was a reminder to engineers to maintain constant vigilance over every step in assembling a complex structure.[24]

Of course, not only do the engineers try to make the building safe for those who will use it, they also try to make the workplace safe for those who must build it in the first place. As noted earlier, there was a chaplain for the safety program recruited from a nearby church. There was also a Port Authority safety supervisor on the site, Don Herbstman, an engineer with a master's degree in safety from New York University. "There's no reason for people to get killed or hurt on the job," he told a reporter. "If they do, it's because they didn't respect their job, their surroundings, or themselves." Reaching for a yellow hard hat on a nearby shelf, he asked, "See this dent? It was made recently by a one-pound bolt which hit a guy. If he didn't have his hat on, it would have put him in the hospital with a fractured skull." Herbstman nominated the man for the Turtle Club—a national organization of people whose lives have been saved by hard hats.[25]

Despite Herbstman's best efforts and pious pronouncements, some serious accidents did occur that could not be blamed on worker carelessness or lack of respect. For example, Domenico Dellicarpini was a thirty-year-old, $140-a-week laborer, married and the father of four children. While working on the construction of the World Trade Center on May 15, 1969, he plunged thirty feet when some planking gave way. He has been incapacitated ever since, never able to work again: Mr. Dellicarpini had landed on his head, fractured his neck, and injured his spinal cord. He was awarded a settlement of $500,000 by the State Supreme Court in the Bronx in a case against the Port Authority, the Tishman Construction Company, and two subcontractors.[26]

Safety was a constant nagging problem and concern for the World Trade Center project, but let us go back to the matter of steel acquisition. When the Port Authority decided to break off negotiations with Bethlehem and U.S. Steel and farm out orders to a number of relatively small producers throughout the country, the agency had hoped that the matter would come to an end. But rumors began to circulate that the 192,000 tons of structural steel the Port Authority had purchased for the World Trade Center tower buildings was made up largely, if not totally, of steel manufactured in Japan.

A spokesman for an American firm said, "The importation for the World Trade Center of Japanese steel is causing deep anguish and concern with major domestic producers who are losing a fortune and it is costing jobs for thousands of American workers."[27] The story was picked up and circulated in a number of newspapers throughout the country.

Austin Tobin was furious that the story got such widespread circulation and that so few journalists were interested in checking the facts. About 75 percent of the 192,000 tons of steel was fabricated entirely from "raw" steel made in the United States and all of the steel was fabricated in this country. In order to ensure the most reasonable price, the Port Authority did not stipulate to the bidding fabricators any restriction on the use of foreign steel. The fabricators were free to choose whatever sources of supply would result in the best price. So it was true that some of the raw steel was coming from Japan, but the majority of it came from the United States. In his confidential report to the commissioners, Austin Tobin attributed the circulation of the "malicious rumors" to U.S. Steel or Bethlehem, or both.[28]

Later, a Port Authority spokesman explained, "Since the World Trade Center will represent foreign trade, it fits into this category that some of the steel comes from foreign sources. All but two of the successful bidders have told us that they won't use imported steel."[29] The two exceptions were both understandably on the West Coast. One was Pacific Car and Foundry Company of Seattle, which supplied 55,000 tons of high strength, intricately welded structural steel for the exterior wall. The other was the Stanray Pacific Corporation of Los Angeles, which provided steel for the core box-shaped columns and box beam framing.[30]

Regardless of whether the steel was domestic or foreign, it still had to be erected. Little by little the towers began to rise (fig. 3.3). With a project of the enormous scope of the World Trade Center, all kinds of special arrangements had to be made, including planning for the feeding of the workers. As the work proceeded into the peak construction period of 1970 and 1971, provision had to be

Figure 3.3. Raising the Tower Walls

made to supply lunch for the equivalent of the Radio City Music Hall audience with standing room only. It had to be done within a lunch period of only thirty minutes with the people spread out over sixteen acres horizontally and a thousand feet vertically.

Nothing like this had been attempted before in building construction. Earlier there had been no need. Usually, the general contractor would solve the problem by having an operator arrange to deliver food to the workers. Or workers could just pick up a sandwich across the street. But in this case, "across the street" might mean a descent of a quarter mile followed by a long walk each way. So the Port Authority contracted with the American News Company to feed construction crews at the World Trade Center by means of a systematic, large-scale operation. American News had a commissary at 120 Broadway that made it possible for items to be easily delivered and heated on the site using mobile equipment.[31]

During the peak period of construction, thousands of workers were employed and paid millions of dollars. Since New York was known to be a high-cost and high-wage area with unionized labor, none of this was particularly remarkable.[32] However, some workers at the top of the pay scale did make extraordinary amounts of money. None attracted more attention than Tom Dowd, a thirty-nine-year-old foreman of the operating engineers, from Spring Valley, New York, whom *Time Magazine* called "The $94,000 Hardhat." The operating engineers were the workers who handled the hoisting and excavation equipment at the construction site. It seems that during his six years of scheduled work on the project, Dowd was able to earn more than $500,000 in wages. The reason for this large sum had to do with the work rules governing overtime pay.

Dowd, as a master mechanic, had to be kept on the job whenever three or more operating engineers were on duty. Since operating engineers ran all the cranes, bulldozers, and hoisting equipment, this meant in practical terms that there were three or more union members on duty around the clock.

In order to stay on the job for all these hours, Dowd had private quarters at the site equipped with a bed and a refrigerator. By his own description, he seldom operated any actual machinery himself. Instead, he saw himself as a labor mediator, someone who could solve problems and disputes right on the spot. Most of the media excoriated the unions over the Tom Dowd case. *Time* criticized "sky-high paychecks like Dowd's."[33] However, the *New York Times* took a more balanced position, saying, "Whether Mr. Dowd's overtime is viewed as an extreme example of featherbedding as some construction officials contend, or as legitimate pay for a crucial position that entails far more than his work title implies, he is an example of a new class of what might be termed executive union workers."[34]

We shall be better able to put the question of high wages to labor into perspective if we recognize the fact that most of the cost increases for the project were due to the political delays discussed in the previous chapter. To be sure, the work was interrupted by a number of strikes, but the fact is that for the most part labor did its job in an efficient manner. Once the foundations were in place, work started on the North Tower. Next came the South Tower and then the other outlying structures. The whole operation was paced, using the critical path method, to make the best use of time, materials, and manpower. The exciting visual drama of erecting the Twin Towers may be analyzed in four steps.

First, there was the construction of the core or rectangular elevator-service area where all the interior columns are clustered together. From the core, the floor system reaches in a clear and unobstructed clean sweep to the exterior wall. Although few tenants subsequently took full advantage of the dramatic interior layout potential, the fact remains that the architecture offers great possibilities. It was at the core that the giant kangaroo cranes lifted the steel from the outside.

Second, there was the construction of the exterior wall. Naturally, the placement of the load-bearing outer columns proceeded at the same pace as the erection of the core columns. The wall was put up in prefabricated panels with the vertical columns already welded to the horizontal beams called spandrels. Each unit weighed about twenty-two tons and was three modules wide, or about ten feet. The units came in two sizes; they were either two or three stories high. The finished wall presents a series of columns at intervals of three feet, four inches, a fairly narrow spacing designed to accommodate even narrower windows of twenty-two inches that make the occupants, even acrophobes, feel secure. Even if you stand right at the windows, you do not feel as if you might fall out.

Third, there was the installation of the floor (fig. 3.4). As the columns and walls rose, the floor was installed in preassembled sections that spanned from the elevator core to the exteriors walls. The floor sections were thirty-two-inch-deep trusses, or triangular metal frameworks, made by the Laclede Steel Company of St. Louis. The floor trusses had a corrugated metal lid on top designed to accept the poured concrete floor slab. The end result was a solid, smooth, and safe floor. To simplify later work, the ductwork for the telephone and electrical distribution lines, made by Granite Steel Company of Granite City, Illinois, was built into the corrugated deck. Below the truss decking, sheet-metal workers, or "tin knockers,"

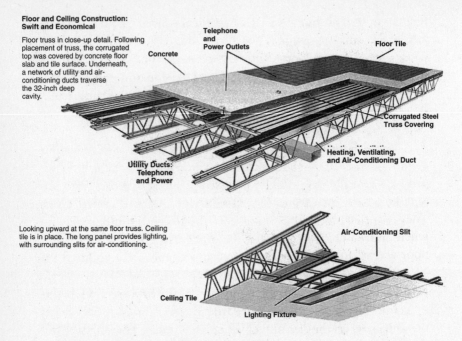

Floor and Ceiling Construction: Swift and Economical

Floor truss in close-up detail. Following placement of truss, the corrugated top was covered by concrete floor slab and tile surface. Underneath, a network of utility and air-conditioning ducts traverse the 32-inch deep cavity.

Telephone and Power Outlets

Concrete

Floor Tile

Corrugated Steel Truss Covering

Heating, Ventilating, and Air-Conditioning Duct

Utility Ducts: Telephone and Power

Looking upward at the same floor truss. Ceiling tile is in place. The long panel provides lighting, with surrounding slits for air-conditioning.

Air-Conditioning Slit

Ceiling Tile

Lighting Fixture

Figure 3.4. Floor and Ceiling Construction

placed the air-conditioning ducts, which were to be covered by the ceiling underneath. The work of floor framing kept pace with the erection of the exterior wall.

The fourth and final step for the Twin Towers was the installation of the curtain wall cover. Metalworkers put up a skin of aluminum with stainless steel trim that enclosed the structural steel. The contract for fabricating the aluminum had gone to the Aluminum Company of America (Alcoa). The practical purpose of the curtain wall is to keep water out and to keep either cooled or heated air inside. But the curtain wall is also the face that the building presents to the world, so it is supposed to be handsome as well. Other workers sprayed a slushy gray fire-proofing mixture containing asbestos on each steel column before placing the outside curtain walls. Of course, the curtain wall is also supposed to let in some light. The twenty-two-inch spaces between the columns are for the windows, which are recessed ten inches in order to shade them from all but direct sunlight. The architect specified a bronze-tinted, heat-reflective glass for the 43,600 windows.[35]

Of course, this brief summary of the four-step process makes the whole operation sound much simpler than it actually was. In any large-scale construction project, with so many people involved, there are bound to be numerous conflicts. One predictable stress point is the interaction between the architect and the construction manager. On the one hand, the architect regards his building as a monument. The construction manager, on the other hand, is likely to see it as just another tall building.

As we have explained, once the job of erecting the steel was complete, the external skin of the building had to be put into place. The skin was made up of large panels of anodized aluminum. The architect, Minoru Yamasaki, was keeping an eye on the process. They had gone about twenty floors up with the aluminum panels, when Yamasaki got it in his mind that one panel on the fifteenth floor was off in color.

Yamasaki insisted that the construction people remove and re-place the unsightly, faulty panel. Ray Monti refused, saying that it would be too costly to remove five floors of paneling just to get at one panel. Yamasaki continued to complain. Finally, an afternoon meeting was called for final resolution of the dispute. Everyone concerned was gathered together, including Jack Kyle, the chief engineer, and Ray Monti, the construction manager.

But first the disputants had to go out for lunch. Yamasaki had his usual three or four martinis at lunch. Afterward, they walked back to the site. Yamasaki looked up and pointed at the offending panel.

"You see that panel? It's just not right."

Everyone else had difficulty identifying the offending panel. They looked and looked.

Finally, Jack Kyle laughed and said, "Yama, you're standing on the wrong corner. This is the southeast corner! It's not where you were before."

Yamasaki quietly dropped his objection, and the matter never came up again.[36]

During the period of the construction of the World Trade Center, the commissioners of the Port Authority were not terribly worried about building the towers. What really concerned them was finding and retaining tenants. How would they find tenants for ten million square feet of office space? Even the Pentagon, which up until then had been the world's largest office building, had only 6.5 million square feet. Efforts were made to identify prospective tenants and to sign them up for long-term leases. From time to time, the Port Authority's tireless promoter, Guy Tozzoli, hosted special events for these prospects. One such event was an on-the-spot construction progress report held on September 10, 1968, for some four hundred guests. At that time, less than half the rentable space in the Twin Towers was under contract. It was very important to keep those who had signed up happy, and even more important to seek out new prospects.

The guests were invited for a walk on a trestle that crossed the World Trade Center construction site. Austin Tobin gave a brief account of rental progress and explained the construction activity that was going on all around them. Ironworkers hoisted steel girders into place for the elevator core of the North Tower. Bulldozers moved across the floor of the site, some fifty feet down. To their right, crews were demolishing the remaining three floors of the old building at 50 Church Street. Five trucks filled with earth were ready to drive across the trestle to the landfill area as soon as the guests had departed. A Port Authority helicopter hovered at 1,350 feet, the projected height of the tower buildings. Port Authority chairman James C. Kellogg III gave a speech and told the assemblage, "Today, you are looking down onto construction activity. Tomorrow millions will look up to a new landmark." It was a brave show in the American tradition of ballyhoo.[37]

While the Port Authority was trying to recruit new tenants from the business community with one hand, it was trying to maintain labor peace with the other. A low point was reached during July 1969 when construction progress was slowed by three separate strikes. The first strike, by Local 20 of the Sheet Metal Workers, had very little disruptive effect before it was settled. The second strike by the International Brotherhood of Teamsters was settled on July 31 after it had delayed construction operations by cutting off deliveries of materials.[38]

The most serious was the third, the strike by the International Union of Elevator Constructors which began July 1, 1969, and dragged on for three and a half months. During that time, all workers had to walk up the stairs to their work areas, which in some instances were as high as the twenty-seventh floor. They then had to walk down the stairs every time they needed to return to the ground. Although the Port Authority made every effort to deliver food and tools to the affected workers, the strike did have an adverse effect on the construction schedule. Full-scale work could not resume until the strike was settled on October 19.[39]

With the settlement of the elevator strike, Otis Elevator sent its sixty-six constructors back to work. At the insistence of the general contractor, another twenty constructors were added to the work force. This enabled all work at the World Trade Center construction site to resume at a "full speed ahead" basis. Construction elevator service was quickly restored to the ninth, thirteenth, and twenty-first floors.[40] Otis's work was somewhat hampered by the failure of the electrical contractor, Nager Electric, to provide an adequate power supply to drive the elevators to the heights they were capable of reaching. Nager's problem was caused mainly by its inability to obtain sufficient numbers of qualified electricians from the union to proceed with the electrical installation. Gradually, as new electricians became available, this problem was solved.[41]

Six months after the elevator strike was settled, another big unexpected problem presented itself. It had been standard industry practice for years in the steel buildings to use a spray-on fireproofing containing asbestos. The technique was to mix dry asbestos with water and shoot the mixture through a nozzle onto beams, floors, and ceilings. This step was regarded as necessary because steel, in a fire, will bend and warp. But just as work was well under way on the North Tower, the use of fireproofing materials containing asbestos had come under scrutiny by Dr. Irving J. Selikoff, director of the environmental sciences laboratory at the Mount Sinai School of Medicine. Dr. Selikoff's research proved what medical researchers had long suspected, that asbestos caused cancer. As a result of this work, the Environmental Protection Agency issued a restrictive set of standards covering the spraying of asbestos-containing materials. The EPA was especially concerned because in the spraying process as much as 50 percent of the asbestos escapes into the air.[42]

Ironically, the World Trade Center building was the first and only project in New York City where the spray contractor, Mario and DiBono, had taken precautions to prevent the scattering of dried asbestos as well as planning elaborate cleanup and disposal procedures. The building's exterior on the floors where asbestos was being sprayed was tightly enclosed by canvas, and the asbestos-spray work area was closed off from other interior areas. However, the job lacked a vacuum-cleaning operation as required by the new regulations.[43]

By this time, construction had already reached the thirty-fourth floor. A difficult decision was made to stop using fireproofing with asbestos. Meanwhile, an initial search to find alternatives came up with nothing. Fortunately, a new material came on the market, introduced by U.S. Mineral Products of Stanhope, New Jersey. Independent laboratory tests showed that the new material was as effective, from the standpoint of fireproofing survivability, as the older one containing asbestos fibers. Then a difficult decision was made to change all of the spray in the World Trade Center, at the huge cost of $300,000. However, in retrospect, the decision to shift to the new material was the right one. To remove asbestos from just one floor of the center now would cost more than a million dollars.[44]

While the public controversy about asbestos was making the evening television news, much of the routine work inside the skyscraper was proceeding without notice. This work would be invisible to the tenants of the completed skyscraper. They would care, of course, that the building was warm enough or cool enough. They would want water when they turned on the tap. They would want power when they plugged in an appliance. It was up to the mechanical engineers to worry about how to install all the necessary piping. Some of this work was on an unbelievably large scale. In January 1970, for example, they began installing the huge, *sixty-inch-diameter* pipes necessary to carry the Hudson River water into the site to be used for cooling. The work would have to be completed in time to test the refrigeration equipment, the largest in the world, which was simultaneously being installed in the basement levels. These giant machines were being placed in a two-acre area, five floors below street level. The air-conditioning system would provide a total refrigeration capacity of 49,000 tons—enough to serve a city of more than 15,000 homes.[45]

It is interesting to note how demands on the mechanical engineers in tall building construction have increased over time. For example, Karl Sabbagh, author of *Skyscraper*, explained: "Over the last fifty years air conditioning in office buildings has been transformed from a luxury to a necessity as buildings have grown larger. Before World War II even the most famous skyscrapers such as the Woolworth Building and the Empire State Building did not have central air conditioning. The only way to stay cool in your office on a hot summer day was to open a window—always assuming you were close enough to a window to obtain the benefit. This was fine in, say, the Empire State Building, where no office was farther than twenty or thirty feet from a window, but as ambitions became grander and buildings became wider, this was impossible."[46]

Later in 1970, an important milestone was reached. It was on Monday, October 19, that a single piece of steel thirty-six feet high, ten feet wide, and weighing four tons, was quietly hoisted into place somewhere in the vicinity of what would become the 103rd floor. By this simple act, the Empire State Building at 1,250 feet was eclipsed by the World Trade Center—by four feet. The Empire State Building had been the record holder for forty years, so the Port Authority had planned to publicize the record-breaking event. There had even been plans to rent a helicopter to take up newspaper photographers and television crews; but the general contractor, the Tishman Company, put the critical piece of steel up a day early without notifying the Port Authority public relations staff.

By the end of construction, the North Tower would reach 1,368 feet, six feet taller than the South Tower at 1,362 feet. Because it was the headquarters of the Port Authority, Austin Tobin specified that the North Tower would have higher ceilings, by three feet each, at the PA executive offices on the 67th floor and at the PA cafeteria on the 43rd floor. The higher ceilings, of course, made for more impressive spaces, befitting the flagship headquarters of a powerful agency. In any event, both towers were more than 100 feet above the top of the Empire State Building. But it was a running joke at the time that the World Trade Center would be the world's tallest building for the world's shortest time, since Sears was already planning to build a 1,450-foot structure in Chicago to be completed in 1974. The irony was not lost on the hardhats working at the top of the World Trade Center.

"I'm happy now—it seems like I'm working on one of the great wonders of the world," said ironworker Philip Blaske from Brooklyn. "But I'd rather be on that one in Chicago. It won't be long until I'll be feeling left out."

But there were other workers who were unconcerned about the race for height.

"This is just another building," said George Nelson of Park Ridge, New Jersey, nonchalantly. "I worked on the Empire State Building too, and that was just another routine job."[47]

As the steelworkers kept pushing the structure skyward, on the lower floors others pushed ahead with routine interior work. Tile workers installed travertine in local elevator lobbies and regular floor tiles up to the fifty-third floor. Local elevators were made operational. Automatic temperature controls were installed. Lobby marble was installed. Building directories were completed. The tenant areas were painted. Drapes were installed.[48]

Unlike most other Port Authority projects such as a bridge or a tunnel, there was no one date set for a grand opening or ribbon cutting. Instead, the World Trade Center would open bit by bit, floor by floor. Some tenants would move in while the upper floors were still incomplete. It was mid-December of 1970 when the first two tenants moved in. One was Irving R. Boody and Company, importers and exporters of raw materials. The other was Export-Import Services, freight forwarders and customs house brokers.[49]

It was on a Tuesday, December 15, that the moving vans pulled up and started unloading. Boxes of files and papers, tables and chairs, pictures and plants were carted up to the tenth and eleventh floors of the North Tower. Wednesday was the first day of business, which opened without ceremony in the new building. Reporters stopped by to see how they were doing. At the firm of Irving R. Boody, on the eleventh floor, the proprietor, Mr. Boody, and his vice president, Thomas Edward Kelley, were getting settled into their brand-new executive suite. The firm had been located previously at 42 Broadway. They, like everyone else in downtown New York, had received solicitations from the Port Authority to move into the new building. They were invited to move in at about the same time as their earlier lease had come up for renewal. The World Trade Center was supposed to have been completed just in time for a smooth transition. So they agreed to sign on with the proviso that they would be protected. Since they were not going to renegotiate a new lease, they had to have some guarantees that the new building would be ready for them. Otherwise, they would be left in limbo.

Both Boody and Kelley were eager to move in because they felt that the new address would give their company's image a boost.[50]

Meanwhile, in the outer office, Margaret Siss, a secretary from Astoria, was busy hanging pictures. In an adjoining room, Frank Ramirez was busy checking out invoices. In the background were sounds of riveting, the clang of metal, and workers shouting. The first incoming message to the World Trade Center arrived over a direct teleprinter circuit. The telex message, a confirmation of a sale of spices from Ceylon to Colombia, was received at 9:54 A.M. (EST), within an hour after the New York import-export firm had opened for business.[51]

Meanwhile, there was also activity at Export-Import Services on the tenth floor. One clerk was mimeographing form letters while other office personnel were preparing bills. The head of the company, James Farrell, Jr., was on the phone with his wife receiving the good news that they had just become grandparents of James Farrell IV. Later that week the two pioneers were joined by Petroleos Mexicanos, representatives of the Mexican government's oil industry authority. Meanwhile, construction on the North Tower continued high above their heads.[52]

The biggest problem those early tenants had was that, when they went to work, they were never sure what the situation would be at the World Trade Center. Some days the construction workers would have to move things around so they would have to go through a different entrance or get off at a different floor and walk up or walk down. They never knew what the temperature was going to be. Sometimes they would go into the office and the temperature was much too hot and they could not get cool enough. Other times, it would be freezing cold.

How were these pioneer firms able to move in before everything was in good working order? The usual procedure was that you had to have a certificate of occupancy, which meant that the building was fully ready to be occupied. However, the Port Authority was an independent operating agency, and any property that they owned was exempt from local zoning laws and local building code regulations— one of which required a certificate of occupancy. So they were permitted by law to move tenants in even though the building under normal standards might not be ready for occupancy.[53]

As the first tenants moved in, the end was really in sight for the steel erectors. This symbolic achievement was to be marked by a "topping-out" ceremony and party, organized by the public affairs department of the Port Authority and originally scheduled for Tuesday, December 22, 1970. Though Karl Sabbagh wrote about another building, his remarks aptly describe the ceremony: "Much of life has rituals, conscious or unconscious, and the construction industry is no exception. The practical significance of topping out is virtually nil. There was certainly no specific significance in the date chosen. . . . Topping out is meant to mark the emplacement of the final piece of the steel in a steel structure, but—with a schedule that was continually changing by a day here and a day there, an erection crew that were to stay on to put up the metal framework of the roof, and the need to set a date for the ceremony several weeks ahead—the actual date had very little to do with the stage the building had reached."[54]

Significant or not, in accordance with long-standing construction tradition, ironworkers of the Karl Koch Erecting Company of Carteret, New Jersey, attached an American flag to a thirty-six-foot-long, four-ton column. A giant kangaroo crane then hoisted the column to the top of the structure at 11:30 A.M. on Wednesday, December 23. (The ceremony had been postponed one day because of weather.) Immediately following this lift, a thirty-foot Christmas tree attached to a three-story-high exterior wall section was raised to the southeast corner of the building.[55] Port Authority archives are silent on how much beer was ordered or consumed, but the industry standard is three cans per guest. We may assume that this standard was upheld.

Four months later, on April 30, 1971, the Port Authority celebrated its fiftieth birthday. It was the anniversary of the day in 1921 when representatives of New Jersey and New York met in New York City and signed a compact between the states to develop terminal and transportation facilities in the New York Harbor area—a 1,500-square-mile sector within a 25-mile radius of the Statue of Liberty. For Austin Tobin, this golden anniversary was a bittersweet occasion. He could point with pride to his domain with six interstate tunnels and bridges, a regional system of four airports and two heliports, six marine terminals, the world's largest bus terminal, and two motor truck terminals. He had just finished topping out the North Tower of the World Trade Center, a crowning accomplishment. In addition, he could look forward to topping out the South Tower in less than three months. Despite all this, the fun had gone out of the job for Austin Tobin. Governor William T. Cahill of New Jersey was constantly insisting that the Port Authority go beyond its announced plan to invest $200 million in improving existing PATH facilities. There had been a series of public hearings in Albany, Trenton, and Newark bringing almost unbearable pressure on the authority and its director. Increasingly, Tobin found the demands on his beloved agency to be more shrill and strident and unreasonable.[56]

Soon it was summer, and time for the topping out of the South Tower. The ceremony was held on Monday, July 19, 1971, with rain and mist obscuring the peak of the tower. As in a Shakespearean drama, the weather mirrored Austin Tobin's gloomy mood. Yet as before, ironworkers attached an American flag, this time to an even larger seventy-foot-long, ten-ton steel beam. Once again, a kangaroo crane hoisted the beam to the top of the structure. Next came the usual self-congratulatory speeches.

On this occasion, the American Society of Civil Engineers' national award for outstanding achievement was presented to the World Trade Center. Samuel S. Baxter, president of the ASCE, presented the plaque to Port Authority chairman James C. Kellogg III, honoring the facility judged "the engineering project that demonstrates the greatest engineering skills and represents the greatest contribution to engineering progress and mankind." The chairman, acknowledging the plaque as a tribute to all the men and women at the Port Authority involved in the Trade Center's design and construction, promised it would be placed in a prominent public location within the center after construction was complete.

Raymond Corbett, business manager of Ironworkers Local 40 and president of the New York State AFL-CIO, speaking at the ceremonies, said that the Trade Center's record of *no fatalities among the ironworkers during construction* was a phenomenal achievement in a project of this size and scope. The statement was reiterated by the

Koch Erecting Company, which reported it had realized a safety record far surpassing that of any other project they had built. The Port Authority presented Mr. Corbett with a framed Solovioff print, depicting ironworkers handling a massive steel beam, as a tribute to the ironworkers who helped to build the World Trade Center.[57]

After placing the final pieces of steel atop the last 1,350-foot tower, the kangaroo cranes had finished all their slewing, luffing, and lifting. Getting the huge construction cranes down from the top of the building presented a tricky problem. Each kangaroo crane was dismantled and lowered to the ground by another, until finally there was a fourth and last crane left. How to get this last one down? The answer was a guy derrick, which the last kangaroo crane raised from the street. Workers then took the fifty-ton kangaroo crane apart and used the guy derrick to lower its components down to the ground level. Then the guy derrick was dismantled, and the parts were taken through a roof hatch and brought down by freight elevator.[58]

With the Twin Towers substantially completed, Austin J. Tobin, at sixty-eight years of age, was ready to retire. In announcing his retirement in December 1971, the silver-haired Tobin noted that he had been with the agency for forty-five years and had served as its executive director for thirty. Tobin had built the organization into the most powerful agency of its kind in the world. When Tobin joined the Port Authority as a law clerk, it had 300 employees. On the eve of his retirement, it had 8,000 employees and an investment of $2.6 billion in bridges, airports, ship terminals, and other facilities, including the World Trade Center. Now, upon his retirement, Tobin was said to be the highest-paid public official in the United States, except for the president.

The retirement was described by one source as the "normal retirement of a man who has been in office for a long time." Tobin told his associates that he was looking forward to spending more time at his second home in Quogue, Long Island. There he would be able to indulge his interests in classical musical and bird-watching. Those who knew him well believed he would be unhappy in giving up the job where he had routinely worked twelve to eighteen hours a day, yet insiders privately said that Tobin was simply worn out from all the controversy swirling about the Port Authority projects. There had been the unsuccessful fight to build a fourth jetport for the New York City area. There had been the bitter private real-estate opposition to the World Trade Center, which would not have to pay local property taxes. But worst of all had been the pressure to shoulder more and more rail transit responsibilities that Tobin saw as a drain on profitable operations. It was time to quit.[59]

The work of the Port Authority continued, of course, but it would never be quite the same. Much of the old can-do spirit of the post–World War II period was lost. Then in September 1972 came more bad news. The people of the Port Authority were saddened to learn of the untimely death of Martin S. Kapp, who had been appointed as chief engineer just two years earlier. Kapp, who was only forty-eight years old, was carrying on the great tradition of the four men who had held that post in the Port Authority since its creation in 1921—General George Goethals, Othmar H. Ammann, John C. Evans, and John M. Kyle. Kapp's specialization in soils and foundations had earned him the highest recognition in the engineering profession. It had been Kapp's research that had led the Port Authority to adopt the slurry trench method of foundation construction for the World Trade Center, resulting in substantial savings in construction time and cost.[60]

Despite the retirement of the executive director and the death of the chief engineer, the project kept going. By now it had a life of its own. The person responsible for keeping it on budget and on schedule was the construction manager, Ray Monti. The complexity of his task invites the use of metaphor. Some observers compared Monti's building of the Twin Towers to his playing a game called "Build the World Trade Center." He is given $600 million worth of steel, concrete, plate glass, aluminum, woodwork, pipes, flooring, various nuts and bolts, and other construction materials. The object of the game is to use his engineering staff and a computer to arrange all these pieces to form the largest office complex ever built. The game is plagued with obstacles—labor strikes, parts shortages, transportation snarls, expensive accidents, and terrible weather. Monti has to put these pieces together within seven years or pay steep financial penalties.[61]

Ray Monti himself preferred a military metaphor to explain the monstrous logistical problem of directing construction of the twin towers. "It's like the D-Day invasion in terms of the intricacy of planning and coordination," explained Monti, his choice of words reflecting his service in the navy's construction battalions, or Seabees. The highly detailed plans called for the just-in-time delivery of component parts so that the whole job would never be held up by a missing detail. "If the steel is not up, it delays laying the concrete floors, which follow 10 stories behind the steel, and both affect the wall men, ceiling men, floor-tile men, plumbers, electricians, sheetmetal men, and the rest."

Ray Monti continued the military metaphor in explaining his organizational structure. His office was the "headquarters company" which included a "war room," which held charts and graphs and a conference table. This "headquarters company" controlled the scheduling and costs and directed the activities of the resident engineers, or "line commanders." There were four line commanders to manage the two towers. Monti's language suggested a management style built on the kind of discipline and structure that led to camaraderie and a sense of belonging. He had to have the ability to bring all the contractors and subcontractors together and get them to work the way they should.

Whether the metaphor was one of gamesmanship or war, the real engineering process at the heart of the matter was the critical path method, which Monti had put into practice for building the Heliport and Exhibition Building at the 1964–1965 New York World's Fair, one of the few pavilions of 1964 that attempted to use fresh technology. The heliport was a kind of elevated platform that resembled a table with the legs at the centers of each side, rather than at the corners. The building is one of the few that remain in Flushing Meadows–Corona Park. Monti recalled with a sigh of nostalgia: "Myself and five other guys managed the World's Fair Building and knew every nut and bolt in the place. That was a nice, simple $5 million project."[62]

During the busiest periods of putting up the World Trade Center, they might have spent that sum in two weeks. It was during one of those busy periods, October 1972, that Ray Monti received some welcome news: he had been named chief engineer of the Port Authority. It was a great American success story, and Hollywood could not have scripted it any better. For twenty years, Monti had been deeply engrossed in the agency's power game. He had chosen his projects carefully and had gotten himself onto Guy Tozzoli's team. And no one was closer to the center of power than Tozzoli. If Monti had worn campaign ribbons for Port Authority projects, they would have represented work on Kennedy International Airport, the bus terminal, several piers, and (most important) the Exhibit Building for the New York World's Fair of 1964–1965. Through a combination of charm, savvy, and timing, he was now at the top of the career ladder.[63]

As construction proceeded, the monumental size of the Twin Towers invoked a number of comparisons. Sixteen football games could be played simultaneously in its excavation. Its towers would be more than 300 feet taller than the ocean liner *Queen Mary* upended. It would have more office space than the Pentagon. Comparisons were also made with the Great Pyramid of Cheops at Giza in Egypt, built in 3000 B.C. In sheer weight of material, mostly granite and limestone, Pharaoh Cheops was still ahead. In width, at thirteen solid acres, the Great Pyramid was also ahead. When asked by a reporter what people of a future era might examine in wonder as they compared the Great Pyramid with the Twin Towers, Ray Monti said modestly, "The World Trade Center holds no engineering puzzles to compare with those of ancient times, but if men should come upon it, preserved into a distant age, I imagine they would simply note that 20th-century man took a lot of little pieces and put them together in a logical order."[64]

Step by step, the Twin Towers were nearing completion. Guy Tozzoli, who had overseen every step along the way, was fond of telling his staff, only half in jest, that every project can be broken down into six phases: (1) enthusiasm, (2) disillusionment, (3) panic, (4) search for the guilty, (5) punishment of the innocent, and (6) praise and honors for the nonparticipants. Indeed, these sweeping generalizations do fit the story of the building of the Twin Towers. We have seen in these pages the early enthusiasm of David Rockefeller and others as well as the later disillusionment of officials from both states as they watched the slow process of political approval unfold. There was genuine panic when word of huge cost overruns became public. There was a search for the guilty when the project was characterized as a white elephant. There was punishment of the innocent as Austin Tobin retired before he was really ready to step down. Now it was time for praise and honors for the nonparticipants.[65]

Indeed, many of the dignitaries at the official dedication of the World Trade Center in early April 1973 had themselves very little to do with the completion of the complex. A heavy rain cut the size of the crowd and forced the ceremony indoors to the lobby of the North Tower. The main speaker, U.S. Secretary of Labor Peter J. Brennan, did not appear. It was believed that Brennan did not wish to cross the picket line against the PATH trains. Mayor John Lindsay was out of town, and officials got the name of his substitute wrong. The basement levels were a half-finished mess. Water from the street flooded into a connecting subway entrance, forcing some visitors to wade through deep puddles.[66]

There were many ironies accompanying the official dedication. There was the fact that tenants had started moving into the complex two and one-half years earlier. At the time of the dedication, the buildings were more than half filled with rent-paying occupants. Why then was the dedication so late? According to James C. Kellogg III, the chairman of the Port Authority, the dedication had to wait until the sculptural works of art had been installed. There was also the matter of trying to coordinate the schedules of the dignitaries. Even with all the delay, some schedules never did get coordinated. Only eight out of the twelve Port Authority commissioners were able to show up for the dedication. Yet all twelve (including the nonparticipants) had their names inscribed in gold on the lobby wall at the plaza level of the North Tower where the ceremony was held.[67]

The dignity of the occasion was saved, however, by the presence of both governors. "Another great day in a great city," said New Jersey's governor, William T. Cahill, in a conciliatory tone befitting a bistate ceremony.

"It's not often that we see a dream come true," said New York's governor, Nelson A. Rockefeller. "Today we have." He commended the men and women who had made the Trade Center possible, "and at the head of the list," he said, "has got to be Austin Tobin." The crowd applauded loudly.[68]

But Austin J. Tobin was not there. "It was raining," he said when asked why he had been absent from the dedication ceremony. Aside from his comment on the weather, Tobin declined to say anything further.[69]

But four years later, in 1977, when Austin Tobin was dying of cancer, he got his old lieutenant, Guy Tozzoli, to take him from his Manhattan apartment to visit the site. Tozzoli explained: "It was his dying wish. He had me take him down in a wheelchair and he sat all alone looking at the plaza and the twin towers for about two hours. Nobody talked to him. This was important to him because it was an incredible thing that he had done. True, he was a lawyer and a great executive; but, in his heart, he was an architect. He loved architecture."[70]

For thirty years, Austin Tobin had fought and struggled to make the New York and New Jersey region dominant in world affairs. And the Twin Towers symbolized this dominance. With this last gaze at all he had wrought, the old warrior perhaps found peace. The following year, on February 8, 1978, Austin Tobin died in Manhattan, the city he had loved. In 1982, the Port Authority named the plaza—site of summertime concerts—the Austin J. Tobin Plaza.[71]

4
Winning
Acceptance

How a White Elephant
Became Prime Real Estate

The story goes that a student once asked the architect, "O master, why did you build two 100-story buildings instead of one 200-story building?" And he answered, "Ah, to keep the human scale."

—GAEL GREENE, *NEW YORK*, MAY 31, 1976

THE TWIN Towers of the World Trade Center are now an accepted part of the Manhattan skyline. They appear in establishing shots for movies, on tour bus brochures, and as part of corporate logos. Tourists buy postcards with the image of the Twin Towers and send them back home. For those with a sense of history, the outcome is quite remarkable because the Twin Towers were born in controversy. From the start, the project had enemies who tried to make sure it would never be built. Even after they were built, the Twin Towers had fierce critics who regarded them as an ugly blight on the landscape. Now a full generation later, the Twin Towers have won the war of public relations. The project is not just grudgingly accepted, it is warmly embraced. How this victory was achieved makes a fascinating story.

The World Trade Center was constructed during the late 1960s and early 1970s amid a drumbeat of criticism. The Port Authority was blasted for being too arrogant. The project was too big, too expensive, and too wasteful. It would generate too much pollution and too much traffic. Port Authority spokespeople had answers for all these objections, but they were always on the defensive. It seemed that the agency was good at building things, but weak in explaining itself and its purposes. On the face of things, no rational person in the late 1960s would have guessed at the eventual public relations triumph of the World Trade Center. The Port Authority was under assault from both Albany and Trenton for not spending its resources wisely. The Port Authority got the blame for everything that went wrong in the region.

Of course, one problem was the nature of the World Trade Center project. It was so big and so grandiose that it acted as a lightning rod to attract criticism. It was one thing for the Port Authority to labor in obscurity as a transportation agency; it was something else to be constructing the world's tallest building. Most criticism took an obvious form: "If they have the money for the trade center, why don't they have the money for my project?" The Port Authority had clearly favored motor vehicles with bridges and tunnels, not to mention favoring air travel with airports. It was evident to everyone that the agency had not paid much attention to maritime properties and railroads. Criticism of the agency filtered down from editorial writers to the proverbial man in the street. In 1969 a newspaperman reported a conversation with a New York City taxi driver. As they pulled away from the World Trade Center construction site and drove along the Hudson, the driver pointed out the decaying finger piers along the Hudson and said, "It's the Porta Tority. It's the fault of the big fellows. They're running the docks down allatime. They got their reasons, and they ain't good ones."[1] Of course, the criticism was unfair since the docks belonged to New York City, not the Port Authority, but the damage was done, anyway. The public believed, right or wrong, that the agency, with its unlimited resources, was all-powerful. So why, they asked, didn't the agency just step in and fix things?

Meanwhile, the World Trade Center project was panned by editorial writers, architectural critics, not to mention taxicab drivers. Why did public attitudes soften and change? One explanation is based on the passage of time: the older generation never did accept it, but their attitude no longer matters. This idea was best expressed by Eric Nash, author of *New York's 50 Best Skyscrapers*. Nash wrote, "Not even a remake of *King Kong*, Philippe Petit on a tightrope, or an attack by mad bombers could endear these twin aluminum and glass behemoths to old-time New Yorkers. But for the generation born after they were built, it is a different story, and the twin towers appear on bus tour logos and posters for the Rangers and Yankees, in the Channel 11 logo, and on such tourist gimcracks as thermometers, pencil sharpeners, and key chains."[2]

Certainly in the battle for public acceptance, time was on the side of the Twin Towers. But a favorable outcome was neither natural nor inevitable. It required patience, persistence, and a consistency of effort—not to mention a bit of luck. Somewhere between the low point of 1969 and the present lies the answer to our question of how the World Trade Center won the acceptance of New Yorkers in particular and Americans in general.

The explanation for the public relations victory of the Twin Towers requires a big canvas and a broad brush. In the discussion that follows, we will examine the 1976 remake of *King Kong* with Jeff Bridges and Jessica Lange. This film shifted attention away from the Empire State Building, the symbol of an earlier era, and it endeared the newer Twin Towers to the public. We will also look into a series of daredevil exploits in the 1970s that riveted nationwide attention on the Twin Towers. To be sure, neither the filmmaking nor the daredevil deeds were initiated by the Port Authority. One could argue that these events were just a matter of luck. But, in both cases, the agency responded deftly and adroitly to get the best possible publicity from these incidents.

Even more important in the battle for public acceptance was the underlying master plan for the Twin Towers project. It is natural for people, when confronted with a tall building, to want to get to the very top. Yet it must be remembered that the Port Authority gave people two ways to get there. For those who wanted an inexpensive visit of short duration to get a magnificent view, there was the observation deck on the South Tower. For those who wanted a leisurely and elegant meal to entertain either a client or an out-of-town guest, there was Windows on the World atop the North Tower. This simple scheme was designed to please nearly everyone: the democratic masses had their view, and the power elite had their exclusive restaurant. It was a win-win formula. As we shall see, to make it work, the Port Authority had to get people to roll up their sleeves and deliver good service to both constituencies—day in and day out, year after year.

BORN IN CONTROVERSY

It was an ordinary Wednesday in New York City. For Austin Tobin, April 12, 1967, started like any other day. He arrived in a chauffeur-driven Cadillac at the Port Authority Building, 111 Eighth Avenue, in the Chelsea district of Manhattan. He was greeted by a nattily uniformed elevator operator who took him up to the top floor, the executive floor. Tobin felt good as he sat down at his desk; excavation at the site was well under way. Imagine his surprise and shock when he picked up his copy of the *New York Times*. There was an editorial calling for a review of the World Trade Center. Up until this point the newspaper had supported the idea as a symbol of the city's stake in international trade. But here was an editorial describing the project as "enormously expensive and grandiose." It called for "cutting it down to realistic and efficient size."[3]

The *Times* editorial was the opening shot in a decade-long war between the Port Authority and its critics. Tobin was especially upset because the editorial went to the heart of the matter, questioning the premises and assumptions of the project. Over the next few years, the project would be attacked from every viewpoint—the political, the economic, the environmental, and the architectural. As each new argument was raised, Port Authority spokespeople would patiently answer the objections. But the process took a heavy toll on the morale of the agency. Tobin became weary and dispirited. It was no surprise when he resigned in 1972, before the Trade Center was formally dedicated.

The most vigorous and energetic political critic of the Port Authority during this period was Theodore W. Kheel, a labor mediator, who was identified with efforts to support the New York City subway system and avoid fare increases. In the late 1960s, Kheel constantly argued that the Port Authority should get out of the real estate business and shoulder responsibility for mass transit. Kheel was a formidable adversary because he was both a powerful speaker and a gifted writer. In November 1969, Kheel gathered together all of his arguments against the Twin Towers for a major article that appeared in *New York* magazine. Basically what Kheel wanted was for the Port Authority to double its tolls on interstate bridges and tunnels, and then turn the profits realized over to New York and New Jersey to subsidize mass transit. Whatever the public policy merits of his argument, Kheel could not resist attacking, with rhetorical zeal, the Port Authority in general and the Trade Center in particular. Kheel described the Port Authority as "a dangerously short-sighted and rigid conservative money machine harnessed to

serve, not the public interest, but the private vision of an oppor-
tunistic management." Later in the article, he described the World
Trade Center as "the clearest sign of the Port Authority's intellectual bankruptcy and arrogant indifference to the real needs of this
community."[4]

At the same time the World Trade Center was being criticized
as poor public policy, it was being attacked as a bad economic proposition. Particularly embarrassing for the Port Authority was the
ever-changing cost estimate for the project: $350 million in January
1964, $525 million in September 1965, and $575 million in January 1967.[5]

Of course, there was an explanation. Port Authority spokespeople were able to point out that the earlier figures were *construction* cost estimates, while the newer ones were overall *project*
cost estimates. The revised estimates included not only construction
costs but also allowances for escalation, site acquisition, engineering and design, and staff.[6] The explanation made sense; but, in the
battle for public opinion, it was tactically weak for the Port Authority to be constantly on the defensive.

Later in 1967, the Twin Towers project was criticized for lack
of patriotism. Critics attacked the Port Authority for buying 25 percent of the steel needed for the project from Japan, losing money for
domestic producers and jobs for American workers. A Port Authority spokesperson defended the decision by saying, "When we place
specific orders, we don't know where the steel originates. We don't
specify where the material comes from. We have not placed any restrictions on any of the producers but we know that all of the finished steel will be fabricated in this country."[7]

Just as the first tenants were moving into the North Tower of
the World Trade Center, another problem emerged. The market for
office space suddenly went soft. Because of a business slowdown,
few firms were seeking new space. Even if the Port Authority were
able to rent all of its space, there was still a problem because its
competition in the private sector was stuck with floors of empty
space. Once again, the Port Authority got the blame. Sol G. Atlas,
a private builder of office buildings, complained, "There would not
be any excess of office space downtown if not for the Port Authority. Listen, the Port Authority doesn't pay any sales tax for con-

struction material; they get their financing through low-interest bond rates, and worse, they're autonomous. They're a law unto themselves. They say who they want to get space in the trade center, offer them lower floor space rates than we pay and in the end, it's we, the private sector, who is subsidizing the Port Authority."[8]

The apparent glut of office space in downtown Manhattan gave Theodore Kheel another opportunity to attack. In a 1970 newspaper interview, Kheel said, "The World Trade Center is the Port Authority's Berlin Wall. It shields the Port Authority from doing what it was set up to do and that is to help move people and goods by developing and coordinating all forms of transportation. Instead, the PA uses government subsidies to finance the largest office building—real estate project in history to compete with private industry where private industry is supplying all the space we need without government help."[9]

The newspaper attacks on the World Trade Center continued throughout the early 1970s, leaving the public with the distinct impression that the project was a white elephant. Then in late 1974, it was revealed that the Port Authority's transportation facilities were subsidizing the World Trade Center, the exact opposite of the agency's original intentions. Official figures for 1973 showed that the Twin Towers returned $7 million in net operating revenues on an investment of $700 million. This accounting did not take into consideration the debt service on the project, which would be many times the modest profit. Meanwhile, Theodore Kheel recommended that the World Trade Center be turned over to private management.[10]

In addition to the mounting political and economic arguments against the World Trade Center, a rash of environmental arguments began to emerge. The most embarrassing episode occurred in the summer of 1971 when New Jersey newspapers began to report that the World Trade Center was dumping 170,000 gallons daily of raw sewage into the Hudson River.[11] People living along the Jersey shore felt especially threatened. Politicians and public health officials made dire comments to broadcasters and journalists. One New Jersey physician, Dr. Ira Ross, said, "And yet with the limitless resources of the great Port of New York Authority, no more imaginative solution has been engineered than to dump untreated sewage into the very waters that bathe the foot of the Statue of Liberty."[12]

The problem was that the original report was true, but it was not the whole truth. The fact of the matter was that at the time all Manhattan sewage from 72nd Street down to the Battery was being discharged through the city's sewer system into either the Hudson or the East River. There was a plan for the city to pipe all the sewage from lower Manhattan to the Newtown Creek Sewage Treatment Plant in Brooklyn. But at the time the World Trade Center came on line, that facility was not yet ready for operation. So it was true that the World Trade Center was adding to the sewage that the city was discharging daily into rivers, but that amounted to only about one-twentieth of one percent of the total.[13] Nonetheless, it was another public relations fiasco.

Another environmental embarrassment in the early 1970s had to do with wasted energy. At that time, there was an increasing public campaign to save energy. Meanwhile at the Twin Towers construction site, anyone could readily see for miles around that the lights were blazing all night long. Of course, there was an official explanation. Port Authority officials assured people that the lights were "required for fire safety as well as for security considerations. In addition, much of the material used in trade center construction is delivered to the work sites on various floors at night, and lighting is required for the safety of the workmen involved."[14] Whether or not people fully believed the explanation, they did seem to accept it.

But when the building was finished, the situation went from bad to worse. It seemed that there was no way for tenants to turn off the lights because there were no light switches. The lights burned all day, even in areas of the building where plenty of daylight came through the windows. Those who insisted on having a light switch were billed $142. One of the tenants, Public Service Commission chairman Joseph Swidler, said, "This building just wasn't built with energy conservation in mind. I now have no option but to waste electricity."[15]

In addition to the substantive issues of sewage and energy, other environmental issues pertaining to quality of life began to emerge. There were real concerns about increased congestion as the Twin Towers brought an additional 50,000 office workers into the financial district. One reporter envisioned a kind of doomsday scenario: "Someday the Wall Street area is going to grind to a stop. Motionless, bumper-to-bumper traffic will clog the narrow streets. Pedestrians won't be able to budge on the jammed sidewalks. Crowds struggling to get into restaurants, shops, elevators will fight to a standstill against the crowds trying to get out."[16] Of course, things never got quite that bad, but the fear was real.

In the early stages of the World Trade Center project, there were concerns about the impact of the project on television reception. Television engineers warned that the planned smooth aluminum finish of the Twin Towers would cripple reception for a sixty-mile range of programs originating from the Empire State Building. It was predicted that viewers would receive the original television waves and then a bounce-back microseconds later off the Twin Towers, causing ghosts, double images, snow effects, and double talk—since the audio portion would rebound along with the pictures.[17] The problem of fuzzy television reception presented yet another headache for the Port Authority. Additional studies were made and press releases were issued to deal with angry viewers. In fact, none of these problems actually occurred because after long negotiations the broadcasting masts were moved from the Empire State Building to the North Tower of the World Trade Center.

Even bird lovers raised an objection to the World Trade Center. They argued that the Twin Towers would "do incalculable damage to our night-migrating birds, an invaluable natural resource." That argument was raised by the Linnaean Society of the American Museum of Natural History. They pointed out that New York City was "at a major junction of flyways" and that there were records of migratory birds crashing into tall buildings. It was true that hundreds of birds had been killed back in 1948 when fog on the Hudson River drove flight after flight of warblers and red-eyed vireos headed for Central and South America into the Empire State Building.[18] One can only imagine the consternation and surprise at Port Authority headquarters when officials learned of this new objection to their favorite project. It must have seemed that the whole world was against them.

NO ENDORSEMENT FROM ARCHITECTURAL CRITICS

We have briefly examined the political, economic, and environmental arguments mustered against the project. To these must now be added perhaps the most painful of all—the architectural arguments. It was difficult in the early 1970s to find a single architectural critic who really liked the Twin Towers. Most expressed some grudging admiration for their size, but then went on to disapprove of their appearance. Here is what Wolf von Eckardt of the *Washington Post* had to say: "There is the fascination of the towers' ugliness. Man's tallest buildings to date defy their surroundings, man's most wondrous, skyscraping community. The 110-story Brobdingnagian shafts stand with blunt, graceless arrogance at the western edge of Manhattan island, seeming to tilt that wonder with overbearing size and hubris."[19] This kind of criticism was hurtful to Austin Tobin, who considered himself a knowledgeable patron of art and architecture. But in this arena, there was little that he could do to counter the bad publicity. Spokespeople at the Port Authority had answers for most public policy objections, but in matters of taste it is difficult to rebut the critics. In private, Austin Tobin fumed, but publicly he maintained a stoic silence.

Perhaps the lowest point for the World Trade Center in terms of public esteem and agency morale came on Wednesday, April 4, 1973. It should have been a joyous occasion since it was the date for the formal dedication, but the event was bittersweet. The weather mirrored the mood of the proceedings. Rain reduced the size of the crowd and forced the ceremony indoors. The basement was half-finished and messy. Runoff rainwater from the street flooded down into a connecting subway entrance, soaking the feet of many visitors.

Strangely enough, from this gloomy and inauspicious day forward, things became better for the World Trade Center. Slowly, the Port Authority got credit for its efforts in running the PATH. It was not everything critics wanted in terms of mass transit, but it was enough. The trains were clean, they ran on time, and the fare was low. Slowly, the World Trade Center shook its reputation as a white elephant. More tenants came, and rental rates were increased. In time, the complex became remarkably profitable. Even the environmentalists were mollified when the sewage was hooked up to a system where it was properly treated before discharge. And the World Trade Center took a pioneering role in recycling, winning several awards for its efforts.

There was one remaining problem where the Port Authority could not satisfy its critics: the matter of esthetics. I have looked into this matter in some detail, and I have been forced to the conclusion that some problems have no solution. In the process of preparing this chapter, I attended a session on "American Art and Architecture" at a meeting of the American Culture Association held in Philadelphia. At this session, I made a presentation on the World Trade Center that included many images of the Twin Towers not from works of architectural history but from fashion advertising, travel posters, tourist postcards, and corporate logos. I made the argument that the building was a landmark in American architecture and that the widespread image of the Twin Towers in commercial art proved that it had a place in the hearts of people worldwide.

While everyone in this group was too polite to laugh aloud, most felt that I was too far out on a limb. This was a sophisticated group, and they knew that architectural critics had widely denounced the World Trade Center as a self-glorifying monument built by an unaccountable public authority. Professor David M. Sokol of the College of Architecture, Art, and Urban Planning of the University of Illinois at Chicago, who had organized the session in the first place, advised me against pursuing the topic any further. "At my college," he said, "we take the history of architecture very seriously, and the World Trade Center never comes up. It simply is not discussed."[20]

I should point out that Professor Sokol was not being in the least bit hostile; he was simply stating the case as a matter of fact. Indeed, as I reviewed the literature I could find very few defenders of the World Trade Center. Years earlier, I had studied the history of American architecture as an undergraduate at Yale under

Professor Vincent Scully. When I consulted his latest book, I found that he, too, strongly disapproved of the project. Scully wrote, "In New York the rising spires of the skyscrapers of lower Manhattan were finally invaded by the flat slabs of the International Style, of which the Chase Manhattan Bank was the first. These instantly reduced the scale and quelled the wonderfully competitive action of the earlier towers. The whole pyramidal grouping of spires began to die. The tall but inert twin chunks of the World Trade Center seemed to kill the whole thing off. So big and dead were they that all the dynamic interrelationships of the earlier buildings came to seem lilliputian, inconsequential in scale."[21]

GENERAL ACCEPTANCE BY THE PUBLIC

It is likely that the World Trade Center will never win approval from professionally trained architectural historians and critics. Yet there remains a cultural paradox. If the Twin Towers are so ugly as to be beneath notice, why do they keep appearing in the background of so many ads for upscale products in glossy magazines? Week after week, we find the Twin Towers in ads for expensive women's clothing and accessories. Fashion models are often photographed from promenades at either Brooklyn Heights or Jersey City. Of course, advertisers are not interested in reflecting the tastes of highbrow intellectual esthetics. Rather, they are interested in selling to consumers. And from all available evidence, consumers respond favorably to the Twin Towers.

All of this is an old problem in the study of American esthetics. The intellectual elite disapprove of the World Trade Center because of its massive scale, its stripped-down, no-frills look. For this group, the project is simply outside recent architectural history. But there is something about it in its spare and minimalist look that resonates from our Puritan and frontier past. No matter what the critics say, the people have accepted it, perhaps for its sheer size.

The proof is that the World Trade Center has earned a listing in the controversial *Dictionary of Cultural Literacy* in the category of Fine Arts. The authors of this dictionary are educational reformers who argue that communication and thinking depend on our knowledge of the common stock of people, places, sayings, happenings, and ideas that "all truly literate Americans know and recognize." The World Trade Center is right there along with the Taj Mahal. Conspicuously absent are many other New York buildings favored by architectural critics. Among the missing are the Lever House of 1952 by Skidmore, Owings, and Merrill, as well as the Seagram Building of 1958 by Mies van der Rohe and Philip Johnson. The authors of the dictionary explain, "Our principle for inclusion is not personal opinion about the merits of a particular art or artists, but our judgment of their established status as enduring points of reference in our culture. Everything that is included here is a classic—not because it is old or new, but because it has achieved broad currency. People refer to these works and artists without explanation, assuming that we will understand their reference."[22]

In the late 1980s I had the pleasure of watching on public television the series *Pride of Place* sponsored by Mobil and hosted by architect Robert A. M. Stern. The host, always well dressed and hyperactive, led the viewers on location to various architectural masterpieces. The programs were arranged by topics such as college campuses, dreamhouses, suburbs, resorts, and so on. The key to the series was that Stern, in the manner established years earlier by Alistair Cooke, would personally be filmed at the site of each important structure, thus holding the whole thing together not just through narration, but through the force of his personality and image.

The program that I remember best was one on skyscrapers called "Proud Towers." For me it was significant that Stern was concerned not only with the ultimate truth and beauty of each skyscraper, but also with its popular reception. For example, he pointed out that Daniel Burnham's Flatiron Building of 1902 was the sensation of its time, "joining the Statue of Liberty and the Brooklyn Bridge as one of the foremost postcard souvenirs of the city." As if to prove the point, Stern would then *on camera* mail a postcard picturing that very skyscraper by dropping it in a mailbox in the building's own lobby. It was a dramatic gesture, suggesting that portrayal on a postcard represents popular vindication. He did this again for Cass Gilbert's Woolworth Building of 1913 and for William Van Alen's Chrysler Building of 1930. What bothered me is that Stern never visited the World Trade Center because it is by far and away the postcard favorite of tourists, both domestic and foreign. Any visitor to New York City can participate in this experiment. Go to a postcard rack anywhere tourists frequent and see which building is most heavily represented. Chances are good that the winner will be the World Trade Center. In fact, if you are downtown, the chances are excellent. If Stern had started with postcards rather than using them as an afterthought, he would not have been able to ignore the World Trade Center.

Taking my own advice, the day I conducted this admittedly unscientific experiment at a souvenir shop on Fulton Street I picked up four different views of the World Trade Center. It was the *only building* at my rack that had multiple representations. Purchasers of postcards want to impress their friends back home with splendid scenes, so it is reasonable to assume that postcard photographers do their best to come up with flattering shots. The World Trade Center has many good sides, but the best views are all from a distance. Postcards are an ephemeral kind of document usually not taken seriously and often discarded, but they provide valuable clues to popular iconography. In a word, the people who buy postcards may not know much about architecture, but they know what they like.

Picture postcards of the World Trade Center have been sent to people all over the world, and they keep showing up among the meager possessions of desperate illegal aliens and stowaways trying to come to the United States. Over the years, there have been persistent reports and rumors of immigration officials who find people, with no official papers, clinging to a postcard of the World Trade Center as a symbol for their hopes for a better world.

I think it is fair to say that a listing in the *Dictionary of Cultural Literacy* in 1988 may be taken as evidence of popular acceptance of the World Trade Center. It is also reasonable to assume that its continuing popularity as a postcard image at the present time is further evidence of that trend. But these things are simply *signs* of that popularity. We must continue this discussion further to find out the *causes* of that popularity.

THE MAKING OF *KING KONG* IN 1976

When director John Guillerman took on the challenge of remaking the classic 1933 movie *King Kong* some forty years later in 1976, he substituted in the concluding scenes the Twin Towers for the Empire State Building. Just as in the original film, Kong is captured on a remote island and brought back to New York Harbor on a ship. Plans are made to launch a showbiz spectacular. On opening night, an international television satellite network covers the event. As in the original film, Kong goes berserk and breaks free. The giant ape starts to wreak havoc on New York City. The army sets up a command post to track Kong's path of destruction. Where will he strike next? No one is sure, no one except the hero, Professor Jack Prescott, who contacts army headquarters and speaks with the man in charge. The conversation is charged with tension.

"Excuse me, Professor, you say you know where Kong is headed?"

"Yes, I do. It's a place where you can trap him without danger. Now, can you get a couple of big helicopters and some steel blasting nets to drop on top of him?"

"Sure, no problem. Where is Kong headed, Professor Prescott?"

"We deal for that. You promise to capture him without injury, and I'll tell you where."

Here there is an excruciatingly long pause while those in the command post contemplate the proposal. The hero, at long last, becomes impatient.

"Dammit, do we have a deal?"

"Yes, Professor, we have a deal. Where is Kong headed?"

"There is one place in Manhattan that looks exactly like a certain part of his native habitat. Let him through to it, and you can trap him there. Let him climb . . . to the top of the World Trade Center."

Of course, in the end the army betrays the professor's trust, and the mortally wounded King Kong falls 110 stories from a ledge onto the plaza below. The final fall was a five-minute scene filmed on location in June 1976. The filming took place over three consecutive nights at a cost of a quarter of a million dollars. Production officials said that the total cost of the film came to $23 million. A crowd of more than 5,000 New Yorkers surged past police lines and fought its way to the place where the giant gorilla lay dead. The ape was constructed of Styrofoam covered with horsehair. He was bleeding with a mixture of Karo syrup and vegetable coloring. The crowd was made up of unpaid extras who had responded to newspaper ads. The scene, illuminated by two dozen 40,000-watt arc lights, was filmed again and again until director Guillerman, perched atop a thirty-foot hydraulic crane and directing the crowd with a megaphone, was satisfied. At the very end, Jessica Lange, wearing an evening dress, surrounded by photographers, is pictured by a mounted camera that pulls slowly back, fulfilling the requirements of the last page of the script that called for "a weeping sequined star."[23]

I think that it is a terribly significant development in American popular culture that *King Kong II* switched buildings. It showed our continuing fascination with architecture, and it served to validate the Twin Towers as *the* new American icon, at least among the masses of American people. So popular was the first full-page ad for the 1976 *King Kong* that the producers were deluged with 25,000 requests for full-color reprints. They worked 'round the clock to fill orders. The ad showed King Kong breaking up airplanes with his right hand and clutching Jessica Lange in his left hand, standing astride the Twin Towers. At the time, even architectural critic Ada Louise Huxtable was swept up in the excitement of the film. With benign good humor, she said of the poster, "While this may provide less of a nostalgic kick, it is vastly elevated high camp. And it also gives King Kong an infinitely superior footing. Instead of perilously grabbing the famous Art Deco spire, he has each leg firmly planted on one of the two new flattop towers."[24]

THE FEATS OF DAREDEVILS

In the 1970s the newly completed Twin Towers became the premiere attraction for daredevils from all over the world. Like mountains and other tall buildings, they became irresistible magnets. In a few short years, the Twin Towers were walked between by tightrope, parachuted from, and finally climbed. The stories of these accomplishments were widely disseminated through the mass media and became part of the lore of the World Trade Center. Long-term tenants of the building old enough to remember the 1970s keep the memory of the daredevils' deeds fresh in the hearts and minds of a new generation of office workers. The stories underscore the infinite vulnerability of the daredevils coupled with their awareness of the danger and their willingness to take risks. Consciousness of their deeds makes even the ordinary office worker in the towers a partner in this heroic arena.

The first of these recklessly bold heroes was high-wire artist Philippe Petit, twenty-four years of age at the time, from Nemours, France. Previously he had walked a tightrope between the towers of Notre Dame Cathedral in Paris in 1971 and between the towers of the Sydney Harbor Bridge in Australia in 1973. His next challenge was the World Trade Center, where he eluded guards, ran a slender tightrope across the tops of the Twin Towers, and walked across it early in the morning of August 7, 1974. People gathered by the hundreds on the streets below starting at about 7:15 A.M. to look up some 1,350 feet at the Frenchman dressed in black, outlined against the gray morning sky. A contemporary account in the *New York Times* described how Petit was able to accomplish this feat. A day earlier, he and three others disguised themselves as construction workers, wearing blue jeans, work boots, shirts with pencils in the pockets, and hard hats. They split up. Two went to the uppermost floors of the North Tower; the other two went to the uppermost floors of the South Tower.

According to Petit, they were able to load their supplies without challenge onto a freight elevator, store them just nineteen steps below the roof, and move about freely. Two assistants took up positions on the roof of the North Tower. On the night before the walk, Petit and one associate stationed themselves on the roof of the South Tower. Using a five-foot bow, they shot an arrow with a strand of fishing line across to the other tower. They passed progressively heavier lines until the 200-foot cable was strung across the 131-foot gap.

Once the main cable was in place, the men attached guy lines from the cable to the roof to keep swaying to a minimum. At one end the cable was attached to a steel stanchion on the roof. At the other they used a come-along, similar in function to a winch, to regulate the tension. On the morning of the walk, Petit paused before starting because he was in awe of the view offered to him. He told reporters later, "I couldn't help laughing—it was so beautiful." Then he started off. As he walked, a crowd of office workers, construction men, and police officers gathered below. Soon there were so many spectators that they created a massive traffic jam.

"After the first crossing, I look at the people and that was fantastic," Petit said. "New York wake up and what did they discover? There was a high walker on the twin towers. I was not scared because it was a precise thing. I was dying of happiness."[25]

Petit kept the crowd enthralled for nearly seventy-five minutes. During that time he made as many as seven or eight daring trips across the tightrope aided only by his thirty-eight-foot-long balancing pole. He stopped several times to lie down or sit down. Another contemporary report in the Newark *Star-Ledger* explained how the performance came to an end. Accounts of what happened that day differ. The police say that they persuaded the high-wire artist to stop, but Petit himself says that he was coerced. Charles Daniels, a sergeant with the Port Authority police, was sent up to the roof. Daniels called Petit a "tightrope dancer—because you couldn't call him a walker." Daniels, of East Orange, New Jersey, said, "He was laughing and smiling to himself—he had complete confidence in his ability—so that he started jumping. He was bouncing up and down—his feet were actually leaving the wire. He even lay down as if he wanted to take a nap . . . he was absolutely fearless. I figured I was watching something that no one else would ever see again."

Sergeant Daniels, drawing on his two years of college French, was able to communicate haltingly with Petit's accomplice, Jean François. Daniels persuaded (or coerced) Petit to give up after threatening to send a helicopter to pluck him off. Petit was worried that the downdraft from the craft might blow him off the tightrope. It was, a Port Authority spokesman sighed, "a very interesting day."[26]

Nearly a year after Philippe Petit surprised everyone by walking between the towers of the World Trade Center, he was on the highwire with the Ringling Brothers and Barnum & Bailey Circus. If anyone thought about the World Trade Center, it was mainly a concern about how they were going to find enough tenants to fill all those offices. Then, all of a sudden, the Twin Towers were back in the news again, on Tuesday, July 22, 1975, thanks to another daredevil. The attempt might have been predicted since parachuting from fixed objects had long been a recognized activity. There is even a specialized term for it, "BASE jumping," which is an acronym for jumping from fixed objects—Building, Antenna, Span, and Earth.

A skydiver from Queens, the largest borough of New York City, on Long Island, grabbed attention by parachuting from the North Tower to the plaza 1,350 feet below. Lee Dembart, a *New York Times* reporter, described how it was done: "With his white parachute concealed in a green bag, 34-year-old Owen J. Quinn of 30–42 23rd Street, Astoria, eluded security guards on the 78th floor of the north tower, walked to the roof above the 110th floor, jumped off at 4:45 P.M. and landed less than two minutes later on the raised ceremonial plaza between the buildings."[27]

Quinn free-fell 600 feet, then the chute opened, and he glided down the rest of the way to the ground. On the way down, the wind pushed him into the building, causing some cuts and bruises on his left leg. It all happened so fast that few people saw the drop, but Gerry Lewinter, working for the State Department of Social Services on the twenty-ninth floor of the South Tower, had a good view. According to Lewinter, "I saw a white blur outside and looked up to see a parachute going down. It was going quite fast. The guy was wearing a silver helmet. He seemed to hit very hard. He got up and started walking, limping for about 25 steps. Then he sat down. He seemed to be in pain."[28]

Port Authority Police took Quinn for a psychiatric examination at Elmhurst General Hospital in Queens. Later they booked him on charges of criminal trespass and reckless endangerment. Quinn said he jumped to draw attention not so much to himself but to the plight of the poor. He said, "If people decided not to eat once a month and to send the money to the needy poor, then it would help the situation." He received a flurry of congratulatory letters, some with donations for CARE, and one from the lieutenant governor of Ohio.[29]

The Sunday after his jump, the *New York Times* covered Quinn's accomplishment in the "Week in Review" section. The story reviewed the details of the feat and went on to report that Quinn wore gray cutoff shorts and a blue football jersey that bore a biblical inscription from Matthew 19:26 which read, "But Jesus beheld them and said unto them, With men this is impossible; but with God all things are possible."[30]

If the Twin Towers had been tightrope walked and jumped from, what was left to do? Why, to climb straight up the face of the building! It happened on May 27, 1977, almost two years after Quinn's stunning jump. The climber was George H. Willig, who was then a twenty-seven-year-old professional toy designer and amateur climber from Queens. Willig had plenty of mountain-climbing experience. All his life he had climbed trees, rocks, cliffs, and mountains. Among his more difficult climbs had been scaling the 300-foot-long route up Reed's Pinnacle in Yosemite Valley in eastern central California.

Of all the feats taking place at the World Trade Center, Willig's was the one that received the most attention. The celebrated "human fly" was watched by thousands on the ground and by millions on television. The reason was simple. The feat took three and a half hours to complete, giving crowds time to assemble and television news crews time to arrive on the scene and broadcast it all over the world.

Willig used equipment he had designed and built himself and tested in secret at night. For his climb, he used nylon rope and special metal clamps that fit into the metal grooves that run up and down the building to accommodate window-washing equipment. It was a fitting accomplishment for a man who spent his professional hours as a model maker, toy inventor, and "think tank" participant for the Ideal Toy Company in Hollis, Queens.

Willig designed the clamps so that they locked into place when pulled down by his body weight of 155 pounds, but released freely when he chose to raise them. He had started visiting the Twin Towers a year earlier. He made measurements and thought about the problem. He began to make the equipment that he would need. After about two months, he had something to test. He went there four or five times at night, and started testing at the base. He never went up until the day he started to climb. Willig explained the climb to Edith Evans Asbury, a reporter with the *New York Times*: "I was never scared, but a little nervous at the beginning, because I was afraid the Fire Department would send a cherry picker before I got too high for it to get me. That made me nervous, and I went up as fast as I could. But once I knew I was out of range of a cherry picker, I knew I was safe, so I slowed down and relaxed."[31]

The heroic climb started at 6:30 A.M. According to contemporary accounts, Willig wore denim trousers, ankle-high leather climbing boots, a T-shirt, and a little blue neckerchief. He carried a small red nylon knapsack with a canteen of water, a nylon jacket, sunglasses, and his specially designed climbing clamps and wrenches. He used a royal blue nylon line with a test strength of 3,500 pounds. He had it hooked through equipment on his waist and attached

to the metal devices that fit into the window-washing equipment
tracks. Gradually, thousands of pedestrians gathered at the scene to
watch Willig's gymnastic grace. News helicopters from various networks started hovering near the area. Then police helicopters had
to be dispatched to prevent them from getting too close to the
building.

Two police officers were dispatched on a window-washing
scaffold lowered from the roof. Their assignment was to try to
draw Willig onto the window-washing rig with them. From the
New York City police came Officer Dewitt C. Allen, a member of
Emergency Service Squad 1, who had previously rescued potential
suicides from and been as high as the towers of the George Washington Bridge in his work. Officer Allen was joined by Port Authority police officer Glenn Kildare. Reporter Mary Breasted of the *New
York Times* described the police actions in a front-page story the
next day. In less than three minutes of conversation, Officer Allen
realized that Willig was not insane: "I judged by his responses to
my questions, by the type of equipment he was using and I guess
you could say by the look in his eyes. Every response he gave me
was reasonable. The only thing unreasonable about it was the fact
that he was on the outside of the building."

The police decided not to attempt to grab him, and they simply
accompanied him the rest of the way up. Along the way, they established rapport. The two officers, supplying both a pad and pen, got
autographed notes from him at the seventy-fifth floor.

"Best wishes to my co-ascender," said each note.[32]

Meanwhile, back on the ground, a Port Authority spokesman worried about what might happen to Willig since the tracks
for the window-washing equipment had been designed as guides,
but not supports. Because of this, nobody knew how much weight
they could hold. The tower panel that Willig climbed was sheeted
with aluminum, held on by screws, which had never been tested
for strength. Afterward, Officer Allen said that the only difficulty
that Willig ran into was occasional irregularity in the grooves. For
this problem, Willig was prepared. He had brought a little hammer
along.[33]

When the time came to prepare for the peak, Willig handed
his knapsack to Officer Allen. Other police on the roof lowered a
line about fifteen feet below. With the eyes of the world on him,

Willig hooked that line to his harness and allowed himself to be pulled to the top through a tiny hatch window normally used for the window-washing equipment. He had commanded three full hours of media time, and the newsmen on the roof all cheered.[34]

At first the glory of Willig's accomplishment was marred by the fact that the city of New York sued him for a quarter of a million dollars because they estimated that the caper had cost that much in terms of the use of helicopters and police overtime. When Mayor Abraham Beame learned of the lawsuit, he was angry. The mayor saw that going after a folk hero would be a public relations disaster. The mayor met with Willig's lawyer, and they settled on a fine of $1.10, which represented a penny a floor. At a mobbed press conference, Willig gave the mayor a dollar bill and a dime. The Mayor, not to mention Port Authority officials, was happy to have a graceful way out of a bureaucratic snafu.[35]

Perhaps the last word on this affair should go to poet John P. McNett, who wrote a quatrain in the style of Lewis Carroll:

'Twas Willig and slithy tower
Did gyre and gimble in the wind;
All mimsy were the bureaucrate
But the Toymaker outgrabe.[36]

The exploits of the daredevils, like the remaking of *King Kong*, were lucky events that helped to humanize the Twin Towers. Perhaps the real value of the film was that it connected the upstart World Trade Center of the 1970s with the familiar Empire State Building of the 1930s. By means of the image of the giant ape, the World Trade Center had the good fortune to be bathed in the warm glow of nostalgia. Even if it was just instant nostalgia, or camp, people loved it nonetheless. The film helped to link the present to the past, to provide a sense of continuity. Viewers drew hope and comfort from their happy memories of the original *King Kong*.

Similarly, the three daredevils of the 1970s were able to use the massive, impersonal Twin Towers in ways that helped to humanize them. The daredevils with their honor and courage asserted a human stamp on an artifact that was almost, but not quite, beyond human scale and comprehension. The net effect of these three officially unplanned and unscheduled but wonderful events was to increase the public approval ratings of the World Trade Center, which had hit the bottom of the abyss on the day of the dedication back in April 1973. It turned out that the Twin Towers were amazingly resilient in the battle for public approval.

There remain two additional aspects of the rehabilitation of the World Trade Center that must be discussed. We now turn our attention to the opening of the World Trade Center observation deck in 1975 and the opening of the Windows on the World restaurant in 1976. Reaching out to different constituencies, these two rooftop attractions helped to endear the Twin Towers to people everywhere.

THE OBSERVATION DECK

The observation deck had been part of the original plan for the World Trade Center all along. There was a reasonable expectation of success. Port Authority planners studied other similar facilities, such as the one at the Empire State Building with its eighty-sixth-floor view and the Rockefeller Center observatory atop the RCA Building, to gather as much useful information as possible. The Port Authority was eager to learn from the experiences of others, borrowing their good ideas and avoiding their mistakes. The plan called for an enclosed, indoor observation deck with extra-wide windows on the 107th floor, which would offer good views even on very cold and windy days. On this floor would be educational exhibits, food service, souvenir shops, and restrooms. From there, weather permitting, visitors could take escalators to the open-air promenade which was set back thirty-one feet from the edge of the roof.[37] Careful market studies projected a potential attendance of two million visitors a year. When the facility opened, they came close, running around 1.8 million visitors a year.[38]

Nearly everyone liked the observation deck from the very beginning. The press wrote favorable reviews, travel writers endorsed the idea of making a visit, and ordinary people recommended it to their friends. At last, the Port Authority had a hit on its hands. Laudatory reviews of the new observation deck started to appear in the press even before the facility was officially opened to the public in December 1975.

As early as April 1972, Paul J. C. Friedlander, a travel writer for the *New York Times*, got permission to make a preview visit to the site. Wearing a bright yellow plastic hard hat, he slowly rode a construction elevator up to the top. With clear excitement, Friedlander compared the view with that seen from a helicopter. He said the view from the World Trade Center was better "because both you and the view are standing still and you have the time requisite to look, identify, and be thrilled."

Friedlander pointed out that, on a clear day with good visibility, it was possible to see forty-five miles in all directions. To the south, it was possible to see the Ambrose Light; to the west, Newark Airport; to the north, the Tappan Zee Bridge. But closer in, he said, "You see a majestic New York without perceiving the dirty sidewalks and streets, the pushing and shoving you fight your way through at sidewalk level; nor hear the traffic horns nor choke on diesel fumes and unconsumed hydrocarbons. There is magic in altitude—crime and ghetto and politics and corruption become invisible."[39]

Just prior to the opening of the observation deck, the Port Authority launched a big advertising campaign to attract visitors. An advertising company came up with a theme and a jingle: "It's hard to be down when you're up." There were thirty-second television commercials showing the Twin Towers from a circling helicopter. Particularly striking was their eastern side glowing gold from the rising sun, with the shadow reaching into New Jersey. Advertisements also appeared on the sides of buses and on posters in mass transit facilities.[40]

The Port Authority opened the observation deck on Monday, December 15, 1975, at 9:30 A.M. About two hundred schoolchildren were invited to the occasion because they represented the wave of the future. The children were treated to a special performance by the cast of the Broadway production of *The Magic Show*. There were Dixieland music, clowns, magic tricks, and treats. The opening generated a windfall of favorable publicity. Newspapers throughout the region carried advance stories. While every local television channel covered the event, NBC broadcast it nationally on their network.[41] For an agency accustomed to dealing with bad news and hostile critics, this was a long-awaited public relations triumph.

One of the reasons that the observation deck was so well received was that it was open for long hours, from 9:30 A.M. to 9:30 P.M., seven days a week. Even more important was the reasonable price of admission at $1.70 for adults and 85 cents for children, with group rates for ten or more.[42] The idea of holding the line on prices came from Guy Tozzoli, director of the World Trade Center. Tozzoli told the manager of the observation deck, "As the father of six children, I don't want this place to become a tourist trap. I want it to be a good value for families."[43]

Even the architectural critic Paul Goldberger, who soundly detested the World Trade Center, found himself admiring the observation deck. He praised both the design of the 107th floor viewing gallery, calling it "thoughtful," and that of the open rooftop on the 110th floor, "where a raised walkway permits a stroll around all four sides. It has been set in from the edge of the building, a clever design device that virtually eliminates any feeling of vertigo." Echoing the remarks of Friedlander, three years earlier, Goldberger noted that the towers were so high "that the city below is completely silent—the only noise comes from the airplanes above."[44]

Less than a year after opening, the observation deck hosted its one millionth visitor. It was on October 22, 1976, that Elaine Seib and her husband, Michael, made their visit. To their surprise, the turnstile to the deck clicked an even million as Elaine passed through. One month later, she and her husband were honored at a luncheon where she was given a lifetime pass to the observation deck. In addition, the Hillside, New Jersey, couple was invited to a night on the town, with dinner at Windows on the World, followed by a Broadway show.[45] This story was a publicist's dream come true. Through the magic of careful record keeping, a predictable nonevent could be turned into a celebratory occasion that cost very little money and made everyone feel good about the observation deck. And the best part was that these events could be repeated over and over again as new milestones were reached.

Sure enough, three years later, in October 1979, Gerald and Eleanor Grover left their home in Brooklyn, New York, to visit the World Trade Center. Though both were lifelong New Yorkers, neither had yet visited the observation deck. As they entered the 107th floor, the turnstile clicked to an even five million. One month later, a ceremony was held at the World Trade Center. Mrs. Grover received (surprise!) a lifetime pass to the observation deck as well as dinner for two at Windows on the World. What was different this time is that the honoree received gifts or gift certificates from thirty-six different merchants located at the World Trade Center. There was candy from Fanny Farmer and games from F.A.O. Schwarz, not to mention three days and two nights of deluxe accommodations from the soon-to-be-opened Vista Hotel.[46] The Port Authority was well on its way to perfecting a surefire publicity device that was totally benign and noncontroversial.

As much as the Port Authority might have wanted to control all of the news coming out of the observation deck, it was not always possible. In 1984 the *New York Times* ran a story on August Lind, a seventy-eight-year-old retired ConEdison employee who was a frequent visitor to the World Trade Center. Without any official encouragement from the Port Authority, the newspaper took note of Lind's 2,400th visit to the observation deck. On that occasion, Lind took along a big cake for the employees, who regarded him with great affection.[47] The reason why the Port Authority tried to suppress the story? It seems that observation deck employees sometimes looked the other way and failed to charge Lind admission, which by then was up to $2.95, for his almost daily visits.[48]

As the observation deck became an established institution in the 1980s, certain patterns of usage became predictable. Normally, the busiest day was the day after Thanksgiving, the day when New Yorkers had to find something to do with their out-of-town guests. On such a day, they might get 12,000 people over a twelve-hour period. The slowest period consisted of the winter months of January, February, and March. During those months, it was often too cold to go up to the platform on the 110th floor. The busiest month was usually August, when many people take their vacations. A typical day in August might attract 8,000 visitors. Surprisingly, a factor that turned out not to be very important was visibility. Because the observation deck was basically selling a view, managers felt obliged to post signs at the downstairs ticket window advising patrons of adverse visibility conditions. Even if the weather was poor, many visitors went ahead and bought tickets anyway in order to say that they had been there.[49]

Despite this apparent success, the observation deck at the World Trade Center always trailed behind the Empire State Building in attendance. The Empire State Building had the advantage of a midtown location where more of the tourist and convention people had their hotels. In addition, the observation deck of the Empire

State Building routinely stayed open until midnight. In fact, the World Trade Center apparently had no impact on attendance at the Empire State whatsoever. The Empire State stopped advertising itself as "the highest" and simply called itself "the most famous." No one seemed bothered by the change.[50]

Surveys were conducted to find out the demographics of those who visited the observation deck. These studies indicated that about 50 percent of the visitors came from foreign countries, about 30 percent from the local surrounding tristate region, and about 20 percent from the rest of the United States. Some of the local visitors represented repeat business, of course. Of the foreign visitors, the most heavy representation came from Germany and Japan. In follow-up questions, the Germans often expressed an interest in the engineering aspects of the building and the Japanese were intrigued by the architect, Minoru Yamasaki.[51]

The observation deck of the World Trade Center turned out to be a profit center for the Port Authority. In a typical year in the 1980s, the deck might gross $8 million and net the agency $4 million in profits, which would simply be added to the overall revenues coming in from the tunnels, bridges, and airports. But even more important than the money was the endless goodwill that it created. People kept coming up with ideas for using the space in meaningful ways. Rather than stand in the way, the Port Authority came up with streamlined rules and procedures to allow the observation deck to be used creatively.

Fashion photographers scheduled photo sessions with their models on the rooftop. Couples scheduled their weddings. The armed forces scheduled military reenlistment ceremonies. In general, the Port Authority reasonably asked that people seek written permission in advance and that such activities not interfere with the customary flow of tourists. For example, simple wedding ceremonies with bride, groom, clergy, and witnesses were allowed and encouraged, especially on Valentine's Day. But reception parties were not allowed.[52]

In much the same way, the observation deck also generated goodwill for international visitors and dignitaries. When the General Assembly of the United Nations was in session in New York City, foreign dignitaries often scheduled VIP visits. From time to time, the State Department would request VIP tours for foreign ambassadors and diplomats. Normally, these VIP tours were conducted by giving the visitor "the red carpet treatment" without disrupting the tourist trade, but when Mikhail S. Gorbachev visited in 1990 the deck was cleared of other visitors for security reasons.[53] The enthusiastic public embrace of the observation deck helped gain fame and appreciation for the World Trade Center.

Certainly, Port Authority management, more accustomed to fending off criticism, was delighted with this turn of events. Most of the credit, of course, is given to the sublime view from the top. But some of the credit should be given to the rank-and-file employees at the observation deck who make visitors feel welcome. One such employee is Morris Miller, a window cleaner. Like others of his job description, Miller is a member of Local No. 2 of the Window Cleaners Union and an employee of Modern Sanitation Systems who contracts for the work with the Port Authority.

I first met Miller in December 1994 while I was looking around the observation deck, trying to get a sense of the place. I was lost in a world of my own, reading the captions on the exhibits, looking out the windows, and thinking about what it all meant. All of a sudden Miller came up in his blue coveralls with bucket and water, squeegee and sponge. I was jarred out of my reverie. In a booming voice, he accosted me, "How you doing? How's everything? Okay? Good! I'm glad to hear it." We talked for a while, and I learned that he had been working as a window cleaner at the World Trade Center for twenty years and that he was now sixty-four years of age. He had joined the air force as a young man back in 1948 and was trained as a cook. When he got out of the service in 1952, he tried his hand at professional boxing, vaudeville acting, and working construction. Finally, he drifted into window cleaning at the World Trade Center in 1974.[54]

I learned that on a typical day Miller, who lives uptown, will get up by 3:30 A.M. and take the subway to work, getting off like so many others at Cortlandt Street. He takes the elevator up to work, and he is on the job by 6 A.M. Since visitors do not arrive until 9:30 A.M., he has plenty of time to concentrate on the task at hand. He starts cleaning the insides, top to bottom, of the 232 windows of the Observation Deck. This is the professional part of his job. When he was younger, Miller also went outdoors "over the side" to clean the outsides as well. But now, because of his advancing age, not to mention his hip replacement, he concentrates on inside work. Cleaning the windows must be done, but he can get most of it out of the way before the visitors begin to arrive. In effect, Miller has redefined the job. What he really enjoys is entertaining the visitors, especially the children. Miller says, "I love it here. This is my place."

Because of his acting background and his irrepressible personality, Miller often volunteered to dress up in holiday costumes to entertain visiting children. But it did not require a holiday or special occasion for Miller to radiate his unique brand of cheerful optimism. In subsequent visits, I had the chance to watch Miller work the crowd. Many young children who visit are afraid at first. It's too high up for them, and it's a strange environment. Miller deals with their fears and anxieties by entertaining them and distracting them with balloons. He may approach a group of three young children, obviously unhappy and perhaps crying, and he will say, "Believe me when I tell you this. Look what I got here for you [holding balloons in his hands]. Let me see [pondering who will get the balloons]. You? You? Or you? How old are you? Anybody here over four? Over five? Tell me! Show me! Show me your fingers. Okay, my name is Moe, okay? You tell me what is your name? What is your name? What is your name? Okay, I'm going to give you each a balloon, but first you gotta tell me something. Is everybody happy up here on the 107th floor?" Lo and behold, the children stop crying. One cannot put a cash value on Miller's genius at creating goodwill.

At the same time, there are elderly visitors to the observation deck who may be cautious and frail. They may well hesitate to take the escalator from the 107th floor up to the outdoor platform on the 110th floor. Typically, Miller will approach them and say with a twinkle in his eye, "I'll tell you what. You go upstairs. If you don't like it, come down and I'll buy you a new car. Okay?" Miller then shakes their hands. They go up and they love it. Miller has yet to buy a new car for anyone.

After watching a few of his masterful performances as Mr. Hospitality, I worry a little about Miller's continuing employment as a glass cleaner. I ask him, "Aren't you concerned about spending so much time with the visitors?"

"Don't worry. The Port Authority loves me, and I love them. They never bother me. Why should I want for anything?"

"Yes, but isn't your job title 'window cleaner'?"

"I do my job. I do my glass. There's no complaints, thank God."

"But what about the supervisors?"

"I'm doing a good job, right? Am I doing a good job? Is the glow of the sun coming through the glass?"

"Yes, I guess so."

"Look, the main thing is I talk to the people. I give them love. I love to get a laugh out of a child."[55]

There was not much I could say. Apparently, his union and his company and the Port Authority itself have all recognized that here is a person who makes a favorable impression on the visitors and is best left alone to do things his way.

WINDOWS ON THE WORLD

Many important design aspects flowed from Minoru Yamasaki's original decision to create two separate towers. Very early in the process, it was decided to place the observation deck for the ordinary visitor on top of the South Tower and a private club and restaurant for the elite on top of the North Tower. The plan seemed to make sense. Guy Tozzoli, in his travels around the world, noticed that most other trade centers had some sort of private club for their tenants to entertain visitors and prospective business partners. The idea was to devote the entire 107th floor of the North Tower to the club primarily as an amenity to business tenants. Though functioning as a luncheon club by day, it would be open as a public restaurant in the evenings and on weekends.

The main dining room had an imaginatively tiered physical plan, affording everyone a view. A series of eighteen private suites suitable for board meetings, sales presentations, and cocktail receptions would be located along the west wall. Toward the east would be a magnificent bar. Coordinating everything was Joe Baum, a top restaurateur. In the summer of 1975, the Port Authority began to brief tenants about the forthcoming club's facilities and services. Tenants were invited to view a model of the club in a preview room located on the 102nd floor.

Port Authority officials came up with a scheme that seemed reasonable at the time. Dues for tenants of the World Trade Center were set at a modest $360 per year. Memberships were also offered to nontenants whose principal place of business was South of Canal

Street at $420 per year. The fee for nontenant members north of Canal Street, but within the twenty-five-mile port district, was set at $100 per year. Those whose businesses were located more than twenty-five miles away would be charged only $50 per year.[56] The fees were quite fair and reasonable, especially in view of the fact that, unlike most other private clubs downtown, there was no heavy initial fee for joining. Port Authority officials were also careful to be nondiscriminatory. There was no old school tie, no need to come from old money, no restriction based on race or religion. Prospective members simply had to be creditworthy; anyone who could get a credit card could join this club. Thus the club was not in any traditional sense "elite," though it did have that appearance.[57]

Unlike the observation deck, which was universally well received, the plan for the club met an unexpected firestorm of criticism. There was one fundamental problem with Guy Tozzoli's plan. It failed to take into account the deep underlying democratic values of American society. Even something with the mere appearance of being "elite" would attract bitter hostility. Because of this lack of foresight, the plan for an elegant restaurant on top of the North Tower nearly failed. It took desperate last-minute maneuvering and a compromise to save it. But before discussing that controversy, we need to go back to the beginning of the story.

In his essay "Self-Reliance," Ralph Waldo Emerson wrote: "An institution is the lengthened shadow of one man . . . and all history resolves itself easily into the biography of a few stout and earnest persons." If the Port Authority is the lengthened shadow of Austin Tobin and if the World Trade Center is the lengthened shadow of Guy Tozzoli, then surely Windows on the World is the lengthened shadow of Joe Baum. He was born in 1920 at Saratoga Springs, New York, where his family ran a hotel for fifty-five years. He grew up in a town of racetracks and nightclubs. His father taught him, "When you have customers in the house, give them— give them everything they want. Just *know* what they want." Building on that idea, Baum pioneered the concept of restaurants as entertainment. No attention to detail is spared in order to make a place accessible and inviting.[58] In 1943 Joe Baum graduated with a Bachelor of Science degree from the School of Hotel Administration at Cornell University. Almost immediately, he joined the navy and served as the supply officer aboard the U.S.S. *Lindsey*, a destroyerminelayer in the Pacific. The day President Franklin Roosevelt died, April 12, 1945, the *Lindsey* was bombed and nearly sunk by two kamikaze pilots. After a third of the ship was demolished, the crew abandoned it. As most of the crew headed for the lifeboats, Joe Baum had to stay behind to do his duty. As supply officer, he had one last moral obligation before he could leave the ship. At great risk to himself, he went below to his office for the last time, where he carefully removed the $75,000 in the safe for which he was responsible. He quickly stashed the money in a garment bag, ran for the last lifeboat, and in time was able to return honorably every penny to the government. He was later commended for his conscientiousness and bravery.[59]

In the late 1940s, Joe Baum worked for Norman Bel Geddes, the well-known theatrical and industrial designer. Bel Geddes designed stages for Broadway plays, and his film sets were remarkable for their innovative lighting. Under Bel Geddes, Joe Baum learned a great deal about the technical side of esthetics. These lessons he would later apply to the restaurant business.

In the early 1950s, Joe Baum joined Restaurant Associates, which operated a chain of twenty-four coffee shops. The company, however, was about to launch a white-tablecloth restaurant, called the Newarker, at the Newark Airport, a Port Authority facility in New Jersey. The assignment, considered risky because of its location in the unfashionable swamps, was given to Joe Baum in 1953. At the start, the situation looked grim since the Newarker lost $25,000 the first year. Baum explained: "Initially, we lost lots of money, but God, the things we did! Specially made china, graphically exciting menus, extra oysters on the plate, lobsters with three claws [i.e. a lobster and a half per portion], flaming dishes, brandied coffee, the dessert sparkler—we originated all those things that would eventually become clichés."[60]

Joe Baum hired teams of big-name consulting architects, decorators, and graphic artists (Philip Johnson, Ludwig Mies van der Rohe, Milton Glaser, Alexander Girard). Baum was lavish; he spent six figures a year on flowers, an outlandish sum compared to other first-class restaurants of the day. Baum was a perfectionist; he rejected tons of wood paneling with imperfect grains. Somehow it all worked. "People don't come to fine restaurants just because they're hungry," Baum explained. "They come for a civilized ritual involving hospitality, imagination, harmony, graciousness, and warmth."[61]

By the second year, the Newarker turned a profit, with seven hundred customers a night. Amazingly, at the time, about half of the customers came to the airport to dine, not to fly. It was at this point that Joe Baum's stunning success first came to the favorable attention of Port Authority officials. It was the beginning of a life-long relationship.

As the years went by, Baum became known for his inventiveness and flair. He made his mark not by operating New York City restaurants but by dreaming them up and opening them, one after another. There was the Forum of the Twelve Caesars, not just an Italian restaurant, but a reflection of the Roman Empire. There was La Fonda del Sol, a high-quality Latin American restaurant. The most ambitious of all was the Four Seasons, where the menus changed every quarter; it cost $4.5 million to build and took two and a half years of planning.[62]

In the mid-1970s, Joe Baum was named head of Inhilco, a subsidiary of Hilton International. His job was to open and operate twenty-two different food and drink outlets at the World Trade Center, including Windows on the World, which was scheduled to open in April 1976. The preceding fall, Baum was busy planning the menus, recruiting the chefs, selecting the china patterns, and taking care of thousands of details to ensure that the new club restaurant—Windows on the World—would be the best ever. Then in October 1975, the sky fell in. The state legislature in Albany discovered that the Port Authority was spending $20 million to outfit the new restaurants at the World Trade Center, including $6 million for the private club. Two legislators grabbed headlines by calling this expenditure "extravagance at a time when the mass-transit system of the metropolitan area is in desperate need of help."[63]

As usual, there was an explanation for the apparent extravagance. But the charges of wastefulness got the headlines, while the explanation was buried deep in the story. The fact of the matter was that the Port Authority had tried to recruit every major restaurant operator in the country to put up their own money to launch the new restaurants in the World Trade Center. Not one was willing to do so, because the venture was considered too risky, given its downtown location, considered to be out of the mainstream for restaurants. Only Hilton International was willing to pay a portion of the initial construction, and it was a small portion at that. The contract called for the Port Authority to pay 93 percent of the cost of construction and Hilton 7 percent. In lieu of annual rent, the Port Authority would accept 85 percent of the net profits. While PA officials argued that they would recoup the $20 million over twenty years at a rate of at least $1 million per year, the state legislature in Albany was skeptical.[64]

Having once drawn blood, the press went into a feeding frenzy attacking the Port Authority for its restaurant plan in general and the private club in particular. The criticism centered around the planned decorations, which made easy targets. These included such lavish features as gold leaf, pink marble lavatory walls trimmed with fur, cowhide, and silk-covered ceilings. The bill for the decorations came to $311,000. But the *pièce de résistance* was the bill for four chairs at $3,500 each, though this feature was quickly eliminated as a result of the criticism.[65] The New York *Daily News* regaled its readers with stories about the cost of fabrics, wall-to-wall carpeting, draperies, railings, lighting, and a rug costing $5,000, not to mention a credenza for the office manager's office at $3,075.[66] It appeared to the man in the street that the Port Authority was using the money collected from tolls on its bridges and tunnels to provide extravagant furnishings for a private club.[67]

The New York state assembly held a public hearing on the matter in December 1975. Port Authority chairman William T. Ronan defended the agency's construction of the club, saying that it was necessary to attract and hold tenants and that, in the long run, it would be profitable. Ronan said, "I think it not only is appropriate, I think it's good business. You have to spend money to make money." The assemblymen hammered Ronan with criticisms and tough questions, but Ronan was unflappable. He even managed to joke about the expensive chairs, which helped to defuse the situation.[68]

At the end of 1975, it seemed that the way was clear for the Port Authority to push ahead with its plans for a club and restaurant on top of the North Tower. But suddenly there came an unexpected setback. The New York State Liquor Authority (SLA) issued a "stop order" on the PA's request for a liquor license and ordered a "thorough review" of the application. Thomas Spencer, head of the SLA, said, "Unless the public is granted equal access to the restaurant, it is very doubtful a license would be approved." The Port Authority argued that the facility would only be a private club at lunch and that it would be a public restaurant at night. Spencer seemed 'unmoved by that argument and said, "It is a general policy of the liquor authority that the public must be accommodated."[69]

The key to the controversy was that the Port Authority wanted to exclude the public between noon and 3:00 P.M. Neither the State Liquor Authority nor the Port Authority would budge. The argument dragged on all winter and into the spring of 1976. Opening day was scheduled for Monday, April 12, 1976, but that day came and went with no opening.[70] Behind the scenes, there were frantic negotiations. Finally, one week later, an agreement was hammered out. The nine-hundred-seat restaurant would set aside some sixty seats at lunch for public patrons, though they would pay a special surcharge of ten dollars for the host and three dollars for each guest in addition to the normal luncheon cost. Meanwhile, the Port Authority could take satisfaction in the fact that on opening day, Monday, April 19, 1976, they had already accepted 1,300 members, of whom 837 were World Trade Center tenants and executives of downtown Manhattan firms.[71]

Windows on the World caught on with the public immediately. Not only did it offer spectacular views of the city, it had James Beard as a menu consultant and an unmatched wine cellar. It was a popular restaurant, a tourist attraction, and a business sensation.[72] The following month, in May, Gael Greene, restaurant critic for *New York* magazine, wrote an eleven-page cover story calling Windows "the most spectacular restaurant in the world." She went on to say, "Windows on the World is a triumph. No other sky-high restaurant quite prepares you for the astonishment of these horizons."[73]

Greene's article was better than a million dollars' worth of publicity. Her endorsement was priceless. Windows on the World seemed to have the ability to melt the hearts of the Port Authority's critics. People could begin to forget all the controversies surrounding the construction of the Twin Towers—the delays, the strikes, the lawsuits, the waste, the extravagance, the pollution, and so on. None of that seemed to matter so much anymore.

The greatest compliment for Windows on the World was paid by attorney Theodore Kheel, an outspoken critic of the Port Authority. Kheel had once suggested that the World Trade Center be torn down. Confronted while savoring a dish at the restaurant, Kheel said he was revising his suggestion. "They should tear it down," he said, "all but the 107th floor."[74]

5
Architecture

Beloved by All
Except the Experts

I believe that buildings should have ornament.

—Minoru Yamasaki, architect, cited in
Oral History of Modern Architecture, 1994

PICK UP almost any serious book on American architecture, and you will look in vain for mention of the World Trade Center. The few books that do mention the building do so with disparaging language. How did it happen that something so important, a universally recognized symbol of American abundance, came to be disregarded and disrespected by those who take architecture most seriously? There is a disconnection between elite culture and popular culture because nearly every guidebook to New York City lists the Twin Towers among the city's top ten attractions.

We should not be terribly surprised by the contradiction between the highbrow and the lowbrow assessments of the World Trade Center. This same elite-popular conflict has been played out in debate over other controversial structures such as the Guggenheim Museum and the St. Louis Arch. In all these cases, the debate has been fueled by the fact that the critics and the public have different modes of education and expectations. To paraphrase French social theorist Pierre Bourdieu, the prestige of an architectural critic depends on the rigor of his exclusions. The critic, or tastemaker, brings to the problem a whole set of nuances that only the experienced eye can perceive. The status of the critic depends on his mastery of a perfectly up-to-date set of ever-changing classifications.[1]

One important key to explaining the contradiction between highbrow architecture books and lowbrow guidebooks is to take a close look at the project's architect, Minoru Yamasaki. In the first place, we must remember that for his whole life in America, he was an outsider, a foreigner. In overcoming a life subjected to prejudice,

Yamasaki had developed extraordinary qualities of individualism and self-reliance. He was an outsider in at least three important ways. In the first place, he was Japanese, placing him squarely outside the world of elite WASP architects. Second, he was from the Midwest. His most productive years of architectural practice had taken place in Michigan, unconnected to the world of wealthy clients in New York. But most important, there was a matter of style. Yamasaki was working in an architectural idiom perhaps best described as the New Formalism, which never caught on. The New Formalism was an attempt to get away from the International Style, which had dominated the 1920s and 1930s. What no one knew for sure at the time was that the next style to become fashionable would not be the New Formalism but postmodernism, which came to dominate the 1970s and 1980s.

Delicate political negotiations between New York and New Jersey paved the way for the construction of the World Trade Center. The Port Authority asked Richard Adler to work out a basic architectural conception with the help of the "Genius Committee" consisting of Gordon Bunshaft, Wallace K. Harrison, and Edward Durell Stone. As negotiations proceeded, it became clear to Port Authority managers that there were two problems with this arrangement. In the first place, dealing with a committee was impossibly unwieldy. And besides, these big-name architects would hold out for the highest possible fee. By 1962 the Port Authority had a specific plan for the creation of millions of square feet of space but not a specific design.

Frustration with the establishment architects in general and the Genius Committee in particular led the Port Authority to consider alternatives. Malcolm Levy and Richard Sullivan recommended to Guy Tozzoli that a single architect be chosen for the project. They conducted an extensive review process during which some ten nationally prominent architects were considered. The process included correspondence, interviews, and field visits to the selected examples of each architect's work. They began to ask themselves questions. Why not take a chance on an architect out of the mainstream? Why not consider something other than the prevailing International Style? It was a gamble which might lead to greatness. And in time Minoru Yamasaki was chosen as architect. Let us examine in more detail how Yamasaki was chosen and how he formulated his design.[2]

Architectural historian Anthony Robins conducted a careful review of the Port Authority archives to reconstruct the decision-making process that led to the selection of Yamasaki as architect. Robins points out that Yamasaki, in his correspondence with the potential clients, was warm and personable. He met with officials from the World Trade Department of the Port Authority, including the deputy, Richard Sullivan, and the chief of planning, Malcolm Levy. Later he wrote them a letter in which he explained his approach to the project:

> If we should be so fortunate as to receive the commission, we would build a large scale model of the entire neighborhood surrounding your complex in sufficient detail to enable you and us to understand exactly how various schemes would relate to the surrounding area. We do this for every job which we undertake. Then, using this model, we would try various solutions in block form, working out rough plans considering aesthetics, utility, and overall economy.[3]

The clients were impressed with Yamasaki's grasp of the many engineering problems such as sun control and the relationship of glass to wall. They were impressed with his previous work, especially with his McGregor Memorial Conference Center (1955–1958) at Wayne State University in Detroit. It was a simple, two-story building of meeting rooms, but it was dramatized by a central two-story atrium with a massive skylight. Yamasaki attempted "to create a beautiful silhouette against the sky, a richness of texture and form, and a sense of peace and serenity through interior spatial arrangement and sensitive landscaping." Set in the surrounding landscape was a large reflecting pool with three sculpture-pebble islands. So it was in late August 1962 that Minoru Yamasaki got the job.[4]

It was a bold choice. Yamasaki had once been a disciple of Mies van der Rohe and his International Style, but by the early 1960s Yamasaki had moved on to something new. Yamasaki had been frustrated by Mies's insistence on limiting himself to a few simple shapes. Yamasaki's change of esthetic direction stemmed from a trip to Europe and Japan in 1954. Shortly afterward, Yamasaki began to embrace a style that drew on historical forms, a style that was more decorative and ornamental. At that time it was a lonely path to follow. The only other architect of the day who shared Yamasaki's thinking was Edward Durell Stone. The reason that this kind of change was so difficult was that American architects had embraced the International Style almost as a religion. Mainstream architects believed that they had something profound to say about the nature of man and the built environment, and they regarded Yamasaki as an apostate. Because Yamasaki had forsaken his principles, they called him a "kitsch-monger" and worse.[5]

Yamasaki was turning away from the flat, glassy buildings of the International Style. His travels led him to embrace tradition and history. He became fascinated with one of the oldest preoccupations of classical architecture: How do you design a building so as to take maximum advantage of the change in light experienced from sunrise to sunset? He began to speak out against the monotony of the facades of the International Style. At first Yamasaki was not sure how to solve the problem of buildings with dull faces. An early idea was to come up with some kind of stamping and precasting of metal to yield more interesting surfaces. It took some time to come up with a distinguishing treatment for the faces of his buildings.[6]

Yamasaki's distancing himself from the International Style stemmed from his dislike of the "all-glass" building, which was actually about 60 percent glass. In such buildings, Yamasaki had an intense feeling of acrophobia, especially when standing next to a large pane of glass in a tall building. Instead of having the secure feeling of being inside a building, he felt as if he could just tumble through the glass and fall. At the same time, he realized that with no windows at all occupants would have a sense of claustrophobia. The challenge was to provide people with the pleasure of looking out the windows and enjoying the view while still having the security of being inside a structure and enjoying its protection. By the time he designed the World Trade Center, Yamasaki had worked this problem out to his satisfaction. He gave the building windows that were shoulder-width and spanned from floor to ceiling. A person could lean right up against the frame of the windows and look out and down with no fear of falling. The percentage of glass in the World Trade Center is thirty, about half that of an International Style building.

Another concept he embraced in the years before taking up the World Trade Center project was an idea already discovered years earlier by Frank Lloyd Wright. That was the element of surprise.

Both Wright and Yamasaki were fascinated by the historical architecture of Japan. There one constantly passes from one space to another. For example, in a Japanese temple one might pass from a sunlit courtyard of carefully placed stones through a dark hallway to yet another courtyard filled with lush leafy plants creating interesting patterns of shadows. Yamasaki calculated that similar effects might be achieved by raising and lowering the ceiling heights of various spaces to vary the spaciousness of rooms.[7]

All these ideas were worked out by Yamasaki in his Michigan studios during his forties so that when he got the World Trade Center commission at age fifty in 1962, he had a mature sense of himself and a well-developed design vocabulary to draw upon. After securing the contract, the first thing he did was to become completely acquainted with the project site. It extended from Vesey Street south to Liberty Street and from Church Street to West Street, an area of about seventeen acres near Wall Street. This section was cut up into fourteen small, odd-shaped blocks. Yamasaki took many walks through the area, and concluded that there was not a single building worth saving. This decision opened the way to eliminating the interior streets and creating a superblock out of the whole site. He decided to use this opportunity to create a group of tall and low buildings, combined with a significant courtyard of open space at ground level.

Once Yamasaki was thoroughly familiar with the site, he went back to his Michigan studios to begin work. The Port Authority had given him a list of specifications but no particular plan. The specifications called for about ten million square feet of space to accommodate various government agencies, world trade services and exhibit areas, and private businesses. Of the total space in the center, about four million feet were to be made available for rental to businesses engaged in foreign trade.

World Trade Department deputy director Richard Sullivan told Yamasaki, "Look, these are the studies, we expect there to be a large population. We expect there to be consumer services. It's got to be a great space in the City of New York."[8] So Yamasaki did what he had said he would do. He had his staff of professional model makers construct a mock-up of the site and surrounding area. Then he was ready to make a series of cardboard models of his various ideas to see what they would actually look like. It was very much a trial and error process. The need for so many square feet of office space and so many square feet of retail space can be [pressed]. However, when it comes to the esthetics of w[hat] space should take, there is no substitute for looking at [it]. tried one large tower. He tried three square towers. [He tried] identical square towers. All in all, there were more th[an a hun]dred schemes in this subjective process.

Somewhere between the twentieth and fortieth attempt, he hit upon the idea of a pair of towers. He felt that he was on the right track, but he continued on with another sixty schemes just to be sure. At first the two buildings were only eighty or ninety stories high. Only later did Yamasaki agree to push the design to 110 stories. It took fifteen months from getting his commission to presenting a detailed plan to Austin Tobin and the Port Authority commissioners. Next came the enormous task of designing the buildings in detail.[9]

In large measure Yamasaki's design followed logically from engineering considerations. We have already seen in the previous chapter that the World Trade Center used an innovative construction technique. The exterior walls carry the weight of the structure as well as providing bracing against the stress and strain of lateral winds. The entire building perimeter acts as a strong tube. The outer wall consists of closely spaced vertical columns. This kind of construction would have been a terrible problem for a conventional International Style building, because there is no way for the architect to achieve the "all-glass" look. For Yamasaki, it was not a problem because for esthetic reasons he preferred less glass. He came up with a module size of three feet and four inches, made up of eighteen-inch-wide columns and twenty-two-inch-wide windows (including the sash). It was a brilliant decision.

The columns are ten inches deep from the outer skin of the aluminum to the glass, shading much of the glass of these narrow windows. This is particularly important on the south and west facades, saving energy for air-conditioning during daylight hours in the summer. Similarly, the low amount of glass saves on heating in the winter. Yamasaki's accomplishment is all the more remarkable when we recall that he worked out these energy-saving ideas well in advance of the Arab oil embargo of 1973, when energy prices soared.

Some critics felt that the view from Yamasaki's twenty-two-inch windows was too limiting. Yamasaki responded, "The purpose of buildings is to have comfortable working areas and not to be observatories where one stares out the window at the view all day long. The windows are amply wide and sufficiently close together for both a dramatic outlook and little sense of claustrophobia. I have always been against high window sills simply because they prevent the people working at locations further away from the windows from seeing the city or the ground and water below."[10]

Once having decided on narrow windows, the next decision had to do with the choice of exterior wall material. Because the actual weight of the building was supported by closely spaced vertical steel columns, the exterior material could be very thin and lightweight since all it had to do was to keep in heat and keep out cold and dampness. As long as these "curtain walls" were waterproof, they could be made of just about any permanent material. Earlier skyscrapers might have had walls of brick or terra-cotta or even blocks of stone. Cost considerations dictated the use of some lightweight metal. At first Yamasaki contemplated the use of stainless steel. According to his own account, he got a call one day from Fritz Close, who was then chairman of the Aluminum Company of America (Alcoa), the dominant producer of that metal in the United States.

Close said, "Yama, I understand you are going to use stainless steel for the curtain walls of the towers." Yamasaki laughed and admitted it was true.

Close asked, "Why? Aluminum is significantly cheaper." Yamasaki responded that he did not like the silver color of aluminum. It was too cold. Close was not easily discouraged and went on to offer to change the composition of the alloy to provide a choice of several warmer shades. Because aluminum by itself is soft and has very little strength, it is almost always alloyed with small amounts of copper, magnesium, zinc, and other elements; thus, making a customized alloy was not a big problem. Yamasaki insisted that he did not want a color coating, but an alloy that would have a consistent color throughout the panel. Alcoa agreed and came up with a number of colors. Some, like the shades of brown, were serious contenders. Others like the shades of pink were frivolous.

Yamasaki said to Close, "You really aren't serious about making these two large buildings pink, are you?" Close laughed. They finally settled on a silver alloy that had an uncanny ability to reflect different shades of sunlight.[11]

From the very beginning of the planning process, there was an

assumption that building tall office towers on a "supe
the existence of a plaza. Certainly, Yamasaki had vis
he knew that the Piazza San Marco was the yardstic
all other plazas were measured. Saint Mark's Squ
Marco), the center of activity in Venice, has the C
Mark on the east side of the square. A bell tower called the Campanile
stands nearby. Buildings in the Renaissance style of architecture rise
along the other three sides of the square. Cafes in front of these buildings are favorite meeting places for both residents and visitors.

Yamasaki designed his plaza likewise—to be an environment
totally for pedestrians and away from automobiles. There is a broad
opening at Church Street that serves as the main entrance. This entrance, 175 feet wide at the plaza level, is in stark contrast to the narrow streets of lower Manhattan. The Plaza pavement is of beige-gray
Mankato marble, an especially hard marble from Minnesota. In the
central area of the five-acre plaza is a great spherical bronze sculpture
and ninety-foot-diameter fountain by Fritz Koenig of Munich to give
a focal point and unifying element of design. Off-white lines radiate
out from the fountain. There are other sculptures on the plaza, including a black granite grouping by Masayuki Nagare of Japan and
a stainless steel assemblage by James Rosati of New York. Surrounding the fountain are rings of benches and a circle of flower boxes
whose colors should change with the seasons. The silver-colored
gleaming towers, each 209 feet square, as the main attractions were
placed at the south and west corners of the plaza. The four detached
lower plaza buildings—the U.S. Customs building, the northeast and
southeast plaza buildings, and the hotel—are in a darker brown-col-
ored aluminum cladding as if to emphasize their subordinate role in
the composition. The plaza is at its best during weekdays in the summer months from about noon until two in the afternoon, when activities and concerts are often planned for office workers on their
lunch breaks. The whole idea was to provide an interesting mix of
low and high structures around a great open space.[12]

Yamasaki devoted considerable attention to the question of
how people would approach his complex. Perhaps the best way and
certainly the most impressive is for the pedestrian to come into the
plaza from the east off Church Street. After crossing the plaza, one
can enter either tower at the mezzanine (upper) level of the tower's
lobby and take the escalator down into the main (lower) level of the

lobby. For most visitors, the mezzanine level of the South Tower is the more interesting of the two since here we find discount theater tickets for Broadway shows and the ticket counter for the observation deck. Another approach to the North Tower is for the pedestrian to come off West Street and enter the building at the main lobby level, a full story below the plaza. Similiarly, one may come off Liberty Street to enter the South Tower at its main lobby level. In actual fact, however, most people enter from the concourse level arriving by subway or PATH trains well below the whole complex.

The practical advantage of this arrangement was that people had a protected, all-weather connection to all of the Trade Center buildings. Though not esthetically attractive, the concourse is a welcome space for getting from one place to another during the severe winter months. People arriving by PATH come up by means of a very wide bank of escalators into a central square. Until the budget cuts of the mid-1990s, the Port Authority had an information person stationed at the top of the escalators who could point visitors and tourists in the right direction. They could then pass through the wide corridors either to exit to the streets or to enter the lobbies of the towers.

The shopping area in the concourse was designed by Arcop, a group of Canadian architects who had earlier designed Place Bonaventure in Montreal. It was a difficult assignment because the concourse itself is not an inviting area, especially in the warmer months when the outdoors beckon. The ceiling is low and the lighting is artificial so that the visitor feels confined. There is a strong desire in most people to keep moving in order to get their bearings and see some real daylight. There are such large numbers of people passing through so quickly that browsing seems out of the question. There is a sense of being swept along by the crowd. Everyone is in a hurry. Anyone stopping to browse at a store window might be knocked down by the swiftly moving tide of humanity. There are no benches for sitting, no place to catch your breath, no nooks and crannies for reading a paper or checking a schedule. There is one nice thing about the arcade. When one passes into either lobby of either tower, a pleasant surprise awaits: the lobbies are extraordinarily high and the Gothic arcade is open to a wide expanse of natural sunlight.[13]

A skyscraper is by definition a tall building. The term suggests that the building will "scrape the sky." From the beginning, Yamasaki planned on very tall buildings. However, as we have already

They Built the Towers

World Trade Center architect Minoru Yamasaki demonstrates where the buildings will go on a model of lower Manhattan. (AFP/CORBIS)

The powerful Port Authority director, Austin Tobin (AP/WIDE WORLD)

New York City mayor John V. Lindsay and New York governor Nelson Rockefeller at the May 12, 1966, press conference unveiling the plan for the World Trade Center and Battery Park City (BETTMANN/CORBIS)

(*Left*) David Rockefeller, chairman and CEO of Chase Manhattan Bank (BETTMANN/CORBIS)
(*Middle*) New Jersey governor Richard J. Hughes (BETTMANN/CORBIS)
(*Right*) Labor leader Theodore Kheel (AP/WIDE WORLD)

(*Left*) Malcolm Levy, deputy director, Planning and Construction, World Trade Department of the Port Authority (AP/WIDE WORLD)
(*Middle*) Guy Tozzoli, director of the World Trade Center (AP/WIDE WORLD)
(*Right*) Fortune Pope of Colonial Concrete (BETTMANN/CORBIS)

Under Construction

By April 1968 the concrete bathtub keeping out the waters of the Hudson River has been poured. Note the steel rods protruding from the wall at right. (AP/WIDE WORLD)

An excellent view of the kangaroo cranes at work on the construction of the North Tower. (AP/WIDE WORLD)

French aerialist Philippe Petit provides thrills to the crowds below as he calmly walks a tightrope stretched between the two towers of the World Trade Center, August 7, 1974.
(AP/WIDE WORLD)

George Willig, the "human fly," is barely visible as the daredevil from Queens climbs the outside of the South Tower on May 27, 1977. Port Authority and NYC policemen follow his ascent in a window washer's scaffold. (AP/WIDE WORLD)

Willig (l.) and Petit (r.) compare notes at the base of the Twin Towers in April 1978.
(AP/WIDE WORLD)

Towers Famous

Owen Quinn parachutes off the roof of the WTC on July 23, 1975.
(AP/WIDE WORLD)

A crowd gathers around the fallen King Kong at the base of the Twin Towers on June 21, 1976, during the filming of the Dino De Laurentiis remake starring Jessica Lange.
(ROBERT ROSAMILIO, *New York Daily News*)

Daily Life at the Twin Towers

Austin Tobin Plaza was a popular lunch and gathering spot for many office workers. The sculpture at the center is *The Sphere* by Fritz Koenig. (GAIL MOONEY/CORBIS)

From the outdoor observation deck at the South Tower of the World Trade Center, you not only got a great view of the rest of Manhattan, but of the North Tower and its huge TV broadcast antenna. (GAIL MOONEY/CORBIS)

Diners enjoy the romantic view from the 107th floor of the swanky Windows on the World restaurant in the North Tower, one of New York's must-see spaces. (KELLY-MOONEY PHOTOGRAPHY/CORBIS)

The Collapse

The beginning of the end. The South Tower begins to collapse. (AP/WIDE WORLD)

Firefighters make their way through the rubble of the collapsed Twin Towers (left). The portions of the facade that remained standing are eerily similar to that shown in the right-hand photo, as construction workers erect the towers from the inside out. (AP/WIDE WORLD)

The World Trade Center will live on in our memories. (AP/WIDE WORLD)

seen in chapter 2, the initial idea for making the World Trade Center "the tallest in the world" was not Yamasaki's. The idea originated with Lee K. Jaffe, in the public relations office of the Port Authority. Jaffe knew the idea would appeal to her bosses, Austin Tobin and Guy Tozzoli, because the culture of the agency promoted a sense of manliness and an almost compulsive competitiveness. The contest to build the tallest skyscraper in the world was an American pre-occupation for the first three-quarters of the twentieth century. For most of that period, the tallest skyscrapers were found in New York City, although in the end Chicago took the prize. As we approach the end of the twentieth century, Americans seem to have given up the fight as the battle has shifted to the Pacific Rim.

For a long time, the Empire State Building was secure in its title of "the world's tallest skyscraper." Serious challenges were not attempted during the Depression and were not possible during World War II. The Empire State Building became a landmark and a familiar yardstick against which big things like ocean liners were measured. There was an office building boom in the 1950s, but nothing particularly tall was built. "As a result," according to architectural historian Anthony Robins, "the Empire State held the title for so long that, unlike its predecessors, it seemed to have a permanent claim. The World Trade Center proposal in 1964 came as a rude shock."[14]

The World Trade Center's bid to surpass the Empire State Building in height was opposed by the threatened owners of the older landmark. They put up a good fight and succeeded in delaying the new project for months. Of course, in the end the World Trade Center won the battle, measuring 1,368 feet in height. What is amazing to most people is the intensity of emotion surrounding New York's battle of the skyscrapers. Devotees of the Empire State Building have never forgiven the Port Authority for topping the classic midtown skyscraper. For example, consider what distinguished architectural historian John Tauranac wrote. In dealing with the Empire State Building's loss of its record—a full twenty-five years after the fact—Tauranac's prose sounds angry. He cannot resist slamming the real winner with invective. Tauranac writes, "Its fans certainly felt unlucky in the early 1970s, as they stood by and watched helplessly as the World's Tallest record went to the World Trade Towers. It was like a Brooklyn Dodger fan watching his beloved team go to Los Angeles. If the Empire State Building wasn't going

to remain champ—and it had won the record fair and square, just
as the Dodgers had finally won the Series—why did it have to lose
to something so big, so boring, so banal?"[15]

By way of contrast, those on the World Trade Center team,
whatever their private feelings may have been, were much more
decorous in their public statements when they in turn were defeated
by the Sears Tower, the national headquarters of Sears, Roebuck,
and Company, on Wacker Drive in Chicago. The Sears Tower was
begun in August 1970. It surpassed the World Trade Center in
height at 2:35 P.M. on March 6, 1973, with the first steel column
reaching to the 104th story. It was "topped out" on May 4, 1973,
one month after the World Trade Center had its formal dedication ceremonies. The Sears Tower was completed in 1974 with a
record-breaking height of 1,454 feet.[16] The architect and designer
of the Sears Tower was Fazlur Khan, who worked for Skidmore,
Owings, and Merrill in Chicago. Khan worked out a structure
called the "bundled tube" in which the perimeter columns brace
the building against the wind. The nine tubes that make up the
building terminate at different heights, giving the Sears Tower a
stepped appearance. A large part of its distinctive appearance is its
overall black color, achieved through the use of a black anodized
coating on the steel and black-tinted glass panels.[17]

Minoru Yamasaki was philosophical about losing the record to
the Sears Tower. In his mind, what was important about the Trade
Center design was not the height of the towers, but the fact there
were two of them. That characteristic became the identifying trait of
the World Trade Center, and it made a distinctive addition to the skyline of Manhattan. Besides, going for the World's Tallest was really
his client's idea. It was Guy Tozzoli who had Malcolm Levy tell Yamasaki, "Let's go higher than the Empire State."[18] But perhaps even
more important was the fact that the World Trade Center only held
the title for the two years between 1972 and 1974. Even before the
World Trade Center was finished, it was widely known that the title
would soon shift to Chicago. So Yamasaki never had enough time to
feel permanent "ownership" of the title. He wrote:

> One source of criticism of the Trade Center has to do
> with its very bigness. I will admit to sharing a measure of
> fascination with the numbers and statistics that this and

other large projects seem to generate, but I had realized long before it happened that it would only be a matter of time before another building would be announced as "tallest in the world." I had never believed that the Trade Center towers would retain that distinction for very long in a society such as ours, which is one of large-scale and grand achievements, and I am content to let the latest new champion, the Sears Building in Chicago, or its successors defend the title for the "tallest" or the "biggest."[19]

Over time, nearly everyone adjusted to the new rankings. The Sears Tower could call itself "world's tallest." The World Trade Center could claim to be "tallest in New York City." At least one guidebook took to calling it "the world's almost-tallest building."[20] It did not seem to matter. People still came in large numbers to enjoy the spectacular views. The public relations department of the Empire State Building now took to calling its own building the "world's most famous." No matter what it was called, crowds still packed the Empire State's observatory, which was considerable consolation to its owners. Once the fight was over, it was peace and prosperity for everyone—the chambers of commerce, the owners, the observatory concessionaires, the makers of postcards and souvenirs, and the tour companies. Everyone, that is, except the architectural critics who thrive on controversy.

Architectural historian Anthony Robins has made a careful study of the critical response to the World Trade Center. Robins found that the project was at first taken seriously by established critics. When the eight-foot model of the sixteen-acre project was first unveiled in the early 1960s, it was acclaimed. But by the late 1960s critical opinion turned against the Twin Towers. Criticism became increasingly harsh in the 1970s and has never swung back to positive.[21] Among serious historians of architecture, the World Trade Center has been given the harshest treatment of all: it is simply ignored.

In the very beginning of the project's development, there were two notable architectural critics in the Northeast. They were Ada Louise Huxtable of the *New York Times* and Wolf von Eckardt of the *Washington Post*. At first both endorsed the World Trade Center with enthusiasm. In January 1964 Huxtable wrote that the World Trade Center "may herald a new era of skyscraper design for the city that has made the big building its trademark."[22] That same month, in another story, she wrote, "From the design aspect this is not only the biggest but the best new building project that New York has seen in a long time. It represents a level of taste and thought that has been distressingly rare in the city's mass of non-descript postwar commercial construction."[23] In February 1964 she wrote, "The Trade Center faces the problems of big city building head-on, and does so with a civic conscience and an imaginative search for new and better solutions. . . . The huge towers are planned as the stupendous focus at the end of a handsome plaza surrounded by lower, arcaded buildings conceived on a sensitively human scale."[24]

During this period of early euphoria, the editorial page of the *New York Times* echoed the enthusiasm of its architectural critic. In its first editorial on the subject, the paper briefly noted the problems of relocating displaced businesses and the planning relationships to the surrounding areas. However, the overall tone was enthusiastic. The editors wrote, "Fortunately, these soaring 110-story skyscrapers with their handsome low buildings enclosing a five-acre plaza, promise to be a civic ornament. . . . It is in the best tradition of city-shaping complexes like Rockefeller Center, which for the past thirty years has demonstrated to be one of the city's outstanding successes. And it carries New York's superb romantic symbol, the skyscraper, to literally new heights through legitimate technological advances. From the delicate Gothic tracery of the nearby Woolworth Tower to the 'modernistic' stainless steel Chrysler spire, these famous shafts are the city's greatest visual drama. The World Trade Center could be a fitting successor."[25]

No less enthusiastic was Wolf von Eckardt, who in the *Washington Post* that same year called the Trade Center "a magnificent work of architecture and urban design." He expressed some mild reservations about the impact of the project on traffic. "But," he continued, "their skillful and handsome design and the magnificent open plaza on which they are to rise can evoke only unqualified admiration." Von Eckardt called Yamasaki "sensitive," and he called the design of the Twin Towers "a stunning tour de force." Von Eckardt was particularly pleased with the plaza. He wrote, "It will be paved, contain planting and reflecting pools and sculpture and presumably pigeons. It promises much of the elegance of the Piazza

San Marco in Venice combined with the grandeur of Rockefeller Plaza, the two most exciting outdoor spaces in the world."[26]

Two years later, it would be difficult to find an architectural critic who had a kind word for the World Trade Center. There was a stunning about-face in critical opinion. What happened? The project itself had not changed. It still had two very tall shining silver towers in a plaza with four low brown buildings. Everything was exactly the same as before, but the critics turned their backs on the whole thing. The culture had changed, and the sixties caught up with the World Trade Center. There were new concerns about environmentalism, grass-roots democracy, and historic preservation. Basic cultural assumptions were being called into question. Was bigger really better?

A striking example of this change of heart can be found in a lengthy article, "The World's Tallest Fiasco," written by Wolf von Eckardt for *Harper's* magazine. In a remarkable flip-flop, he wrote, "As presently designed this fearful instrument of urbicide will be not only the tallest, but unquestionably one of the ugliest buildings in the world." He questioned not only the height, but the design itself. He went on, "Worse, these incredible giants just stand there, artless and dumb, without any relationship to anything, not even to each other." Von Eckardt called Yamasaki "currently the most popular kitsch-monger." He ridiculed the comparison to Piazza San Marco, calling Yamasaki's plaza "a bland, vast expanse of pavement."[27]

Meanwhile, Ada Louise Huxtable continued to defend the project. As an alert cultural observer, she could see that resentment against the project was growing. In the article "Who's Afraid of the Big Bad Buildings," she identified five groups opposed to the Twin Towers: "What has come out of public hearings and protest is: 1. Establishment-baiting, in this case the Port Authority; 2. Yamasaki-baiting, particularly popular among architects; 3. emotional arguments, usually aimed at the project's size; 4. fears of the real estate interests; 5. concern for the destruction of a small but irreplaceable business community."[28] Only one of the five groups was genuinely concerned with architecture as such, and they just did not like Yamasaki.

Huxtable argued that the opponents were against the World Trade Center solely because of its size. As a student of architectural history, she reminded her readers that an earlier generation of critics had opposed the skyscraper boom of the 1920s for the same reasons. Now in the 1960s, she pointed out that the "senseless" towers of the 1920s had become classics. She acknowledged the pain felt by small business owners in the area of development, but she called the area "of minimum interest to preservationists."[29]

But as the 1960s wore on, even Huxtable eventually lost her enthusiasm for the project. Initially, she had reservations about the city-planning implications of what she saw as the Port Authority's unchecked powers of capital formation and eminent domain. By the time the Twin Towers were completed in 1973, she had misgivings about the architecture as well. In an article called "Big but Not So Bold," she wrote: "As design, the World Trade Center is a conundrum. It is a contradiction in terms: the daintiest big buildings in the world. In spite of their size, the towers emphasize an almost miniature module—3 feet 4 inches—and the close grid of their decorative facades has a delicacy that its architect, Minoru Yamasaki, chose deliberately."[30] She then went on to criticize the windows for ruining and fragmenting the view.

Though Huxtable had stood by Yamasaki for a long time, she had clearly changed her mind altogether. She wrote: "These are big buildings but they are not great architecture. The grill-like metal facade stripes are curiously without scale. They taper into the more widely-spaced columns of 'Gothic trees' at ten lower stories, a detail that does not express structure so much as tart it up. The Port Authority has built the ultimate Disneyland fairytale blockbuster. It is General Motors Gothic."[31]

The World Trade Center had lost its last critical defender. It was still popular as a background for fashion photographers, and it was still the postcard favorite of visitors. It was perhaps most familiar nationwide as a studio backdrop for CNN's financial reporters on television. But the intelligentsia rebuked the project at every possible opportunity in public lectures, newspaper columns, and letters to the editor. The official negative opinion was codified by the American Institute of Architects in their *Guide to New York City*, which said, in part, "When completed, these stolid, banal monoliths came to overshadow Lower Manhattan's cluster of filigreed towers, which had previously been the romantic evocation that symbolized the very concept of 'skyline.' . . . Ten million square feet of office space are here offered: 7 times the area of the Empire State Building, 4 times that of the Pan Am. The public agency that built them (Port Authority of New York and New Jersey) ran amok with both money and aesthetics."[32]

In time, Paul Goldberger succeeded Ada Louise Huxtable as architectural critic for the *New York Times*. Like Huxtable, he disapproves of the Twin Towers, calling them "boring, so utterly banal as to be unworthy of the headquarters of a bank in Omaha." He calls the plaza "a windswept football field." Despite all this, he gives Yamasaki credit for the design of the load-bearing walls, which he calls "a remarkable engineering accomplishment—they are, in effect, like a mesh cage supporting the weight of the entire building, making these towers a different breed entirely from conventional steel frame construction." Goldberger also pays tribute to the idea of having a first-class restaurant on the 107th floor of the North Tower, which he says "has served as a magnet to bring thousands of tourists downtown who might otherwise have never crossed 14th Street." Most important, Goldberger acknowledges "there have even been moments when I have seen them from afar and admitted to some small pleasure in the way the two huge forms, when approached from a distance, play off against each other like minimal sculpture."[33]

Why is it so difficult for architectural critics to say anything nice about the World Trade Center? Why is praise given so grudgingly? It is all about timing. The project was too new to be International Style and too old to be postmodern. It fell between the cracks of the critical establishment. If the Port Authority had gone ahead and built the Trade Center in the fashionable style of the day, it might have been the final masterpiece of the formal and disciplined International Style. It would have been the ultimate icy-cool steel-and-glass slab, or pair of slabs. Instead, the Port Authority wanted to go beyond the conventions of the day and reach ahead to a more unusual, more ornamental architect. They wanted something new and different.

What no one knew at the time was that the next trend in architecture was to be postmodern. Had the project come along a dozen years later, it might have been designed by Philip Johnson as twin Chippendale towers. A bit later the two towers might have been designed by Michael Graves. For Graves, each tower would have had a blue base and crown, connected with pink shafts—taking full advantage of Alcoa's ability to come up with multicolored alloys. Still later the Port Authority might have hired Frank Gehry, who would have found innovative ways to use galvanized corrugated steel and chain link fence in his design for the tower facades.

In short, it was bad luck for the project that it occurred when it did. It is the big work at the end of high-rise building in New York. By the time it was built, dissatisfaction was growing out of the anti-establishment movement of the 1970s. There were no champions of the building left at the point when it might have been really celebrated. Architecture was already moving away from that kind of model of high-rise development. Robert Venturi had just published *Complexity and Contradiction*.[34] The book was being read and discussed about the same time that the World Trade Center was being completed. Architectural thought was focusing on how to address the issue of the architect's relevance to society. How could buildings be made more interesting? How could architects address the criticism that was popular at the time? Critics were saying that the buildings of the period were too cold, too inhuman, too dull.

In some ways, the World Trade Center could be considered the first movement into a postmodern condition. Certain things were done against the principles of design prevailing at the time. In most office towers of the 1950s and 1960s, architects made the curtain walls as thin as possible because the rental laws allowed the owner to rent right up to the glass line. The way to optimize one's income was to make the wall thin and to bring columns into the building because columns did not count. Only the exterior wall surface counted. So if Yamasaki had made the curtain wall an inch and a half or two inches thick from the property line or the set-back line, he could have maximized the income on the basis of rentable area. Instead, he designed the buildings with a ten-inch recess from the aluminum shell to the glass, thus losing nearly a square foot of perimeter that could have been allowed for rental all around the building.

Yet in other ways, Yamasaki strictly adhered to the principles of the International Style and modernism in architecture. The World Trade Center is evidence of the idea of repetition and prototype—the floors, the verticality, the columns. There is a great deal of repetition. A floor plan once solved is repeated again and again like a stack of pancakes. The only changes are in the number of elevators or changes in the mechanical equipment as you go higher and higher.[35]

The World Trade Center can be considered from two different points of view—from nearby and from a distance. First, there is the local condition. Here we are right on the ground. From this perspective, most of us are simply not aware of the great height of the building. Second, there is the distant condition. This begins on the level of being in another building in Manhattan and seeing it from across town. The difficulty is that from lower Manhattan itself, one does not have a good platform from which to view the World Trade Center. It is more dramatic when seen from a considerable distance, for example, when seen from New Jersey or Brooklyn. From this more distant point of view, the scale seems appropriate because it is among objects of similiar scale. It can best be appreciated from the water, from the Staten Island Ferry or the Circle Line Cruise. It seems to arise from the base of the island. You can see the changes of light from dawn to sunset. As you circle around the structure, you begin to see that there is a play or a dance of form in the sculptural sense created by the Twin Towers, which are offset from each other.[36]

The most distinctive thing about the project is that there are two towers. According to architect Gaylord Richardson of the University of Kansas, that is the novelty it is based upon, but they are what he calls the "inarticulate two."[37] The towers do not have the quality of texture. They do not lend themselves to multiple readings of scale. There is no reading of small and intermediate and big in the windows. Basically, the building presents us with a surface, a striped surface of aluminum and glass. The Twin Towers thus become ideal objects. The structure draws upon the platonic concept of purity and reduction of information. It is a pair of simple geometric shapes. It allows no multiplicity of readings. What you see is what you get. It is an identifiable object because there are two towers. It has an iconic quality and therefore enters into cognition, but because of the simplicity it doesn't sustain the interest and the multiple readings that critics look for today in buildings. So the building is recognized by ordinary people as an icon for the City of New York, but it does not enjoy the respect of critics in the canon of architecture.

6 The World Trade Center Concept

**Not Just Another
Office Building**

You don't create a World Trade Center by building a building; you build a World Trade Center by having the right tenants and the programs to help them.

—THOMAS J. KEARNEY, *CHICAGO TRIBUNE*, OCTOBER 12, 1987

For a generation of Americans, VJ-Day, the celebration of victory over Japan on September 2, 1945, was the defining moment, proof of American exceptionalism. This moment marked the beginning of America's greatest period of global economic power, a period that lasted for a quarter of a century—from 1945 to about 1971. It was a period that began with the end of World War II and ended with the construction of the World Trade Center. In fact, many of the Trade Center's builders were themselves World War II veterans who had dodged bombs and bullets as they built floating dry docks and airstrips across the Pacific.

During the postwar period, the United States dominated the world's economy, producing 50 percent of the world's goods. The United States did not have to chase after world trade because the world came to this country to buy things. The United States was the only advanced country that had not been wrecked by the war, and so it became the world's largest foreign trader, even though it put less than 12 percent of its gross national product into foreign trade. America became the banker and supplier to the whole world by default.[1]

Yet during this period of unprecedented U.S. economic dominance, the Port of New York and New Jersey was watching its market share slip relative to the rest of the country. Fewer ships were stopping at the port to load and unload goods. Statisticians at the Port Authority were alarmed, and they conveyed their concerns to Austin Tobin. New York was losing out to other ports in the United States for several reasons. In the first place, New York always had

very high labor costs. But research also indicated that other ports
tried to make international trade easier to conduct by concentrat-
ing traders and trade services into specific, dedicated centers. The
first such center was established in Houston in 1927 to encourage
foreign commerce for the Port of Houston and other Texas ports.
New Orleans was another pioneer, setting up its world trade center in 1943 "to promote world peace, trade, and understanding."
The business community in Louisiana understood that they lacked
a manufacturing base, but they did have an excellent year-round
port.[2]

The idea of a World Trade Center for New York City was
controversial from the very beginning. When the project was being
planned in the 1960s, the controversy was over whether the trade
complex was really needed. Would it revitalize the region, as the
Port Authority claimed, by centralizing businesses and public agencies that dealt with international trade? Or was it, as opponents
claimed, just another commercial office building—albeit a huge
one—which would be a monument to the Port Authority while un-
fairly competing with private business?

Austin Tobin's earliest writings in support of the World Trade
Center concept may not have been entirely candid. Tobin did not
dwell on the huge size of the proposed building; instead, he stressed
the functional need for a place to facilitate trade. In an article published in 1964, Tobin argued that the Port of New York was losing
its share of world trade. He wrote: "The years from 1952 to the
present reveal a constant decline in our relative port position. In
1952, the Port of New York was the gateway for 33.8 percent of the
nation's ocean-borne general cargo foreign trade. In 1963, however,
our share had dropped precipitously to 19.8 percent. . . . Clearly,
ports other than New York are the benefactors of the expansion of
our country's international trade, and something needs to be done
about it."

Not surprisingly, Tobin went on to argue that the essential
"something" needed was a world trade center. The theme that he
stressed over and over again was that import-export operations
would be enhanced if they could be housed in a single location. Tobin explained: "The merchandising, financing, insuring, and gov-
ernmental clearing of our foreign commerce is scattered all over

Manhattan. It is the objective of the World Trade Center to become not only the core of these activities but the very structure in which most of them are housed."[3] Tobin's dream was made clear in an early Port Authority brochure distributed to prospective tenants. The planned World Trade Center would have 220 floors (110 in each tower) all nearly the same, with 40,000 square feet per floor. The typical floor was to be a "maritime floor" with a mix of services that included importers, exporters, customs house brokers, freight forwarders, admiralty lawyers, and a shipping company. The plan was never realized because it turned out in practice that these businesspeople, for competitive reasons, preferred less proximity to one another, not more. Still, at first it was the official objective.[4]

Nearly nine years later, at the dedication ceremony on April 4, 1973, an inscription on the marble wall of the lobby at the plaza level of Tower One was unveiled. It was a concise summary of the ideas that Tobin had espoused all along: "Designed to increase world trade by providing at a single location a home for international commerce with the necessary functions and services, an exchange for the sharing and processing of information and a forum for the advancement of world trade education and the encouragement and stimulation of international business cooperation." The 1973 dedication can easily serve as a way of measuring performance against intention, achievements versus goals.

An irony of history is that the World Trade Center was conceived during a period when international trade was thriving, at least on the global level if not necessarily in New York, yet completed at the beginning of a period of adversity. It could be argued that the Trade Center was desirable in the 1960s, but essential in the 1970s, when the New York and New Jersey region would need every competitive advantage possible in a difficult market. In the early 1970s, the collapse of the Bretton Woods system of world finance led to monetary instability, which led to business uncertainty. It became more and more difficult to control worldwide inflation. In addition, the 1970s saw the end of two decades of cheap energy. From 1973 forward, OPEC pushed for increasing oil prices, which had a profound effect on both the industrial and developing worlds. Inflation began to drive up the prices of many other basic materials and products.[5]

Has the Port Authority lived up to its own stated goals? On the whole, it has. Of course, it would be naive to deny that the agency stumbled along the way. It is true that as the World Trade Center's office space came onto the market in the early 1970s, the agency had a terrible time finding tenants to rent the space. During the late 1960s, while the complex was being built, Port Authority leasing agents had canvassed the Lower Manhattan maritime community trying to get people to sign letters of intent to lease space. Of course, such letters were hardly contracts, since no one really knew how long it might take to build the Twin Towers. Because these weakly worded letters were not binding, agents had little trouble signing up prospects. Many of the two hundred letters gathered over the years had been signed over three- and four-martini lunches.[6]

It was then up to Guy F. Tozzoli and others in his world trade department to make follow-up calls on the original letter writers to find out who was sincerely interested. Tozzoli scrambled about signing up banks, freight forwarders, customs brokers, exporters, and manufacturers. Tozzoli pitched his buildings to real estate brokers in ten American cities. He staged photo opportunities with the most prominent politicians, businessmen, and officials of the day. He worked with the diplomatic corps in Washington in an effort to line up foreign consulates and trade offices to rent space in the complex.[7]

During this difficult period, Port Authority leasing agents labored under a unique mandate. They could not just sign up anyone who wanted to open a branch office in New York City, since prospective tenants had to meet eligibility requirements for occupancy. They had to show either that they helped the other tenants that were already in the building, or that they had a demonstrable link to world trade. The eligibility requirement stemmed from the original enabling legislation for the complex.[8]

Despite persistent efforts, as late as 1979 nearly 10 percent of the center's office space had still not been leased, a poor record for Manhattan commercial real estate. In his sixty-third-floor office in the center's North Tower, an embarrassed Tozzoli acknowledged to a reporter from the New York Times that the complex was three years behind in filling up. The renting difficulties, he said, had

stemmed from "market conditions—there wasn't enough demand
for space with all that space available." There was a recession at the
time, and many securities firms went out of business, hurting the
office market in lower Manhattan.[9]

Ironically, the bad market conditions for real estate kept rents
relatively low during the period so that the Port Authority was more
easily able to fulfill its mandate to recruit businesses that were actively engaged in "maritime" enterprises. These were the importers
and exporters, freight forwarders, and so on. In the first ten years
of its operation, now regarded by some old-timers as the "golden
age" of the World Trade Center, there were between 100 and 150
companies involved with the maritime trades. Although they were
never concentrated on a single floor, the owners frequently got together at the WTC Club located at Windows on the World. In those
more easygoing days, business for the owners at least was sometimes wrapped up by one o'clock in the afternoon. Businessmen
could take the elevator up to the WTC Club, where they made deals
and swapped information over cocktails as they whiled away the
afternoon waiting for the trains that would take them to their suburban homes. These idyllic days were swept away with the boom in
the real estate market in New York City of the mid-1980s. As leases
for maritime businesses expired, rents were increased to levels beyond their ability to pay. Suddenly, the selective and favorable rates,
which the maritime industry had always enjoyed, were no longer
available. One by one, the small maritime companies drifted away
from the World Trade Center to be replaced by huge banks, insurance companies, and brokerage houses.[10]

Even under the best of conditions during the "golden age"
of the World Trade Center from the early 1970s to the mid-1980s,
there were a number of unforeseen problems with Austin Tobin's
idea of a "maritime floor." First of all, there were subtle issues of
business politics and personalities. For example, one might imagine
a business situation where a freight-forwarding firm worked closely
with a given steamship line in arranging for shipment of goods. The
arrangement might be going smoothly, and both parties might
ask for a twenty-year lease. But what would happen if, for example, the freight forwarder were to make a number of serious and

costly mistakes? The two parties might end up at odds and still have to meet uncomfortably face to face in the hallway for the next twenty years.

A second problem had to do with the physical layout of the building itself. On any given floor there are some desirable spaces and some undesirable spaces. Each floor is basically a square with 207 feet on each side, but inside that square at the core is a service rectangle with elevators, air shafts, and so forth. Thus the square floor plan with a rectangle at the core yields two desirable shorter sides, not as deep, that provide office space closer to the windows. Conversely, the two longer sides are much less desirable because fewer offices, usually desks with cubicles, can be near windows. Thus, if the goal is to place a group of businesses on a given floor, one in the group is bound to be shortchanged.

A third problem unforeseen by early planners had to do with issues of employee loyalty. Early in the history of the building, all the freight forwarders, about thirty-five in number, formed an association. Rather than negotiate separately with the Port Authority, they decided that there was strength in numbers. As a group, they would need about 100,000 square feet in total. When Port Authority officials tried to quote them "market rates" for rental charges, the freight forwarders balked, citing the enabling legislation that specifically called for the project to strengthen and preserve the maritime industry. So the Port Authority offered not only to give the freight forwarders a break on the rental price, but also to put them together on one floor, which would have been in line with Austin Tobin's original vision. But when the proposal was put to a vote by the freight-forwarding association, it was not accepted by the principals. It turned out that the freight forwarders were fearful that if they were all together on one floor, their key employees would be tempted to use the opportunity to switch jobs. It would be too easy for valuable employees to approach a rival boss at the water cooler or in the restroom.[11]

In any event, though the World Trade Center may have been beneficial to the maritime industry, it was perceived by those in real estate as unfair competition. They argued that the Port Authority had an edifice complex, that these bloated "Tobin Towers" with their ten million square feet of space were symbols of arrogance. In addition, they complained that the Trade Center was costly to New York City, which had given up hundreds of millions of dollars in ratables. Furthermore, hundreds of small retail businesses were either involuntarily relocated or destroyed. Theodore W. Kheel, the labor lawyer and longtime opponent of the project, argued that it was the huge supply of office space created by the Trade Center itself that had destroyed the Manhattan market for several years.

Tozzoli replied that "about 80 or 90 percent" of the center's private companies were directly or indirectly involved in world trade. His argument was evasive since only about 60 percent of the filled center would be occupied by private tenants. Nearly 10 percent of the center housed offices of the Port Authority itself. More than 5 percent was taken by the regional office of the U.S. Customs Service, and nearly 25 percent was used by more than forty agencies from the state of New York.[12]

It was the large state presence, more than anything else, that enraged the critics. Why, they asked, did the Trade Center house the State Department of Banking, the State Workmen's Compensation Board, and the State Department of Social Services? They saw these state offices as proof that Governor Nelson A. Rockefeller had pushed the Trade Center project, not to foster international commerce, but to help his brother David's scheme to redevelop lower Manhattan. These critics went on to suggest that the Twin Towers should be named David and Nelson.

In time, these arguments against the Trade Center faded. For one thing, the Trade Center was a *fait accompli*. But more important, the real estate market improved. As rental rates rose, it was possible to move the state offices to less expensive space and to recruit legitimate leaseholders of all types—small, medium, and large. For example, a small tenant might be a business with a handful of employees on a floor with other small tenants. A medium tenant might have an entire floor. A good example is the law firm of Brown and Wood, located on the 57th floor of One World Trade Center (North Tower). A large tenant, such as the stock brokerage firm Dean Witter Reynolds, might occupy several floors.

From the beginning, the Port Authority has tried to have all three sizes represented. Of course, for those in the business of renting out space, it is easier just to rent to a few big tenants. The reasoning is clear: the larger the tenant, the longer the lease. But this strategy is risky because if one of them leaves, it has drastic consequences for cash flow.

Furthermore, looking closely at the taxonomy of World Trade Center tenants—small, medium, and large—many of the businesses actually engaged in world trade are small tenants. These companies never appear in the Fortune 500 rankings of the biggest firms. They are not brand names that are easily recognizable. Instead, they go about their business quietly—negotiating contracts, arranging for the transportation of the goods, securing risk protection, dealing with rates of exchange of various currencies, and preparing the necessary documents.

The small tenants are typically the ones who are doing the real work of exporting auto parts, flavoring extracts, valves, copper wire, polyvinyl chloride resin, used clothing, and thousands of other things. They are the ones who are importing coffee and bananas from Central America, flower bulbs from Holland, electronic components, frozen meat by the ton, and whatever else it is that Americans need to buy. Historically, the Port Authority has always felt it was part of its responsibility to make room for the small trader. The World Trade Center at its best serves as an incubator for small import and export companies.

Historically, there have been five major categories of tenants—the maritime industry, the commodities brokers, foreign banks, stockbrokers, and insurance companies. Over the years, the first three categories have dwindled. The slack has been picked up by domestic banks, stockbrokers, and insurance companies.

At any one time, the World Trade Center is home to about three hundred prime leaseholders, yet over the last twenty-five years there have been some three thousand different leases. The clear implication of these numbers is that some tenants are always moving out, and new tenants are always moving in. Despite the best efforts of the Port Authority to retain tenants, inevitably some leave for a wide variety of reasons. Some move out because of mergers; perhaps a given company was absorbed by a larger entity. Others move out because a real estate broker steers them to a better deal. Still others move out because their business is slowing and they are looking for less expensive areas. Some may move because they want to relocate the business closer to their homes; for example, some Japanese companies have moved out of the World Trade Center to midtown offices in order to be closer to Grand Central Station, which is convenient for commuting to their employees' homes in Westchester County. Similarly, some Chinese companies have moved out of the World Trade Center to Jersey City and Fort Lee because their employees' homes are in the North Jersey suburbs.

To retain old tenants, the Port Authority, like other major landlords, uses a two-pronged strategy. Tenant-services representatives come around from time to time to take care of routine problems like cleaning and parking and storage. It's their job to keep tenants happy by solving small problems before they become major irritants. Lease representatives talk to established tenants about renewing very early in the game, eighteen to twelve months prior to expiration of the lease. The goal is to keep the old tenants aboard in order to have a continuous cash flow. If a tenant leaves the building, the landlord can expect a six- to twelve-month period with no rent, so it pays to give old tenants some incentives or credits to renew the lease.

Simultaneous with efforts to hold on to old tenants are efforts to recruit new ones. In some ways, selling office space at the World Trade Center is like selling office space anywhere. The Port Authority uses all of the usual marketing tools. They employ telemarketers, they hold open houses for brokers, they place magazine and newspaper ads, and they print fancy brochures and handouts. Like other organizations, the Port Authority can never be entirely sure which marketing devices work best, so they try them all. A perennial dispute within the organization is over the effectiveness of paid ads in newspapers and magazines. Said George Rossi, who handled these matters for many years, "I never had a prospect come into my office with one of those ads stapled to his chest, but I still believe that they work in the long run."[13]

One difference in marketing office space in the World Trade Center from that of other office buildings is that the potential market is global. Thus managers have to learn how to reach out to multinational businesses as well as to understand and respond to a wide range of cultures. An obvious first step is to join international business associations, attend their conferences, and network with their members.

During most periods, the World Trade Center is about 85 percent occupied and 15 percent unoccupied. Of course, during boom times the occupancy rate goes up. For example, from the early 1980s through the mid-1980s the occupancy rate was about 96 percent, which for all practical purposes was considered completely occupied. During that period of time, George Rossi, who was in charge of leasing space, recalls literally selling space over the telephone. He might get a call from a business in France looking for a small office of 5,000 or 6,000 square feet. The prospect would ask if space were available and in which tower and on what floor. If everything seemed right, the prospect would agree to the deal for a five-year lease without ever personally inspecting the property.[14]

During most periods, leasing office space is not so easy. Most of the time, tenants need to be sought out and encouraged to take out offices in the World Trade Center. For example, a print ad in the *Journal of Commerce* in 1996 ran under the headline "A World-Class Address Can Make a World of Difference." The ad featured a dramatic photo of the Twin Towers as seen from the Austin Tobin Plaza looking straight up. In the body of the ad we are told, "The World Trade Center is truly the world's most prestigious address. Today, some 350 companies took advantage of our world-class amenities and unsurpassed value." After listing a number of such amenities, the ad concludes, "The World Trade Center has premium office space designed for your business. Come see for yourself how a World Trade Center address can make a world of difference."[15]

The Port Authority attempts to find tenants engaged in world trade, but the agency has always pushed the idea that the World Trade Center provides more than office space for the international trading community. There are, of course, conference facilities, exhibit spaces, and dining facilities. But more important, the Port Authority stresses the broad array of services, especially information services and education.[16]

The Port Authority devoted considerable support to its World
Trade Institute, an educational organization set up in 1970 specifically to foster international commerce by holding classes at the
Twin Towers complex. The Institute was run by the agency itself
from 1970 to 1997, when it was sold to Pace University, which
has continued to offer these specialized classes. I myself audited a
course there in the fall of 1995.

I took the course taught by Robert T. Kelley called "Introduction to World Trade." Like most World Trade Institute instructors,
Kelley teaches part time. His primary position is president of his
own import-export company, Artek Incorporated, of Bloomfield,
New Jersey. Kelley represents a rare blend of skills. On one hand,
he has the hard-charging stamina and the decisiveness to be a successful businessman. On the other hand, he has the kindliness and
patience of a natural-born teacher. Often wearing a brightly colored necktie decorated with the world's flags, he brings his evening
class to life with firsthand stories about the joys and frustrations of
international trade. His course materials are the actual documents
used in real-life situations.

Kelley has a favorite story about a couple he calls the Bakers.
The story never fails to grab the imagination of his students.
Charles Baker started out in life as a carpenter. With his experience
in the building trade, he eventually became a municipal building inspector. His work as an inspector was easier and he had more regular hours, but he missed working with his hands. For a hobby, he
started making wooden toys in the basement for his grandchildren.
The toys were lovely and soon his friends and neighbors started
asking him to make some. At first, Charlie was too embarrassed to
charge, but demand grew and grew.

Reluctantly, he decided he would have to charge a realistic
price. To his surprise, asking for money did not seem to deter anyone from placing an order. The business grew, and Charlie moved
his shop from his basement to his garage. Still the business grew,
and Charlie rented space in an industrial area. At first most of the
orders were from local retailers, but later he got hooked up with a
national wholesaler. He quit his day job and started making toys
full time.

Meanwhile, his wife, Helene, was handling the office work.

One of her jobs was to go to the post office every day to get the mail. One day, as she was sorting the mail, she noticed an unusual envelope. It was an odd size, an airmail envelope framed by a red-and-blue border, with foreign stamps. She opened it up and found inside a note written in halting English asking for a catalog to be sent to the writer in Japan. Helene Baker put the letter back in her "to do" pile, since she really did not know how to respond. They had never gotten a request from overseas before.

Time went by and still Mrs. Baker kept putting the foreign letter aside. After about a month, she said to herself, "I've got to respond to this request!" So she reached up to a nearby shelf and got a catalog with a price list, which she put in a large envelope. She did not bother with a cover letter. She simply addressed the envelope and mailed it from the post office. Mrs. Baker was relieved because now the request was no longer sitting on her desk.

About a month later, Mrs. Baker got another letter from Japan. This time there was a one-thousand-dollar check inside with a letter requesting samples. The Bakers found a large, sturdy cardboard box and packed it with a thousand dollars' worth of toys taken right off the shelf. They took the box down to the UPS office and sent it off to Japan. The next thing they knew a fax came through from Japan. The company there wanted to buy $50,000 worth of wooden toys.

The Bakers were in consternation. What should they do? They knew nothing about international customs, documents, finance, or transportation. Would they be able to deliver the toys? Would they be able to maintain standards for such a large order? How much time and effort would be needed? Did they have the time? The Bakers had many questions.[17]

At this point, Kelley abruptly stops the story. It is frustrating because, of course, everyone wants to know the ending. But there is a purpose for telling the story this way. Suddenly, the students realize that they don't have the answers to these questions, either. Kelley is one of the instructors for the Evening School of the World Trade Institute, an unusual kind of school that caters to entrepreneurs and people from small business who want to learn the nuts and bolts of international business.

For the most part, Kelley's course deals with basic technical subjects: how to negotiate a contract, how to arrange transportation of the goods, how to arrange insurance and finance, how to prepare letters of credit, and how to prepare necessary government documents. Kelley tries to immerse the class into the world of international trade so that at the end of nine weeks, the student comes out thinking like a trader. To do this successfully, Kelley proceeds on three levels of discourse. The most formal level of instruction is conveyed through handbooks and textbooks; this information is relatively fixed and unchanging. The next level of information is conveyed through magazines and newspapers; actual trading opportunities are short-lived, so getting timely information is crucial. The least formal, but by no means the least important, level of instruction is conveyed through anecdotes—many of them about cross-cultural understanding. The stories might be generated from the instructor, the students, or the recommended reading. Most of the stories are both humorous and didactic. Embedded in the stories is practical advice on how to avoid mistakes and problems.

Courses like the one offered by Kelley are not just entertaining because they are packed with illustrative anecdotes like the examples just given; they are also practical and cost-effective. They typically meet once a week for six to twelve weeks. As I have mentioned earlier, these courses cover export, import, finance, and transportation topics. The approach is generally broad and can be followed by nearly anyone with an interest in the topics, even beginners and entry-level people. Tuition is kept at an affordable level for working people. The course titles are warm, inviting, and user friendly: one can take "Essentials of Establishing an Export Business," or "Understanding Foreign Exchange Trading," or "Fundamentals of Building an Import Business." To be sure, the courses cover specific and vocational topics, but they are not intimidating.

The World Trade Institute, when it was run by the Port Authority, could not grant degrees. Of course, Pace University can give credits and award degrees, but the purpose of most courses is still to provide individuals with specific information to succeed as traders or to make them more competitive. Mainly the clientele for the courses is made up of people who are already involved with international trade. A number of the courses at the Evening School of

World Trade have been recommended for credit by the New York State Education Department.[18] Normally the students for these courses come from the New York and New Jersey region because they have to show up every week for an extended period of time. However, on occasion, students have commuted weekly from as far away as Boston to get the special kind of training they need.

The World Trade Institute also runs daytime seminars and conferences for businesspeople. These programs are quite different since they usually meet all day long for two or three days in a row. Such meetings are usually for well-established midlevel people. These courses, often attended by people from Fortune 1000 companies, are more advanced. Some of the seminars and conferences are offered at the World Trade Institute's conference facility at the World Trade Center in New York, while others are given in many cities throughout the United States. The titles of these programs, while intriguing and perhaps even fascinating, are unwieldy and packed with jargon to scare off the neophyte. How would you like to take "Energy/Commodity Price Risk Management Workshop: Strategies for Enhancing Corporate Financial Viability" for two full days? No appeal? How about "Transfer Pricing and Other International Tax Issues in the Pharmaceutical and Chemical Industries"? Obviously, these courses are highly valuable to particular, narrow constituencies. People who need these courses come from far and wide to attend for two or three full days. They stay in nearby hotels and devote their undivided attention to the task at hand. The tuition fees for these highly specialized seminars and conferences are markedly higher than those charged the Evening School students. More often than not, the employee's company pays the tuition bill as well as traveling expenses.

Many people in international business seek language training to help in their career advancement through employment opportunities or for personal achievement in gaining cultural awareness. The World Trade Institute Language Center teaches ten languages— Arabic, Chinese, English, French, German, Italian, Japanese, Portuguese, Russian, and Spanish. The most affordable way to learn one of these languages is through small group classes (no more than ten). Teachers try to get students to develop confidence by expanding their practical vocabularies. For those who need to learn a language more quickly, there are accelerated executive programs and weekend language immersion programs.

Most of the courses are primarily designed for the benefit of Americans involved in international trade. However, the Institute also has special International Training courses designed for foreigners in both the public and private sectors. Often funded by the United States Agency for International Development, topics include agribusiness management, international purchasing, and management skills development. Also funded by the United Nations are topics including port management, trade promotion, and marketing tourism. For these courses, people typically come from overseas for two or three weeks. Shorter programs, usually four or five days, are held in the host country.[19]

As everyone knows, most educational operations lose money and require subsidies. So why did the Port Authority maintain the World Trade Institute from 1970 to 1997? The answer to this question is to be found in the same enabling legislation that empowered the Port Authority to build the complex in the first place. The two states would never have agreed to build just another office building. The only way for the Port Authority to justify the project was for Austin Tobin to insist that it was *special*, that the project really would foster world trade and increase the use of the port. Hostile critics were watching the Port Authority's every move. There were two main tactics to defuse the arguments of the critics. One was to make sure that the tenants were really involved in world trade; the other was to maintain an educational division. It was a point of pride for the Port Authority to keep the World Trade Institute going whether it made money or not. Of course, the commissioners liked the Institute best when it could at least break even; but they were committed to it in principle because it stood for an ideal.

No one said it better than the Institute's first director, Jack Zwick, who told a reporter, "This is the heart of the World Trade Center. The rest of it, that's just real estate, remarkable real estate and fascinating engineering, but just real estate." Zwick, a former Columbia and Harvard business school professor, went on to explain, "What we are doing is getting people involved in world trade. We have an information retrieval that will provide people with the latest information on such things as tariffs, quota restrictions, where the buyers are and where the sellers are."[20]

The World Trade Institute had a laudable record of reaching out not only to managers and supervisors, but also to beginners and entry-level workers in international trade. I asked Eunice Coleman, a senior program manager at the Institute, how the "Introduction to World Trade" course, which I sat in on, got started. She explained that it, like many other courses, was developed in response to specific requests. She recalled that years ago someone approached her and said, "We run an international operation, and we have a secretary who is going to be in charge of all this kind of stuff, but she has no idea of the terminology or anything else. However, she's very smart. Can you develop a kind of introductory program?" Others approached Coleman and said, "We think that the career future lies in international trade, but we don't know what part of international trade we want to get involved in. Can you help us?"

Coleman said that people really responded to the idea of taking a twelve-hour introductory course. If they completed that course, they would be in touch with all the different pieces of international trade. They could then start focusing on the aspects that really interested them. Certainly a key lesson of the introductory course is that international trade is two-sided. Exporting and importing make up the yin and yang of the field. Most Evening School students who are ready to move on to intermediate and advanced courses pursue either exporting or importing.

On the exporting side, there are thousands of people in the New York and New Jersey region who do the paperwork and the documentation for the traffic leaving the port. These jobs are mostly done by principal clerks. Because these jobs attract people who are careful with details, they make excellent candidates for promotion. As a result, there is a great deal of turnover in those jobs all the time. Consequently there is a real need for courses to train new people.

On the importing side, the focus is more on customs paperwork. The emphasis here is on the voluntary compliance by legitimate business with the regulations. Even the most law-abiding firms have to deal with matters of enormous complexity since Customs is the administrative arm for some four hundred different government agencies whose rules may impact on imports. Just to name a few, the Food and Drug Administration, the Department of Agriculture, and the Fish and Wildlife Service all have something to say about what is allowed into the United States, but Customs is the group that first contacts the importer. For instance, Customs might flag a food product item and direct it to the U.S. Food and Drug Administration's kitchens in Newark where it could be tested.[21]

It is undoubtedly true that the programs of the World Trade Institute helped the Port Authority for many years to convey the message that the World Trade Center was not a trade center in name only. But times change, and by the late 1990s there was a new set of imperatives. The Port Authority commissioners were actively looking for programs and projects that could be privatized when it was in the public interest to do so. The World Trade Institute seemed to be a classic example of something that a private operator could do just as well as, if not better than, a public agency. So the Institute was put up for sale. The agency received seven proposals. The winning bidder at $500,000 was Pace University, a private coeducational New York City university founded in 1906. Not only did the Port Authority make money on the deal, it also gained a tenant—leasing the space for fifteen years to Pace University. Most important, the good work of the Institute could continue without interruption.[22]

Important as education is to the World Trade Center concept, the real test of compliance with its own mission statement is to check the tenant directory. A close examination of the list yields a few questionable tenants. Are all the law firms, personnel, and computer companies engaged exclusively in international commerce? Most of the New York State offices are gone, but a few still remain. And, of course, there are retail stores and restaurants in the concourse that serve the people who work there as well as subway and rail commuters. Granting all these objections, there are still nearly eight hundred firms that would fit nearly anyone's definition of world trade. There are importers, exporters, ship charter brokers, oil traders, trade associations, international merger and acquisitions firms, leasing agents, insurance organizations, freight handlers, steamship lines, commodities brokers, architects and naval architects, and so on.

By all accounts, the Port Authority was initially very successful in getting most of the core international business firms to lease space in the buildings. Some estimate that as many as 90 percent of the lower Manhattan steamship companies and freight forwarders signed lease agreements. But then in the 1980s, these businesses began to drift away. When their leases came up for renewal, they simply went elsewhere.

Why did this happen? There seem to be two broad explanations. One is economic; the other, technological. In the first place, the 1980s were a period of explosive economic growth. Real estate prices were up around the country. Nowhere were prices more sky-high than in Manhattan. Rents in the financial district of lower Manhattan went into the stratosphere. Businesses in international trade, especially small businesses, could not keep up with the new rentals being charged.

A poignant example was given by the son of a proprietor of a small freight-forwarding company that had been one of the World Trade Center's first tenants. Exporters rely on freight forwarders to smooth the path of exporting. The forwarder acts as the exporter's agent or representative in handling air or ocean shipments in preparing all the necessary documents. Albert Cohen, of Mutual International, explained his problem in renting space in the building: "When my father, Leon Cohen, signed the original lease in 1970, he took the space for fifteen years at six dollars a square foot. Most people only signed for five- and ten-year leases. In 1986, when that lease expired, they jumped our rent to thirty-four dollars a square foot. No concession was made for the fact that we were freight forwarders."[23] The Cohen family managed to stay in the World Trade Center by shrinking their space requirements to the bare minimum, but most of the people in the business were not making the kind of profits needed to justify such huge rents. They just moved across the Hudson River to New Jersey. International traders moved out; banks and stockbrokers moved in. That was the trend of the 1980s.

The other broad explanation is technological. Just as rentable office space in the World Trade Center was becoming available in the early 1970s, a communications revolution was just getting started. Over the ensuing twenty-five years, the nature of business communications was to change profoundly with the development of the fax machine, the personal computer, and E-mail. As we all know, it's possible to put a piece of paper in a fax machine in New York City and have everything that is important about that piece of paper be transmitted through telephone lines overseas to Paris where the paper (with the information) is resupplied. It no longer matters where a person's office is physically located. Albert Cohen, who still stubbornly maintains a World Trade Center office, says, "Theoretically, I could run this business from the basement of my home on Staten Island."[24]

He *could* run his business from his home, but he chooses not to do so. Why not? The reasons are difficult to pin down. If all that is needed is a desk and a chair plus a phone, a computer, and a fax machine, then one place is as good as another. But to achieve superior economic performance, firms must carefully choose their environment. The choice of office space makes a statement about the firm's place in the world. A firm projects an image when it is dealing with government agencies, suppliers, distributors, customers, clients, and competitors. All other things being equal, a prestigious business address should help a firm gain respect and thus have a competitive advantage.

In my interviews with World Trade Center tenants, most freely admitted that their business could be conducted elsewhere just as well at a lower cost. But they value the address because it is both prestigious and appropriate. Spending the additional money on rent for them is an expression of a priority. The decision to move into the World Trade Center for the first time or to stay when the lease comes up for renewal is generally justified as the result of careful thought, but underlying the thought process is some degree of emotional commitment. The choice of an impressive office address is closely linked with attitudes toward work, wealth, consumption, and achievement. While the long-term goal of the business is the accumulation of wealth, along the way it may be necessary to spend a little extra on rent to establish the firm's social rank and to validate its achievement. The World Trade Center address is valued not for itself but as a symbol of achievement and power.[25]

What I found most striking in my interviews with World Trade Center tenants is that no one claimed that there was any value in

physical proximity to others engaged in international trade. Austin
Tobin's original idea was to design the building as a cluster of related businesses, but it never really worked out that way. For example, all of Albert Cohen's customers are engaged in the import or
export business. Fully 95 percent of his customers are not located
in the World Trade Center. In fact, they are not located in New
York City or even in New York State. None of the air cargo carriers
that Cohen uses have offices in the World Trade Center; none of the
steamship lines that he uses have offices in the World Trade Center.
In short, the World Trade Center has evolved in ways unforeseen by
its builder. It is a great location for world trade, but it is not really
an exclusive *center* of world trade because the nature of the business has evolved toward decentralization.

7

A City
within
a City

or, A Day in the Life . . .

This world is a place of business. What an infinite bustle! There is no sabbath. . . . It is nothing but work, work, work. I cannot easily buy a blank book to write thoughts in; they are commonly ruled for dollars and cents.

—HENRY DAVID THOREAU, "LIFE WITHOUT PRINCIPLE," 1863

IT IS five o'clock on a Monday morning in mid-June in New York City, and in the distant suburbs people start to wake up. In the hazy morning light, most of the World Trade Center is empty. Rays of sunlight are starting to reach through the glass of corner offices. The weatherman says it's going to be quite sticky, with clouds and some sunshine. Conditions are very warm and humid, with almost no wind. By six o'clock the rush hour has begun. More than three million people commute to Manhattan daily, and forty thousand of them are headed for the World Trade Center complex. Most will regard the trip as daily drudgery. They come via all three New York subway systems (IRT, BMT, and the IND) as well as the Port Authority Trans-Hudson (PATH) rail rapid transit system. Others who cannot part with their automobiles will use bridges and tunnels. Perhaps the most fortunate are those who will arrive by ferry. Because Manhattan is an island, it had ferries long before it had bridges and tunnels. Some people commute by taking the ferry from Hoboken, operating out of the old Lackawana Railroad slip, over to the Battery Park City terminal. These are the lucky ones; they have a few moments of tranquility, fresh air, and breathtakingly beautiful views of the Twin Towers. As the day starts, none of these commuters knows exactly what lies ahead. Maybe it will be a good day.

OPERATIONS SUPERVISORS

While the commuters enjoyed their weekend, some work at the World Trade Center continued. A large commercial office building can never be left unattended. Air-conditioning must be kept going, water and electricity systems maintained, and vital equipment guarded. All these functions are carried out twenty-four hours a day, seven days a week. The headquarters for these activities is the Operations Control Center (OCC) located on the B-1 level, one floor beneath the lobby level of Tower Two, or the South Tower. The OCC is a kind of command post, resembling the damage control center of a warship. Security guards check identification as you pass into the Control Center. These same guards issue the cleaning contractors their keys when they start their shift. Once inside, you encounter the Operations Supervisor seated at a large desk on a raised platform behind a gray Formica counter. In this windowless basement room there are banks of video monitors to watch key security areas. One video camera is focused on the door to the roof of Tower One, which permits access to the television mast. I tell my host that if a daredevil were to try to get to the roof we could see him on the monitor. He says, "Oh, I hope not this morning. As long as it doesn't happen on my shift. There's too much paperwork to fill out as it is." [1]

In the back room is the desk supervisor, who receives all the radio messages from four different two-way radio channels, a variety of other telephones, and the elevator communications system. They say that the desk supervisor has to be an octopus, because you need eight hands to stay on top of everything. The radio crackles with static as messages pour in and are acknowledged. There are walls full of toggle switches, dials, glowing indicator lights. The desk supervisor stays in touch with the fire command stations throughout the complex and with the police desk. As regulations for emergencies have proliferated over the years, so have the monitoring electronics. Additional consoles for additional monitors have been added, so the whole place is of mind-boggling complexity. A large black digital clock ticks off the time, second by second, in red numbers. It's now 7:31:59. If some kind of emergency were to occur, large reels of tape would start recording every word said.

The Port Authority places the day-to-day responsibility for the building on its operations supervisors, comparable to command duty officers on a ship. The general operations supervisor is at liberty to patrol around the complex, troubleshooting here and there as needed. But he is backed up by the operations supervisor, who stays at his post, the Operations Control Center. These supervisors are given twelve-hour shifts. The night supervisor works from seven in the evening until seven in the morning. On this typical Monday morning, the day supervisor arrives at 7 A.M. to relieve his predecessor. But there is a period of about half an hour of overlap to exchange information. The night supervisor will describe any critical work that is going on and needs to be continued on into the day.

During his shift, the general operations supervisor is totally responsible for everything that happens. Much can happen. No two days are alike, and no two shifts are alike. There are situations, emergencies, problems—both major and minor. It takes a certain kind of personality and temperament to succeed at this job, since it is largely reactive. You do not know in advance what the problems are going to be. The only thing you know for sure is that there will be problems.

Today has begun well. The air-conditioning system is functioning without problems. There is very little wind, which is a good thing. When it's too windy, the buildings twist and turn, making it impossible to use the freight elevators. With an elevator shaft 1,350 feet long, you can't have the cables slapping around in the shaft. When the freight elevators are out of action for any period of time, you have to redo the schedule for the removal of trash from the buildings. The general operations supervisor relaxes and takes a sip of coffee. For a moment, he thinks maybe there will be no problems at all today. Then a report comes over the radio about a backup of a drain in the subbasement. There is some flooding on level B-5. The problems have begun, after all. He sends a crew with fifty-five-gallon wet-vacs to the subbasement.[2]

ELEVATORS

Before the commuters arrive in large numbers, elevator inspectors from the Ace Elevator Company check the equipment. Elevators in the Twin Towers have to be in good working order. Engineers estimate conservatively that there are about 450,000 "passenger movements" per day in these elevators. A passenger movement is defined as one person going on one trip. But because of the skylobby system, two-thirds of the people have to make double trips. This includes all those in the second and third zones, because in effect each tower is made up of three skyscrapers, stacked one on top of another.

There are 254 elevators in the World Trade Center, and each has its own drive motor plus its motor-generator set. These are big electric motors, each the size of a small van, each with about 450 horsepower, more powerful than a 911 Porsche, which has only 280 horsepower. Interestingly enough, the original elevator equipment for the World Trade Center was manufactured by the Otis Elevator Company. Of course, it was in the early 1850s that Elisha G. Otis of Yonkers, New York, invented the first automatic safety elevator. Even if the ropes broke, there was a device to prevent the elevator from falling.[3]

Air-Conditioning and Electricity

This particular Monday morning follows a hazy, hot, and humid weekend. The weather forecast calls for more of the same, so engineers will have started the equipment to cool down the building at four or five in the morning. If they tried to conserve energy by cooling it down starting at seven, they would never be able to achieve their objective. People themselves give off about 600 BTUs per person per hour just sitting at a desk.[4] Air-conditioning became widespread in office buildings in the 1950s, so the World Trade Center had the advantage of being designed for central air-conditioning from the start. On a day such as this, the energy usage for the complex is phenomenal.

Down in the fifth subbasement level, between Tower One and Tower Two, is the central refrigeration plant for the complex. It is housed in an enormous room three stories tall, about the size of a small airplane hangar. In this room are seven 7,000-ton machines called "centrifugal liquid chilling units," along with two 2,500-ton parallel compressors that come on line when there are lighter loads to be handled. The workers are so dwarfed by these huge machines that the place resembles a movie set for a science-fiction thriller.

Whereas most office buildings vent the waste heat out by means of a cooling tower on the top of the building, the World

Trade Center uses the Hudson River to expel excess heat. Technicians pump river water into the building through huge pipes, some
as large as sixty-six inches in diameter. The water circulates through
the refrigeration plant and goes through that equipment to transfer
the heat back out to the river. At the peak of the summer season, the
system will use 100.7 million gallons of river water per day. Meanwhile, the machines yield chilled water, which is pumped through
somewhat smaller pipes running up to the mechanical equipment
rooms where heat exchangers are located, to adjust cooling for individual tenants.[5]

At the same time, down in the sixth subbasement level, early-
morning crews are testing the emergency electrical generators, just
in case they might be needed later that day. Originally, there were
five emergency generators rated at 1,000 kilowatts each. Later, in order to accommodate the broadcasters, a sixth generator was added
to the common pool of emergency power. Still later, building operators modified the fuel injection system so that they were able to get
1,200 kilowatts out of each generator. So at present, the system
can yield 7,200 kilowatts (or 7.2 megawatts) of emergency power,
enough power for the needs of about four thousand typical suburban homes.[6] At first glance, this seems like a great deal of power;
but, in fact, it's just barely enough for the building to limp along
until full power can be restored. Even with all six emergency generators running simultaneously, there is not enough power to start
a single refrigeration machine. However, there is enough for such
essentials as stairway lighting, fire alarms, communication systems,
fire pumps, and sprinkler pumps. There is also enough electricity
for one elevator per bank, though nowhere near enough to run all
254 elevators.[7]

POLICE OFFICERS

As the daytime operations supervisor is being briefed, Port Authority police officers are taking up their "image posts" in the concourse.
The origins of the Port Authority police go back to June 1, 1928,
when forty men were selected from two hundred applicants to police the newly opened Goethals Bridge and Outerbridge Crossing.

At that time, collecting tolls was their primary responsi[bility; this] duty was transferred to civilian collectors in 1962. The p[olice ju]risdiction of the Port Authority police is an area within [a] five-mile radius of the Statue of Liberty. This area, know[n as the] Port District, includes airports and marine terminals, bistate bridges and tunnels—and the World Trade Center.[8]

During the morning commuting hours at the World Trade Center, supervisors place a number of uniformed officers at highly visible locations, known as "Fixed Image Posts," to monitor pedestrian traffic. Unless there is a problem, the officer is expected to stay put at his or her post. The officers themselves do not care for this duty. They prefer to move around, to be on patrol, to be "fighting crime." They feel like they are just standing there like wooden soldiers, but in fact they are performing a very valuable function because it is reassuring to commuters to see them there. They are not fighting crime; they are building public confidence and the perception of safety. If any problem arises, the everyday commuter knows right away where to find an officer.

It has been a controversial method of operation because it is easy for critics to say that the police are just standing there. For example, Bob Grant, a popular radio talk show host, has called these police officers "blue asparagus," since they are apparently doing nothing. But police supervisors insist that it makes for a more civilized and orderly society if people feel that they are being watched. Between seven and nine in the morning is the period of time when the maximum traffic is going through the mall area. It's like trying to maneuver through a football field with some people going one way and others going in the opposite direction. Thousands of office workers are trying to get to their own particular spaces. Some of the people in the mall, or concourse level, are just commuters or transients passing through because the World Trade Center is a transportation node within the subways and PATH systems. If you are in a hurry, you are okay. If you try to go slowly, you might have a problem.

The World Trade Center may be the only high-rise building in the United States with its own police department, with forty-two officers. It's a unique situation since Port Authority police have full police powers in two states—New York and New Jersey. Nowhere else in the country is there such a bistate agency. It's a selling factor when leasing space at the World Trade Center to be able to tell prospective tenants that the building has its own police force right there. The police unit also serves as an industrial fire brigade; they are the first responding unit. Police officers at the World Trade Center are cross-trained as firefighters. (At the airports, police officers are cross-trained for fire, crash, and rescue.)

How do they deploy the force? Usually, there are eleven officers on the day shift; five on the evening shift; five on the overnight shift; and five on the weekends. The numbers sound small, but they are proportional to the population served. What is the population? For years, World Trade Center officials said that the complex served 50,000 tenants and 70,000 visitors daily. These figures were bandied about during the design phase of the project and repeated so often that they became part of the standard information released to the public. But since the 1993 bombing, more careful counts have been made. The real figures are closer to 35,000 tenants and 15,000 visitors daily.

From time to time, the Port Authority Police Department has conducted security surveys and risk analyses. Routine problems are street crimes, office theft, and burglary. During the day, there are very few crimes. However, pickpockets operate on the concourse level. They particularly like to work in and out of revolving doors and on escalators (or "motor stairs," as they are customarily called in police jargon). These are places where some bumping is not unusual and may go unnoticed. Pickpockets often operate in teams. The most successful teams are groups that might go almost unnoticed, such as three grandmotherly women. Pickpockets do best in shoe stores during the busy lunchtime period. Their work is almost laughably easy. As women customers come into the shoe stores to shop, they routinely set down their handbags as they try on shoes. As they try on pair after pair, their attention is focused on the search for the perfect shoes, not on the nearby handbag—which disappears.

There is a crime prevention unit. One sergeant is dedicated to this duty. There are programs of crime awareness for tenants, especially as new tenants move in. There are cycles of thefts, often traced to a new employee or a new messenger service. Men are cautioned not to leave their wallets in their coats; women, not to leave their purses in unlocked desks. Police also encourage the ongoing activities of a tenant security council. Large firms have their own security departments. For example, Dean-Witter, the largest tenant of all, has its own security director and staff to patrol its forty floors.

What is the attitude of the Port Authority police who work at the World Trade Center? It's not a place for an officer who wants to be a crimestopper. For real police action, the bus terminal and the airports offer much more opportunity. I talked at length with a senior Port Authority police officer, Joseph Martella, who had served for several years as the captain of the detachment stationed at the World Trade Center. He explained the unusual law enforcement environment there. For example, concerning uniform inspection, he said: "I know their raincoats and overcoats will be in immaculate shape. They never wear them. All the work is indoors." Still, it is regarded as a good job. They get plenty of overtime. It is not all that dangerous as a place to work; it is not cops and robbers. But officers do have to be polite. Visitors get their first impressions from the uniformed police. Martella said, "It's an environment that encourages the customer service approach to policing."[9]

GETTING STARTED

On a Monday morning many workers stop for a cup of coffee and a pastry on their way to work. Most of them stop somewhere for a "grab and go" coffee. For those who have the time, the sit-down restaurant is an inviting choice. Of course, many are reading their own copies of the *Wall Street Journal*, but since this is the World Trade Center there are always a few reading the more specialized *Journal of Commerce*. One television set mounted high on a massive center column in the restaurant is always turned on to CNBC, which has nothing but financial news. CNBC, a General Electric subsidiary based in Fort Lee, New Jersey, is popular with the American financial community because it consistently takes the point of view of a cheerleader for the stock market.

But most breakfast customers don't have time to watch television or read newspapers in the morning. They are really running to their offices. They want to get their coffee, their bagel, their pastry, and their juice. And they want it quickly. Most expect to be served in fifteen to twenty seconds. It's a quick-hit transaction. Studies have shown that they won't stand in line if there are more than five people ahead of them, so the store must have a large number of cash registers.

I asked one coffee-shop executive whose corporate headquarters is located near Seattle, Washington, what it's like serving coffee in the morning at the World Trade Center. He responded with a metaphor right out of the Pacific Northwest. Pointing to the hallway outside his shop, he said, "We call the people that come down that corridor salmon. It's like a salmon run. We're like the bears waiting at the edge of the stream."[10]

GETTING TO WORK

Around seven, as people continue coming into the complex with folded newspapers under their arms, there is a large number of office workers who have forgotten their identification cards. They have had the whole weekend to get out of their daily routines. Large lines start to form at the visitor desks. There are more people than usual in the lobby, with more congestion and confusion.

But by eight o'clock some executives are already ensconced in their large offices, sipping coffee and reading the *Wall Street Journal*. Other workers slip into their windowless cubicles and turn on their computer screens. There is much work to be done: importing, exporting, freight forwarding, banking, publishing, buying, and selling. The Twin Towers have offices for steamship lines, international banks, commodities brokers, insurance companies, and engineering firms.

By nine o'clock work has begun in earnest. Our typical executive first has to open the mail. The pile can be quite large if the person has been out of the office for a while. He or she attacks it in order of importance. First, the express envelopes and then the envelopes that are either handwritten or individually typed without a preprinted mailing label. Then the phones start ringing. The daily routine can be both time consuming and mind numbing.

Tenants start to make trouble calls to building services. On a typical day, there are complaints about space temperatures. "I'm too hot," says one. "I'm too cold," says another. "Good grief, I'm locked out," says yet another. There are cleaning complaints. Some lights are burned out; some electrical receptacles are not working. These calls generate about 40,000 work orders every year. There are enough emergencies to keep five locksmiths at work.[11] But by eleven o'clock most people have burrowed into the day's routine, doing what has to be done.

Flanking the two shimmering 110-story Twin Towers are a number of low brown buildings that frame the five-acre plaza. If the Twin Towers are the stars of the show, these buildings (designated WTC 4, WTC 5, and WTC 6) are the supporting cast. All of these buildings house some activity relevant to world trade. For example, Four World Trade Center, at the southeast corner of the complex, is New York's headquarters for commodities trading. By this time in the morning, it is quite busy. A number of exchanges share a joint trading floor for such goods as coffee, cotton, sugar, potatoes, lumber, and beef. The vast trading floor, about the size of two football fields placed side by side, is all under one unsupported ceiling, not broken by any columns. On my first visit there, I asked one of the floor traders why there were no windows. He said, "It goes back to 1929. That's so nobody can jump out on a bad day."[12]

Lunchtime

When it's time for lunch at the World Trade Center, office workers have little time but many choices. Lunchtime is not just noon to one. There are so many people with such varied schedules that lunchtime could be anytime from around eleven to three. Over the course of recent years, more and more people have been taking shorter lunches. From the people I talked with, it seems that the era of the long, three-martini lunch is over. Many people, especially brokers and traders, order food to be delivered. You may see a pizza delivery man coming up the elevator with fifteen boxes of pizza. There are all kinds of fast foods being delivered, from Chinese to chicken. Brokers often work right through lunch, though they may leave at three or four o'clock in the afternoon.

For those who can get out of the office, even if only for a half-hour, the Austin J. Tobin Plaza is popular in the summertime. Covering almost five acres, an area the size of four football fields, it's good for a bit of fresh air and sunshine. The plaza is dominated by an enormous bronze globe by the German sculptor Fritz Koenig. The seventeen-ton globe was cast and assembled in Ganslberg, Germany. The bronze casting, nearly twenty-five feet in height, is made up of seventy-one welded and six main bolted sections. The statue is set on a turntable that can be set to complete one revolution at variable speeds, from every thirty-six minutes to every twelve hours.[13] The globe's turntable is set on a fountain, which is ringed with stone benches suitable for conversation and something quick to eat. In the 1970s when the World Trade Center first opened, the Port Authority was fond of comparing the Tobin Plaza with the Piazza San Marco in Venice, one of the most celebrated architectural spaces in the world. At first this seemed to be a laughable claim, since the plaza was too vast and empty—totally uninviting. In recent years, however, a real effort has been made to humanize the space, to make it playful and accessible.

Along the north side of the plaza at the foot of Five World Trade Center is a group of wheeled carts painted dark green with thin-line gold trim where sandwiches and salads are sold. Nearby is a roped-off sitting area with dark green lawn furniture, chairs and tables with dark green umbrellas. Along the south side of the plaza at the foot of Two World Trade Center is another cluster of four separate wheeled kiosks, each selling its own line of merchandise: T-shirts, inexpensive prints of local cityscapes, sunglasses, and New York City souvenirs such as pennants and paperweights.

In the summer months, a large portable stage is set up by the Port Authority at the foot of One World Trade Center to provide free lunchtime performances between 12:15 and 2 P.M. Since this is a Monday, we can take a break and bring our lunch while listening to classical music by students and faculty from the Juilliard School of Music. During the rest of the work week, each day will cater to a different taste—Broadway tunes, jazz, country, finishing off the week with rhythm and blues.

As a result of this commendable activity on the plaza level, the shops and restaurants in the lower, indoors concourse mall may be a bit less crowded on a day like today. If it were winter, the place would be packed. But this is summertime, and things have slowed down considerably. Still, some people will always prefer hot food in a sit-down restaurant, and there are several to choose from at the

mall. Most of them are not places for the indecisive. There is no mill-
ing around or confusion. The cashiers take pride in being speedy.

Washing Windows

As office workers in the Twin Towers carry out their duties on this
summer afternoon, they may from time to time enjoy the view from
their windows. Part of the credit for the breathtaking views must go
to the small crew of window cleaners who are now working high
up on the roof of Tower One. Some of the men operate the machinery while others keep it in repair. It's a good assignment for
people who like to work outdoors on their own with a minimum of
supervision.

I meet with Roko Camaj, a window-cleaning-machine operator. I learn that he came to the United States in 1969 as a refugee
from communist Albania. He arrived with his pregnant wife on
September 17, 1969, and on the very next day, September 18, his
daughter was born here in the United States. He started working at
the World Trade Center in March 1975.

Camaj explains to me that there are two automatic, un-
manned window-washing machines—one for each tower. Each
machine has a set of nylon brushes and a squeegee. Water is supplied from a twenty-gallon tank to which detergent is added as
needed. Passersby do not get wet because there is a vacuum unit
that sucks up the dirty water after application to the window, filters
the water, and returns it to the tank for reuse.

Each tower has fifty-eight vertical columns of windows per
side, and each column is numbered. The machine does about twelve
columns of windows per day, so it takes five working days, or one
week, to do one side of the building. There is a turntable at each of
the four corners on the roof, so at the end of the week, the machine
turns the corner to deal with another side. It takes four weeks, or
one month, to do the whole building. Then the process is repeated,
except during the winter months because when it is too cold the
water just freezes. Usually the window-washing operation is shut
down in the beginning of December and resumes in mid-March.

The window-washing machine can handle the "regular" windows, eighteen and a half inches wide, which stretch from the 9th to
the 106th floor. For both towers, it is the 107th floor that requires

special attention because those windows are thirty inches wide to accommodate the spectacular views. The extra-wide windows are needed at the North Tower for the luxury restaurant, Windows on the World. Similarly, extra-wide windows are needed at the South Tower for the observation deck.

These extra-wide windows must be cleaned by hand. Wearing safety belts, Camaj and his colleagues go "over the side" of the building in special scaffolding to do the job. Of course, they can do a much better job than the machine in taking care of small details. This extra care is a justifiable expense since *the view* is what is being sold to both restaurant and observation deck clients.[14]

While up on the roof, Camaj introduces me to Arthur Del-Bianco, a member of Local 94 of the operating engineers, who has been working at the World Trade Center since 1981. He is an operating engineer, one of those responsible for the mechanical maintenance of the seven-building complex. Before coming to this job, he was an aviation machinist mate with the U.S. Navy on an aircraft carrier. Operating engineers maintain all kinds of equipment—steam, refrigeration, domestic water plumbing, and anything else needed to keep the complex going. Right now, DelBianco is assigned to maintaining the window-cleaning machines at the North Tower.

DelBianco recalls being interviewed for his job by Rudy Hoenfeld, another former navy man, who was in charge of mechanical operations at the World Trade Center. After he had passed the interview, Hoenfeld took him aside and said, "Listen, it's a large complex, it's like a little city. It's just like being on a carrier. The only difference between us and a ship is that the buildings don't head into the wind." Of course, he was referring to the fact that aircraft carriers head into the wind during flight operations to facilitate takeoffs and landings.[15]

SHOPPING AT THE WORLD TRADE CENTER

As the window cleaners are going about their daily round of activities, a quarter of a mile below them is a beehive of activity at the World Trade Center. The mall here has won no architectural awards. This esthetically ordinary mall has low ceilings and long corridors with neither a spacious atrium nor skylights. Since the stores in this mall are located along both sides of a grid of corridors, most people experience a sort of tunnel effect as they pass through the place. What it lacks in architectural design, it makes up for in being well situated. Since the 1993 bombing, there is no longer any public parking available at the World Trade Center, but it doesn't seem to matter. Located on the busy concourse level, it is readily accessible by both subway and PATH. Whether they want to or not, hundreds of thousands of people pass through here on a typical weekday.

The mall at the World Trade Center is a group of retail stores built and managed as a unit. The Port Authority is responsible for cleaning, maintenance, security, and fire protection. Its managers are always trying to attract the right mix of retailers. Large numbers of malls were built in the United States after World War II, but most of them were located in the suburbs since it is difficult for most builders to obtain enough land to build in downtown areas. Since this is an *urban* mall, it has a distinct character all its own.

In the first place, the hours are quite different from those of a suburban mall. This mall opens earlier and closes earlier to accommodate the commuters who make up its customers. Most stores located on the concourse are open weekdays as early as 8 A.M., so office workers can do some quick shopping before reporting to work. The stores stay open all morning and all afternoon to accommodate regular customers, most of whom work in the area. Other office workers may stop to do some quick shopping just before their commute home. As a result, most of these stores close at the tail end of the commuting period, around 6:30 P.M. Unlike suburban malls, this one is much busier during the week than on weekends, when hours are sharply cut back. Stores here are generally open on weekends only between 10 A.M. and 5 P.M. on Saturday, and closed on Sunday.

Yet another difference with suburban malls is the striking absence of children, teenagers, and the elderly. They are unlikely to be found in a place that caters to office workers. Just about everybody here is an adult of working age. It's not a good place for teenagers who love video arcades with games like Battle Zone, Space Invaders, or Star Gate. There's not a single video arcade in the complex.

Also, since there are no benches, no places whatsoever to sit in the common areas outside the stores, it's simply not a suitable place for "hanging out." Again, with no place to sit and relax, this mall is not very inviting for older people. And given the sheer volume and congestion created by thousands of fast-footed pedestrians, this is not a safe and comfortable place for mall-walking exercise.[16]

In at least one important aspect, though, the mall at the World Trade Center is similar to its suburban counterparts: the majority of its shoppers are women. About 70 percent of all mall customers are female. Jerry Jacobs of Syracuse University has studied the matter, and he suggests the reason for this is "adult women's endless quest for wearing apparel."[17] Jacobs explains that because women's fashions change so quickly and because women are style conscious, they always need to buy something to wear. This "bottomless pit syndrome" is supported by the ever-changing four seasons. In addition, women shop not only for themselves but also for their children and their husbands. It is also customary for women to do most of the shopping for special occasions such as weddings and birthdays.

The retail mix at the World Trade Center reflects this fact of life, as the majority of stores cater to women. Most of them are local branches of national chain stores, instantly recognizable to suburban Americans everywhere. On a weekday in mid-June, window shopping at the mall reveals that most stores are geared toward women's needs to refurbish their summer wardrobes.

As the afternoon wears on, more pedestrians seem to appear in the mall. Are these more shoppers? Not necessarily. Some office workers are already coming down on the elevators, passing through the concourse, and heading for home.

THE EVENING RUSH HOUR

The evening rush hour is not quite as hectic as the morning rush hour, which tends to be squeezed in between 7:30 A.M. and 9 A.M. The evening rush hour is spread out between four and seven o'clock, about twice as long because many people stay in their offices to work late. People trickle out gradually, which helps to relieve the crunch on the elevators.[18] Soon the Port Authority police will be back at their fixed image posts for the evening rush hour to watch the blur of pedestrians pass by. Research has shown that New Yorkers walk faster than other Americans, about 30 percent faster than people in smaller American cities in the South and West. This creates problems when out-of-town tourists and visitors try window shopping at the mall. Bottlenecks are created whenever visitors pause to look around. Visitors soon learn to keep moving or get out of the way.[19]

In the early days, the World Trade Center practically shut down after five or six in the evening. But since world trade never stops around the globe, there is about a 30 percent occupancy even at night. At ten o'clock at night Eastern Daylight Time in New York City, it's morning business hours in Manila or Tokyo. Still, during the night most offices are closed for business, and things do disappear from time to time. Office machinery, televisions, VCRs, and radios head the list. Typically, the tenants tend to blame the cleaners, but police say they are almost never at fault. Cleaners are most often recently arrived immigrant women, single mothers who desperately need their jobs. The real thieves may actually be white males in dark blue work uniforms, complete with fake photo I.D.s easily obtained from shops along 42nd Street.

Joseph Martella tells the story of video footage recorded on a tenant security camera in the late afternoon. Office workers see a man appropriately dressed, complete with identification badge and alligator clip. He has a toolbox, and he is removing a typewriter. Several office workers pass by him as they are leaving for the day. The surveillance tape resembles something from the old television show *Candid Camera*. Each person sees the man and does a double take, a kind of delayed reaction to this unusual circumstance. But nobody stops the "repairman." Nobody challenges him by saying, "Can I help you?" Everyone accepts the blue uniform and the photo I.D. Finally, the thief is finished unbolting the typewriter and is ready to leave. The last office worker to leave holds the door open for him.[20]

By the end of the day, most office workers are in a hurry to catch a train and go home. Some may stop off at the concourse to do some banking or some quick shopping. And a few will be in need of a good stiff drink in order to unwind.

THE TALL SHIPS BAR

One can find the Tall Ships Bar by passing through the lobby of the Marriott Hotel, all the way at the south end of Three World Trade Center. Passing through the glass doors, you enter a masculine world that evokes the spirit of Old New York. The setting is dominated by mahogany paneling, etched glass, and gleaming brass. On your right, as you enter, is a wall covered from top to bottom with thick strands of manila rope. There are a number of small tables for intimate conversations. Over to your left is the bar. Suspended from the ceiling over the bar are replicas of canvas sails. Behind the bar are five panels of etched glass depicting New York Harbor. Each panel was sandblasted by hand at a cost of $10,000 per panel. The ambience unambiguously suggests that this is a port city with ships and docks and world trade. The menu makes it clear that the name of the bar was taken from a line of the poem "Sea Fever" by John Masefield: "And all I ask is a tall ship and a star to steer her by." From the menu of "the galley" one can order hot sandwiches, cold salads, grilled meats, chicken, and seafood. But on a late Monday afternoon, most businessmen come here to drink. They order vodka martinis, red wine, and single malt Scotches.

I had planned to get a sense of the Tall Ships Bar by talking with one of the bartenders. A senior Port Authority executive suggests that I seek out "one of the top bartenders in New York City," Sal Marciante, who has worked here for seventeen years. Human nature being what it is, most bartenders do not last this long with one employer. Most eventually get fired, either for drinking on the job or for pocketing some of the cash. Sal takes great pride in his honesty and sobriety. He started here "as a kid" at age twenty-three, but he's now forty. He has put on some weight and is turning gray. Sal has been a bartender so long that some of the sons and daughters of his regular customers now stop in for a drink. A connoisseur of fine liquor and perhaps an even better judge of people, Sal Marciante was among the most colorful characters in the World Trade Center and a natural storyteller of the first order. With his ready smile, dry wit, and heavy New York accent, it was impossible not to be charmed by him on first meeting. I ask him to categorize the patrons who come into the Tall Ships Bar.

Sal explains that there's the average working person who comes in for a single drink after work and pays cash, but this is not a neighborhood shot-and-beer establishment. These people cannot afford to sit around and pay top prices.

Then there are the businesspeople or bankers or lawyers who come in and can spend all the money they want because they're not paying for it themselves. It's going on the company credit card: they're entertaining clients, so they can spend money and write it off. These customers, easy to spot because they wear nice clothes, really know how to spend and enjoy themselves after a hard day's work.

The commodities brokers, always living on the edge, dress more casually, often wearing slacks and a sports shirt. Since they are elbow to elbow all day in the trading ring, there's no point in wearing nice clothes. Sal describes them as "streetwise, regular guys." He likes them because they are not cheap; they spend money freely.

Not paying by credit card are those who are having affairs. They pay cash. They want no record of this activity. Sal says they are easy to spot. Usually they are too polite and too friendly. Sal explains, "The man may pull the chair out for her, acting like a gentleman, doing things he wouldn't do for his wife. They kiss and hold hands. Married people usually don't do that at a bar. You can tell they feel guilty because they are constantly looking at their watches. They are worried about the time."

I ask Sal what the most satisfying part of the job is. He explains that he gets to associate with the rich and the famous. He says, "I'm part of the gang. Everybody knows me, and I know them. I'm proud to be affiliated with the World Trade Center, one of the most powerful buildings in the world. It's not like working in some local pub somewhere in the Midwest. This is New York City, where it all happens."

Yet the job does have its frustrations in trying to serve two hundred people at once between five and seven o'clock. Sal says, "During that peak period, I can't even scratch my head, I'm so busy. It's crazy. It's noisy and smoky. It's full of energy because these guys are all hyped up. They need a place to vent and unwind."[21]

As time goes by, some of the customers at the Tall Ships Bar order snacks to go with their drinks: teriyaki beef skewers, spicy buffalo chicken wings with blue-cheese dip, golden-fried mozzarella sticks with spicy tomato sauce, or warm blue corn chips with salsa and avocado dip. Others drift out the door that opens onto Liberty Street to take advantage of the limitless possibilities for dinner that Manhattan has to offer in every price range for every ethnicity. But for those who do not want to leave the hotel, the nearby Greenhouse Cafe is a good choice.

THE GREENHOUSE CAFE

It's easy to walk down the hall from the Tall Ships Bar of the New York Marriott World Trade Center to the soaring atrium lobby and take the spiral staircase up to the second floor and the Greenhouse Cafe adjacent to the plaza, which has a skylight roof affording an unusual view of the lofty nearby Twin Towers. As the lingering summer twilight streams in through the overhead windows, the restaurant has the atmosphere of a cheerful outdoor garden with fresh flowers on the tables. In the summer months, executive chef Walter Plendner takes full advantage of the sunny setting to feature numerous fresh vegetables and salad items.

The chef is continually creating new menus and new dishes. On this typical summer evening, we might find spachtcock on the dinner menu—a small smoked chicken portion with deboned breast and leg served with a light horseradish sauce and julienned carrots. Another selection is blackened salmon, seared in a pan, served on a bed of cucumbers with baby tomatoes and a shallot dressing. Also available is veal schnitzel with sauteed potatoes or halibut with teriyaki and garlic sauce accompanied with stir-fried oriental vegetables.

The restaurant first opened back in 1981 with the opening of the hotel at the World Trade Center complex. The hotel was built under a complex arrangement whereby a Chicago-based developer, Jerrold Wexler, leased the site from the Port Authority, financed the hotel's construction, and then turned it over to another company to manage.[22] The management company was Hilton International, and the hotel was called the Vista International New York. Why was it not called the Hilton International New York, which would seem more logical? Interestingly enough, Conrad Hilton had formed two different companies—Hilton Hotels Corporation in 1946 and Hilton International in 1948. Because of this corporate structure, Hilton International could not use the Hilton name in the United States, hence the new hotel had to have a new name: Vista. This hotel at the World Trade Center was to be the flagship for a series of new Vista hotels in the continental United States.[23] In any event, the executive chef from the very beginning was Walter Plendner, who is widely respected and known to every old-timer at the World Trade Center complex.

When the Vista was built in 1981, the hotel had no direct competition in the financial district, and there was little incentive to refurbish the sleeping rooms or renovate the lobby and public spaces. But later when the Marriott Financial Center and the Millennium Hilton both opened in the same neighborhood, all of a sudden the Vista was forced to compete for guests. In 1989 the Port Authority stepped in to purchase the hotel at a cost of $79 million in an effort to gain control and rejuvenate it, though it was still being operated under contract with Hilton International.[24]

After the bomb blast of February 1993, the hotel was closed for more than twenty months to undergo $65 million in renovations and repairs. But throughout the entire process, Plendner was kept on the payroll to plan the reopening, which took place in November 1994. At the official reopening ceremony, white-jacketed waiters served hors d'oeuvres of liver pâté and smoked salmon on small crackers, with champagne, as a pianist played "Some Enchanted Evening." Four television cameras recorded the event for the local news as Mayor Rudolph Giuliani cut the ribbon.[25]

Six months later, George J. Marlin, then executive director of the Port Authority, announced plans to put the Vista Hotel up for sale. Marlin had been appointed to the post in early 1995 by Governor George E. Pataki of New York and Governor Christine Todd Whitman of New Jersey. The two conservative Republican governors had given Marlin instructions to review the Port Authority's holdings to see what could be sold. Under these circumstances, no one was surprised at the announcement that the Vista would go on the block. Marlin said that the hotel "is a prime example of an area where private expertise can reasonably be expected to deliver better service and efficiency than even the most assiduous efforts of government."[26] In a short time, the Port Authority sold the hotel to Marriott, and it became the New York Marriott World Trade Center.

As we linger over coffee and dessert in the verdant oasis of the Greenhouse Cafe, we see that the sun has set. As night falls, we look up and see light coming from the windows of the Twin Towers. We think briefly of those toiling to clean the offices up there, but first we decide to have a nightcap and check back on what's going on at the Tall Ships Bar.

LATE EVENING AT THE TALL SHIPS BAR

The patrons of this bar wear expensive suits and expensive shoes. They carry expensive briefcases. They have good manners and are well groomed, but after ten o'clock they can become problems. Some of them can't even sign the check. With a sigh, Sal Marciante gives an example, "You could have a banker who runs millions of dollars of business, but this same guy can't add a seventeen-dollar tip on a check because he can't come up with the right total. He's too drunk, and he can't figure it out. In such a case, you usually have to rip up the voucher and try again and be polite about it. You ask them to recheck their addition." But bartenders almost never have to arrange for transportation home for people. Most of them walk out on their own; they would be too proud or to embarrassed to accept help. Besides, they usually have limousine services or company cars to pick them up.

People who have been drinking often leave things behind. They may forget an umbrella, a book, a coat, a briefcase, important papers, an appointment book, wallet, credit card, or some other personal belongings. The staff at the bar turns these items over to the security department of the Marriott Hotel at closing time, one o'clock in the morning.

At about ten o'clock the tourists and the conventioneers staying at the hotel start coming back. They usually go out to dinner or the theater in the early evening, but New York City at night has a bad reputation, so they are terrified about the city. They usually come in for a drink because they do not want to go up to their room all alone. And before you know it, there's another gathering between ten and midnight at the bar.

About this time of night a few "bachelor girls" may drift into the bar. If they are well dressed, they easily slip past Marriott security. They may sit at the bar, sip a martini, and chat idly with bored out-of-town businessmen about sports or politics. They never *say* they are prostitutes. Instead, they are temporarily out-of-work models or waitresses, trying to succeed in the Big Apple, with ambitions to become actresses some day. But it is difficult to realize such ambitions if you are a waitress on the luncheon shift where beginners are assigned. The work is just as difficult as for the dinner meal, but the tips are lower. At the same time, it is difficult to schedule auditions or to afford acting classes. To make ends meet, it is tempting to accept a few "dates" on the side to catch up with credit-card bills or to pay the rent. Sal explains, "They nearly always find a victim or a volunteer. For perhaps an hour's work they can come away with between two hundred and five hundred dollars. Because this bar is part of a hotel, all these men have to do is to go up to their rooms."

On a lighter note, Sal tells of a regular customer, a judge, who liked to play the piano. He happened to be very good at it. He would often start to play at nine or ten o'clock at night, whenever the regular piano player would go out on his break. Most regular customers knew who he was and appreciated his amateur efforts. One particular night, a client went over and put a dollar in an empty glass on the piano. Before the judge was through playing, he had a whole glassful of tips. The judge gave it all to the regular piano player when he came back from his break.

As the evening wears on, even the most vivacious revelers at the bar become drowsy. The need for sleep becomes compelling. Fortunately, since this bar is part of the Marriott Hotel, overnight lodging is just a few steps away.[27]

New York Marriott World Trade Center

In theory, it would be possible to spend years at the World Trade Center without ever leaving. One could live and work and rest entirely within the complex by staying at this hotel. In practice, the hotel is filled during the week with businesspeople who want to be close to Wall Street. On the weekends, the hotel tends to fill up with visitors who have been referred downtown by Marriott's central reservation system after the midtown rooms have been taken. Of course, there are always a few visitors who prefer downtown in order to see old New York and the South Street Seaport. Some say that the unusual semicircular configuration of the hotel makes it resemble a boomerang. Designed in the late 1970s by the Park Avenue firm of Skidmore, Owings, and Merrill, the 818-room hotel of twenty-two stories is located at the southwest corner of the complex at Liberty and West Streets.[28]

The best rooms in the house, which Marriott calls "Concierge Level," are on the twentieth and twenty-first floors. A typical room here facing west is high enough to offer a view of the World Financial Center across West Street as well as the Hudson River and Jersey City off in the distance. The guest rooms themselves are similar in every respect to the regular rooms except that they offer a larger executive leather-covered desk chair, a terrycloth robe, and bathrooms trimmed in black marble. The main difference is in the increased level of service and attention to detail. These guests have fresh flowers in their rooms and a complimentary morning newspaper, either *USA Today,* the *New York Times*, or the *Wall Street Journal.* There is a concierge lounge, an inviting room seating about thirty-six guests, where they enjoy a free continental breakfast in the morning between 6:30 and 9:30 as well as a small reception every evening between 5 and 7:30, with the first cocktail being complimentary.[29]

Construction of the hotel started in 1979, and it was officially opened for business in 1981. The Port Authority had planned for a hotel on the site all along, so the $13 million foundation work was already in place. Completing the hotel cost an additional $43 million. At that time, there was considerable excitement about the project because it was the first hotel to be constructed in lower Manhattan, south of Canal Street, since 1836. Its predecessor, located near City Hall, was the Astor House, a six-story, 309-room building built at a cost of only $400,000. It had "patent locks" and "17 bathing rooms with hot water supplied by our steam engine" and had "more parlor and bedroom suites" than any other hotel in the nation. The Astor House was demolished in 1913 to make room for a new subway.[30]

As hotel guests relax in the evening and finally go to sleep in their comfortable rooms, a small army of workers is busy elsewhere in the World Trade Center fixing things, cleaning the buildings, and making sure the complex is secure throughout the night.

CLEANING, MAINTENANCE, AND SECURITY

In the evening all of the maintenance tradesmen come in, especially those in heating, ventilation, and air-conditioning. Because much of their work is in tenant spaces, their operations are less disruptive at this time. Among the many duties of these technicians is the balancing of the flow of air systems, whether it's heated air in the winter or cooled air in the summer. They make numerous adjustments to damping devices in the ducts, for example, to increase the flow of air to larger offices and reduce it for smaller offices. This work is done from four in the afternoon until midnight. When there is routine maintenance within tenant spaces, building operations become very active because they have to maintain security to protect the property of the tenants.

Cleaning of the World Trade Center is not carried out by Port Authority employees. The work is contracted out, and then monitored and checked by Port Authority supervisors. The contracts themselves run to hundreds of pages and spell out in elaborate detail just what is to be done. Basically, the work falls into two categories. First, there is the routine daily work. For example, the carpets in the main lobbies of both towers are given a "tip shampoo" daily. This means that the "tips" of the carpets are shampooed. The process raises and brightens the surface fibers. Second, there is the so-called exhibit work which is done at regular intervals, such as deep extraction of the underlying carpet dirt.

This second category can be compared to the required maintenance schedule for an automobile. There are certain things you are supposed to do at 7,500 miles and at 15,000 miles and so on. About once a month, or twelve times a year, contractors are required to machine scrub and degrease the 90,000 square feet of roadways and

ramps. Once every season, or four times a year, they have to shampoo the carpets in the elevators. Twice a year they have to steam
clean the 3,500 feet of plaza stone. It is all spelled out in the contract.

It is during the second shift (4 P.M. to 12 midnight) that the
bulk of the cleaning gets done. Like the military, the Port Authority
has a fondness for acronyms. The second shift is devoted to R.O.C.
(routine office cleaning). Basic cleaning calls for vacuuming once a
week, emptying the trash pails every night, and dusting desk tops
every night, with high-intensity dusting done once a week. There is
a routine, and contractors follow a checklist. But most tenants want
more than that. For example, they may have a little kitchen they
want cleaned. In such a case, the cleaning contractor can sell the
tenant additional services. During the third shift (12 midnight to
8 A.M.), they clean the public areas—the lobbies, the elevators, the
truck docks, the PATH facilities, and the concourse.[31]

On this typical night, there are many cleaning people, three or
four on each floor. In effect, they are slowly cleaning all the floors
simultaneously, and all the lights are on. At one point, the Port Authority tried to save energy by turning out all the lights except for
the floor being cleaned. The idea was to have more people assigned
to cleaning a given floor and to have them do the job more quickly.
It was a fine idea in theory, but it did not work in practice. Tenants
prefer to have the same cleaning person every night rather than an
anonymous platoon of cleaners sweeping through in a hurry. The
cleaner who serves the same tenant night after night gets to know
that person's likes and dislikes. It's much better in terms of trust and
responsibility.[32]

Tonight, the general operations supervisor is Eugene "Gene"
J. Raggio, a big man in his fifties, who is in charge of the complex
from 7 P.M. to 7 A.M. He is stuffed into a white shirt with a black
tie. When he speaks, people pay attention. Staying on top of the
maintenance schedule takes constant effort. Raggio says, "I try to
keep the buildings clean. It shows people at least we're trying." I ac-
company him as he takes a walking tour of the complex. Gene no-
tices little things and calls people up on the radio to fix them. Too
much litter in the Chase Manhattan ATM booths. Restaurant
workers at Au Bon Pain hanging around too long after the 9 P.M.
closing. Gene checks up on the guards. They are supposed to be at

particular posts, and not supposed to leave them unless they are relieved. I ask, "What if they are not there?"

"Then we write them up for nonperformance. When the security company presents their bill, we make a deduction."[33]

In general for the evening and nighttime hours, the cleaning
staff works from 4 P.M. to 12 midnight and from 12 midnight to
8 A.M. But the security guards tend to work on shifts that are an
hour earlier. So they might typically work from 3 P.M. to 11 P.M.
and from 11 P.M. to 7 A.M. So at 11 P.M. it's time for us to look in
on the roll call of the security guards. It's a scene reminiscent of the
opening scenes from the long-running TV series *Hill Street Blues*.

Of course, here the assembly is not of police officers, but
of security guards. They are from the Burns Agency. They wear
gray pants, blue blazers, white shirts, and blue-and-white striped
ties. Some are young, some are old. Some are men, some are women.
Some are black, some are white. But having said that, it seems that
young black males are the predominant group among these security
guards. The supervisor is haranguing the assemblage about various
topics, but I find his speech difficult to follow because of the specialized jargon. He is admonishing his troops. "I want you to pay
attention when you're doing your verticals, and make sure your reports are accurate when you're doing your verticals. Don't go writing stuff down because it's been written down before. Make sure it's
up to date, because if it's not, you're going to be in big trouble."[34]

Only slowly do I figure out that there are basically two types
of security guards—those in fixed or permanent posts, such as
those who guard access to the lobby elevators, and those who patrol up and down a number of assigned floors in the office towers,
or "verticals." Security guards are expected to report routine minor
flaws observed during their tours of duty at night. A small crack in
the wall. A light fixture in need of repair. A torn carpet on such-
and-such a floor. Because maintenance personnel give higher priority to major projects than to minor ones, the little things sometimes
are left undone. It's possible for a week or more to go by with the
same little things needing attention. In such a case, security guards
may figure that they really don't need to go on patrol at all. If nothing is getting fixed, all they need to do is to get the report from the
previous shift and write down the same observations. It is certainly

easier than walking around all night. But it is risky when maintenance starts to catch up with the repair work. From time to time,
security guards are embarrassed when confronted with discrepan-
cies between their reports and the actual condition of the building.[35]

As the night wears on into the wee hours of the morning, the
security guards continue to patrol and the cleaners continue to
clean. But nearly everyone else is gone. The commuters have gone
home to the suburbs, and the tourists have gone to bed in their
hotel rooms. Everyone is gone except for those with nowhere else
to go.

THE HOMELESS

No one knows how many homeless people there are in New York
City, but city studies indicate that the number is between 12,000
and 20,000. Some of the homeless are old and some are young, but
experts say that the number of young homeless is growing. Most
homeless youths are black or Hispanic. Some 40 percent are gay,
lesbian, bisexual, or transgender, many of them homeless because
their families kicked them out. Typically, they are unwelcome in
schools and foster homes as well. Most of these homeless young
people use drugs, and many become prostitutes in order to make
money or have a place to sleep.[36] Predictably, some of them turn up
in the World Trade Center every night.

Officially, the Port Authority does not call them "the homeless" but the more politically correct "persons in need." It follows
guidelines, protocols, and procedures, which have significantly reduced the problem. The Port Authority got plenty of experience
in dealing with the homeless at its bus terminal in midtown, which
had become notorious as a place where travelers were harassed and
besieged as they ran the gauntlet of the homeless when they passed
through the terminal. The Port Authority Police were told to deal
with the homeless, but they were in an impossible situation. If they
ignored the problem, they were criticized for being ineffective. If
they pushed the homeless out into the street, they were criticized for
being brutal. Something had to be done.

In December 1991, the Port Authority came up with a program to strike a balance between the needs of the traveling public

and the needs of the homeless. Operation Alternative employed a broad range of new ideas. For example, classical music was piped into the bus terminal, and for reasons that no one fully understands, it drove the homeless out. The program is mainly a mixture of sticks and carrots: the police are the sticks and the social workers are the carrots. The police focus on infractions such as loitering, panhandling, drinking alcoholic beverages, and smoking. People who break these rules are directed to stop or to leave. The homeless or the ill are offered counseling referrals and transportation to social service agencies.[37]

The Port Authority's efforts to regain control of the bus terminal were a striking success. The building was renovated with better lighting, maintenance, and cleaning. The police got rid of the scam artists who lurked about the pay telephones to steal credit card numbers. Secluded spots and corners that harbored drifters and addicts were sealed off. "Places where people would hang out, lying on the floor or leaning up against the walls, we put in up-scale pushcarts," said John F. Brendlen, Jr., the Port Authority's real estate manager. Between 1991 and 1995, referrals and assistance were given to 33,000 people or "persons in need." The efforts paid off in attracting nicely dressed crowds shopping at clean, well-lighted stores. Major national retailers such as the croissant and sandwich chain Au Bon Pain who previously stayed away now started moving in and signing leases.[38]

Operation Alternative was later implemented at the Twin Towers. There used to be about one hundred homeless per night in the World Trade Center, but now there are only about ten. There will always be a few, but officials feel the problem has been brought under control.

The guidelines are helpful, but there is no quick fix. This is a problem that will never be completely solved. From the point of view of the World Trade Center administration, it would be nice if the homeless would just go away. With their shabby appearance and erratic behavior, the homeless hurt the sales of retailers and annoy the rent-paying tenants. There is a constant cat-and-mouse game played out by the homeless and the nighttime supervisors. The homeless look for places to sleep, and the supervisors roust them out. Often the confrontations are good-natured. After all, the adversaries have to deal with each other night after night, so they became acquainted. But sometimes the homeless turn on their tormentors, and the game gets to be more dangerous.

Robert DiChiara, retired assistant director of the World Trade Center, explains that the homeless problem requires several players. You need the building managers and the police and the social workers all working together. Every piece of the puzzle has to be in place or nothing will work. It is not good enough just to push them out of the building onto the street—it is not humane. But just as important, it does not work because the homeless keep coming back. The police are limited in what they can do. They can enforce the rules—no sitting down on the floor and no lying down. Because the concourse of the World Trade Center is a public place, the homeless have a perfect right to be there. But they don't have the right to sleep there. Anyone can be there as long as they keep moving. Social workers from the Volunteers of America are there to offer assistance. But before they can offer assistance, they have to establish a mutual bond of trust. This takes time. If a homeless person can be persuaded to accept service, the case is considered a success.[39]

THE WEE HOURS

As the night wears on, most of the homeless either slip away or grudgingly accept services. The Twin Towers are eerily quiet. In the hotel, visitors are sleeping. The offices have been cleaned, the trash has been collected, and the concourse has been swept. The radios at the Operations Control Center are, for the moment, quiet. The only people awake are those who have to be awake. This busy place is now calm and tranquil.

The plaza is empty and almost silent except for the sound of gently splashing water in the fountain near the North Tower. Dedicated to those who lost their lives in the 1993 terror bombing, the fountain never stops spouting water. The granite circle ties the roughly chiseled names of the victims together forever—John DiGiovanni, Robert Kirkpatrick, Steven Knapp, William Macko, Wilfredo Mercado, Monica Rodriguez Smith and her unborn child. They are sleeping the everlasting sleep of eternal rest. There is a contrast between the broken edges of granite, symbolizing the damage caused by the explosion, and the fountain of water, representing hope and continuity, life and renewal.[40]

But this quiet moment cannot last. At about four in the morning, the delivery trucks start to arrive with fresh food and flowers and ice and all the other things needed for another day. Before long, the cycle repeats itself.

8
Destruction

The Terrorist Attack
and its Aftermath

World trade means world peace and consequently the World Trade Center buildings in New York . . . had a bigger purpose than just to provide room for tenants.

The World Trade Center is a living symbol of man's dedication to world peace.

—MINORU YAMASAKI [1]

THE LANGUAGE of symbols is a tricky business. Back in the early 1970s the architect, Yamasaki, may have sincerely intended the World Trade Center to stand for world peace, but few others saw it that way. Indeed, the building could have been taken to symbolize the Manhattan skyline or the City of New York. Certainly the skyline was important. John A. Kouwenhoven, author of "What's American about America," argued that the skyline was like a jazz performance. Each building goes its own way, and yet the overall effect somehow hangs together in an esthetically satisfying way.[2]

But the Twin Towers came, for nearly everyone at home and abroad, to symbolize something much larger than the esthetics of a single city. It represented American engineering know-how. It showed America reaching for the sky. It stood for American capitalism and, with time, America itself. Indeed, that is the reason it was chosen as a target by the terrorists. Terrorism is a weapon used by the weak against the strong. Because the terrorists were not powerful enough to destroy America, they had to destroy instead an important symbol of America. There should have been no surprise in their choice of target. They had already tried back in 1993 to destroy the Twin Towers. The difference on September 11, 2001, is that they succeeded. There was considerable evidence of careful planning on their part. The hijackers selected airplanes carrying a light load of passengers who might interfere with their efforts, but loaded with plenty of fuel for long flights.

It was a beautiful and clear morning at 8:47 A.M. when American Airlines Flight 11 from Boston to Los Angeles, with some

20,000 gallons of jet fuel and traveling at more than 400 miles per hour, crashed into the 94th floor of the North Tower, killing all 92 people aboard and setting off a huge explosion and appalling fires inside the building. At first, people thought it was an accident.

Somewhere in Afghanistan, Osama bin Laden, listening to the news, told an exuberant group of his followers, "Be patient."

Then at 9:03 a second commercial airliner, United Flight 175, also from Boston to L.A., with 65 passengers and crew, crashed into floors 78 to 87 of the South Tower, ripping through the skin of the building and setting it ablaze. Now we knew that this was no accident.

A bit later, while President George W. Bush was sitting in on a second-grade class in Sarasota, Florida, the White House chief of staff Andrew Card told him, "America's under attack."

Then a third airliner crashed into the Pentagon, the symbol of America's military might, while a fourth crashed in rural Pennsylvania, apparently because passengers overpowered the hijackers.

The attacks were so catastrophic that officials quickly closed all New York airports as well as all bridges and tunnels. The New York Stock Exchange was shut down, and then all the airports and financial markets in the United States followed suit.[3]

Architectural scholars, journalists, and critics quickly discerned the symbolic meaning behind the terrorists' diabolical attack. Michael J. Crosby of *Architecture Week* wrote, "The skyscraper targets in New York City were prominent symbols of our civilization, buildings of American invention that all over the world expressed the spirit of a will to soar above the earth in creations of steel, concrete, and glass. The terrorists chose very carefully. They discerned those skyscrapers as the cathedrals of our age and aimed at their heart."[4]

Within minutes after the attack, brave men and women entered the Twin Towers to extinguish the flames and rescue those inside. Stories emerged of stairwells full of office workers fleeing downstairs to safety, while others rushed upstairs toward the danger, trying to save lives. These selfless people included firefighters, police officers, EMS workers, court officers, and security guards. Their courage and professionalism, in light of what was to follow, has made them the folk heroes of our day.

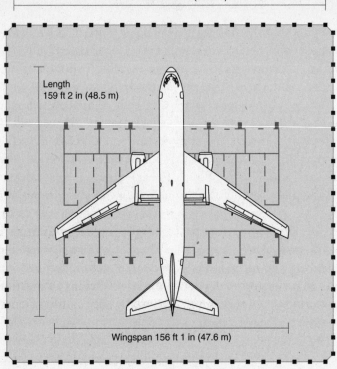

Figure 8.1. Boeing 767 Aircraft Superimposed on Typical Floor Plan

As thousands of gallons of aviation fuel burned, hundreds of firefighters were sent to the scene. The two basic fire-fighting units in the FDNY are engine companies and ladder companies. Engine companies use vehicles called pumpers, which carry powerful pumps and hoses for placing streams of water on the fire. Ladder companies are rescue specialists equipped with special tools; they use ladder trucks, which carry an extension ladder or platform for rescuing people. At the fire scene, their efforts are coordinated by the command structure. Fire officers arriving on the scene must establish a command post, locate and size up the fire, and then begin making life-and-death decisions. In the case of the Twin Towers, fire officers were overwhelmed with the magnitude of the task.

Battalion Chief John A. Jones said, "These were the biggest buildings in New York City. Each floor was one acre in area. And we're looking at this, and we see smoke issuing under pressure from the top twenty floors—maybe more. If we are using the twenty floor figure, you're looking at twenty acres of fire."[5]

When the first airliner hit the North Tower, it seemed at first that the building had withstood the impact and stayed intact. In fact, terrible damage had occurred inside, cutting off key escape routes and starting the process by which the tower fell. If an outline of a Boeing 767 aircraft is superimposed on the plans for a given floor, the actual scale of the impact becomes clear (fig. 8.1). The aircraft had wrecked the central core where stairs and elevators were concentrated. All means of escape were now cut off for those above the impact.

Above floor 93 in the North Tower and above floor 75 in the South Tower, fire officers recognized, there was no way out. The chance of rescuing anyone was slim to none. Eyewitnesses in the floors immediately below said later that the stairwells were blocked with debris and no one was seen coming down. To make matters worse, the elevator cables were severed and tons of aviation fuel was pouring down through the shafts. Deputy Commissioner Tom Fitzpatrick, arriving on the scene, did some simple math in his head. Firefighters in good condition, burdened with heavy equipment, at best can get up the stairs of a burning building at one floor per minute. At that speed, it would take them an hour and a half to reach the fire.[6]

All told, some six hundred of FDNY's bravest were on the scene working the two towers. The firefighters climbing the stairs were equipped with helmet, turnout coat, bunker pants, leather boots, compressed air cylinders, radios, axes, and hand tools weighing about one hundred pounds each. Those arriving on the scene had to duck objects raining down on them—struts, trusses, brake drums, airplane wheels, and shards of glass. Meanwhile, they could not ignore the jumpers. People trapped on the upper floors decided they'd rather jump than burn to death. It was the most disturbing sight of the whole nightmare experience. You could hear bodies rushing through the air, and then there was a frightful thud followed by a splash of red blood.[7]

While no one questions the bravery of the New York City Fire Department, experts now tell us that the job they were given that day was basically impossible. Retired deputy chief Vincent Dunn of the FDNY may be the world's foremost authority on fighting fires in high-rise buildings. Dunn had forty-two years of service with the

FDNY, he has written three fire-fighting textbooks, and he serves as an instructor at the National Fire Academy. Dunn has explained to investigative journalists that a typical fire-fighting hose team can extinguish about 2,500 square feet. That's an area about 25 feet by 100 feet. Two attack hose teams, side by side, may be able to extinguish 5,000 square feet of fire. But the World Trade Center floor areas were 40,000 square feet in size. This high-rise office building with an open floor space design created an area about eight times what firefighters are able to extinguish with conventional hose streams.[8]

In the end, the FDNY lost its fight with the Twin Towers fire, but in terms of the popular culture, they are what Patricia Leigh Brown of the *New York Times* called "knights in shining fire helmets." They are seen as manly and brave and undaunted. We admire them because they are strong, stoic, and competent. Newspaper columns brim with the praise of these new John Waynes.

The whole intellectual establishment, from universities to think tanks, has seen a shift in what constitutes appropriate manhood. Suddenly, it's more important to be strong than to be in touch with your feelings. David Blankenhorn, president of the Institute for American Values, wrote: "A few years ago, a lot of fashionable academics wrote about 'the end of the male project,' the idea that, due to technological advances, men no longer needed physical strength. Doesn't that look different now, when 'the project' at hand is wrestling with hijackers, pulling people out of buildings, and hunting down terrorists in Afghanistan caves?"[9]

One photograph stands out as emblematic of the new male hero. An office worker rushing down the stairs of Tower One from the 71st floor had grabbed his camera and took a photo of Firefighter Mike Kehoe of Engine 28 climbing up the stairs as civilians were going down as fast as they could. Kehoe himself never sought the fame and attention caused by this one photograph that later appeared in the *New York Daily News*. One headline read STAIRWAY TO HELL. When asked how many people he saved that day, Kehoe modestly replies, "I saved one person that day, and that was me, and it was by running for my life."[10]

Suddenly and without warning, at 9:50 A.M., the South Tower

of the World Trade Center collapsed. The prolonged high temperatures of the burning jet fuel had reduced the strength of the steel
structure. Then, with the collapse of an entire floor, the load of the
floors above created a cascading pancake failure as the whole
building fell downward. A building that had taken seven years to
construct collapsed in eleven seconds. The entire neighborhood
was covered with a huge cloud of smoke and debris. Endless pieces
of paper from hundreds of offices—letters, invoices, memos, reports, contracts, proposals—were scattered all over Lower Manhattan and Brooklyn, some drifting out over the Hudson River. The
South Tower had withstood the raging fires for some 48 precious
minutes.

Then, at 10:28 A.M., the North Tower collapsed. Five hundred
thousand tons of steel, concrete, and glass hit the ground at 120 miles
per hour. The North Tower lasted 101 minutes, allowing people a
better length of time to evacuate. It is fortunate that the buildings did
not collapse instantaneously. One tower stood up for more than an
hour and a half, and the other stood up for nearly an hour; because
they survived for as long as they did, some 25,000 people were allowed to escape. Nonetheless, hundreds of firefighters were trapped
and killed there.[11] In all, about 2,870 people perished.

Why did the towers collapse? And why did they collapse so
soon and so suddenly? The answer lies in columns of twisted steel,
melted fireproofing, and aircraft fragments. Only days after the attack, the National Science Foundation made grants to eight separate research teams from universities from across the United States.
These investigations on the structures' fall are being carried out in
cooperation with the American Society of Civil Engineers (ASCE)
and the American Institute of Steel Construction (AISC). We can
take some comfort in the fact that these investigations are going
forward, but there are problems.[12]

It would seem self-evident that all these investigations should
be coordinated by the Federal Emergency Management Agency
(FEMA), but that agency has consistently said that they are not in
the business of conducting investigations. John Czwartacki, a
spokesman for FEMA, said that the agency's main job was to help
victims and emergency workers, as well as to speed the city's re-

covery.[13] It is unfortunate that there is no mechanism in place to investigate high-rise building disasters comparable to the procedures for investigating aircraft disasters. When there is a disaster like the loss of TWA Flight 800 or American Airlines Flight 587, the National Transportation Safety Board (NTSB) conducts a thorough investigation.[14]

In charge of the ASCE investigation is W. Gene Corley, Ph.D., P.E., an expert in building collapse investigations and the principal investigator for the Murrah Federal Office Building Study. No one questions the competence of Corley, but he is burdened by three significant problems. In the first place, the investigation is underfunded. All of his investigators, including structural engineers as well as experts in blast and fire protection, are working pro bono, although the ASCE is paying out-of-pocket costs. It is asking a great deal of these people to work for nothing. As Corley diplomatically explained, "We've asked people to do a lot free of charge while they also try to make a living, and that will somewhat limit how much we can do. . . . We would hope that somebody would come in and provide us with the resources to do more than we plan at the moment."[15]

A second problem with the current investigation is perhaps built in because of the American legal system. There are conflicts of interest in this kind of investigation. For example, the New York City Department of Design and Construction does not want any new regulations to be too strict as the city rebuilds. At the same time, the Port Authority does not want an investigation because it does not want any blame. When asked if he was conducting a forensic investigation, Corley again tactfully replied, "I'd like to avoid the word forensic, because some people might think that we're going to find out things for lawsuits, but that's not what we're doing. We like to refer to it as a Building Performance Assessment."[16]

A third problem is that the clues lie in piles of twisted steel in New Jersey scrap yards, but the evidence is being cut into chunks for export to the Far East to be sold as scrap. The steel beams from the World Trade Center were brought to piers in Lower Manhattan, then carried by barge to a relay point in Brooklyn, and from there they were taken to one of two scrap recyclers—either Metal Management of Newark or Hugo Neu Schnitzer East in Jersey City.

The recycled steel could end up as barbed wire, household appli-
ances, or automobile parts.[17] Much critical evidence of how the
towers collapsed may have been lost. A request to the city by the
ASCE to study the structural steel arrived almost three weeks after
the disaster. By then, much of the steel had already been hauled
away to be cut up. Ironically, one of the investigators accidentally
discovered a key piece of evidence when a flatbed truck loaded with
a contorted mass of columns and beams just happened to park in
front of his hotel in New York.[18]

As this chapter is being written barely four months after the
disaster, it is far too soon to know what conclusions the investigators may reach. However, thanks to the work of investigative journalists, we have a pretty good idea of what the questions are and
where they should lead us. We know that a steel structure can be
damaged by fire. As the fire burns, the steel gets weaker. Though the
steel does not melt, it loses its strength and starts to sag. After a time,
it can no longer support its load. So far, this line of reasoning is little
more than common sense. But what was the exact cause? What was
the collapse mechanism? It is still too soon to know for sure, but two
credible and specific theories have been suggested.

First, we should look at the fireproofing. Professor Abolhas-
san Astaneh of the University of California has focused his attention on this aspect. He points out that, at the point of impact, the
fireproofing was burned and glazed to the steel. In the construction
process, this insulation—a fragile material made of mineral fibers
and concrete-like materials called binders—was sprayed onto the
steel. Though it was designed to insulate and protect the steel from
the heat, much of it was simply blown away by the blasts. Although
construction records would indicate that every piece of steel would
have been treated with the fireproofing, very little of it can actually
be found in the scrap yard. Unfortunately, not much insulation was
left as the building was burning. It was either shaken off or im-
properly installed in the first place.[19] This lack of fireproofing left
the steel vulnerable to the heat from the jet fuel, which leads directly to the next point.

The intense fire may have had a devastating effect on our second point of interest, the supports for the open-plan floors. Professor Eduardo Kausel of the Massachusetts Institute of Technology

has focused his investigation on the connections between the floors and the columns, which he has characterized as relatively weak. Instead of thick steel H-beams, the floors were supported by lightweight trusses made of zigzagging webs of steel rods just over an inch in diameter. The trusses were secured at each end with brackets, or ledges, welded to the wall. The floor was then covered with a four-inch layer of concrete. The advantages of the floor truss system is that it is both swift and economical. (See fig. 3.4.) But there is a drawback to these lightweight trusses: they are very susceptible to fire. One theory is that the weak point was the connection between the truss and the vertical supports. Professor Astaneh says that the heavily distorted brackets found in the scrap yard suggest that this is correct.[20]

On the day after the attack, on September 12, 2001, Americans woke up to a different world. The *Sun Herald* of Biloxi, Mississippi, ran a headline: WHAT NOW?[21] It seemed that no one knew quite what to do or what to expect. The eyes of the nation were on Ground Zero, as the disaster area of sixteen acres in Lower Manhattan with 1.4 million tons of debris, twisted steel, and pulverized concerete is being called. It was a hellish scene of smoke and dust and debris, with the wrecked buildings in a pile about the size of a six-story building and the surrounding streets full of crushed cars and trucks. Rescue workers, hoping to find survivors, were mostly disappointed. What they found were bits and pieces of personal items—wallets, watches, briefcases, keys, and the like. And body parts—a hand or a foot or an ear.[22]

There were few stories with a happy ending. But six firefighters from Ladder Company 6 on Canal Street in Chinatown were very lucky. They had responded to the fire in the North Tower, and they headed up the stairwell, getting as far as the 27th floor, when they heard the South Tower collapse. They knew it was time to evacuate. On their way down they met Josephine Harris, a middle-aged grandmother from Brooklyn who worked for the Port Authority. She had come down from the 73rd floor, so she was tired and unable to walk fast, but the firefighters could not just leave her behind. They helped her and coaxed her to keep moving. They got as far as the fourth floor, when Josephine could not go on. At that point the North Tower collapsed. By a miracle, they were caught in a protected pocket of safety between the second and fourth floors, an intact portion of the stairwell. If they had gone down the stairwell at Josephine's pace, they would have been doomed in the collapsed upper floors. And if they had gone down at their own pace, they would have been crushed in the lobby. Cut, bruised, and covered with dust, they were trapped there for three hours. But in the end, all seven were successfully rescued.[23]

As the days passed, the hope of finding any more survivors dwindled. A week and a day later, Mayor Rudolph W. Giuliani said grimly, "We have to prepare people for the overwhelming reality that the chance of recovering anyone alive is very, very small. We still hope and pray, but the chance is very, very small."[24] In effect, the operation was shifting from rescue mode to demolition removal.

In the weeks that followed, the work at Ground Zero became almost orderly and routine. Heavy construction equipment powered by noisy diesel engines moved back and forth. As steel girders were cut, they fell with a thud and a crash. Amid the confusion and wreckage, a pattern of work, coordinated from the command post, began to emerge. Search and rescue was the responsibility of the firefighters. Cutting up the steel was the job of the ironworkers. Counseling was done by volunteer ministers and the Salvation Army. The crime scene was investigated by FBI agents. Surrounding buildings were protected from looters by state troopers and national guard soldiers. Dan Barry, a reporter from the *New York Times,* described the work of New York City police officers: "Some are lowered into the rubble to search for the living and the dead; others collect DNA samples from relatives of the missing for possible identification of recovered body parts; still others join bucket brigades, where debris is removed pail by pail."[25] It was a busy place, but everyone moved respectfully because it was also a burial ground.

Gradually, Ground Zero also became a tourist attraction. People from all over the country wanted to see it for themselves. In 1819 the English poet John Keats wrote to his brother and sister, "Nothing ever becomes real until it is experienced—Even a proverb is no proverb to you till your life has illustrated it."[26] The urge to see reality up close is a fundamental human need. The tourists came to see the smoking pile of rubble. And when they came, they wanted to take something home as a tangible reminder of the visit.

Some vendors were selling disposable cameras out of a box; others quickly set up card tables with T-shirts, pins, and buttons. Interestingly enough, the biggest-selling items were glossy color photos of the World Trade Center in flames.[27] The photos were, in effect, icons. They were selling just as photos of John F. Kennedy and Martin Luther King, Jr., used to sell after they were assassinated. With great insight, Paul Goldberger, of *The New Yorker,* wrote, "Now that the Trade Center has become a martyr to terrorism, I suspect that architectural criticism of it will cease altogether."[28]

Most Americans have never visited Ground Zero, but they have all been able to see it, thanks to television. There is a video camera on all the time mounted in a window of a building just to the southeast. Mounted on a tripod, it is called REM-7, "Remote Camera 7." It is a pool camera, set up cooperatively by rival news organizations in order to save money. They cannot all afford to keep a permanent crew at the site. Nearly everyone who watches television has seen live images from this camera, which surveys the scene twenty-four hours a day, seven days a week. The images, described by *Star-Ledger* reporter Matt Zoler Seitz, are of "firefighters and construction workers, cranes and steam shovels, dust and smoke and arc-welding sparks."[29]

In the months that followed the attack there were thousands of memorial services and funerals. Some took place without coffins; others, with empty ones. There was one terrible case where the wrong body was in the coffin.[30] Each loss was significant and each loss was unique, yet there was a pattern in the losses. The Associated Press made an analysis of the thousands of missing and dead. They found that three-quarters of the victims were men. Most of those killed were in their thirties and forties, and the average age was forty. Tragically, of course, this is a prime age for parenting, and some were new fathers. Two-thirds of those lost lived in New York or New Jersey.[31]

In a particularly insightful story, reporter Janny Scott of the *New York Times* pointed out that there were many parallels between the World Trade Center victims in neckties and their would-be rescuers in fire helmets. Both groups resembled each other in that they were mostly young, white, and male. Scott described the traders trapped on the top floors of the Twin Towers: "They were men in their 30's and 40's, in the prime of their lives, many of them

Irish- and Italian-Americans, neighborhood guys who made good—college athletes who followed friends to Wall Street, flourished, married, and became soccer-coaching, weekend-golfing, suburban family men."[32]

Then Scott described the firefighters who rushed into the bottom of the World Trade Center to save them: "Many of them men in their 30's and 40's, Irish- and Italian-American, neighborhood guys, athletes who followed fathers and brothers into firefighting. Family men, too."[33] The parallels are eerie. Both jobs demanded a hard-charging vigor, which bred a certain brotherhood and intimacy among the practitioners. To succeed in either job required grace under pressure.

We turn now to the matter of removing the rubble from Ground Zero. As this is written, more than a thousand construction workers, firefighters, and police officers are at work removing tons of debris. The work started with removing a big pile of rubble, and ended by digging down into a deep, dark subterranean pit with a pond of water at the bottom. Mark Loizeau is the president of Controlled Demolition of Phoenix, Maryland, the firm that prepared a demolition plan for New York City's Department of Design and Construction. Describing the plan, Loizeau said, "How do you eat an elephant? Carefully and in small bites."[34]

The job requires at least a dozen different specialized pieces of equipment. The most impressive is the Liebherr crawler crane, a 300-foot crane that can lift up to 800 tons, or the largest pieces of the structure. There are a number of smaller cranes that can lift 400 to 500 tons. A particularly useful demolition machine is the grappler, designed to pull and pick at pieces of the structure; it can lift up to 25 tons. There are cranes equipped with man baskets to lift workers to elevated areas of the structure to cut sections of steel. Water trucks are used to spray work areas to keep down the dust and to suppress smoldering fires until they were finally put out after four months. At night, the area is floodlit from mobile lighting towers powered by diesel generators so the work can continue on a twenty-four-hour basis. More-familiar equipment includes backhoes used to remove pulverized debris. Dump trucks serve to remove smaller pieces of debris, and flatbed trucks transport large sections of steel or concrete.[35] It is a busy place with its own smells and sounds aptly described by the *New York Times* just a month after the attack: "As work progresses, fires still burn deep within the debris, and an acrid smell with a distinctly metallic flavor rises from the ground. It mixes with the cacophony emanating from the site— the beeping of vehicles backing up, the whining of saws cutting steel, the roar of crane engines, the echoing boom of debris being dumped into trucks. And it continues, day and night."[36]

While the flatbed trucks carting away the heavy steel girders were sent to two recycling companies in New Jersey, everything else was taken to the 3,000-acre Fresh Kills Landfill on Staten Island. Here federal and local police go through the rubble, slowly and carefully, looking for telltale bits and pieces. They might find an ear or a finger, a credit card, a wallet, a photograph, or a set of keys— anything that might help to identify one of those people listed as missing. Over the past few months, officials have developed a system for going through the debris, complete with conveyor belts, sifting machines, and grapplers. Says William Allee, the police department's chief of detectives, "These truckloads of destruction are not just being brought here and dumped in a big hole. There is a process. There is a protocol."[37]

At Ground Zero, the excavation work proceeded gingerly because engineers feared anything that might damage "the bathtub," the seventy-foot retaining wall around the basement. The seven-story, sixteen-acre basement is full of debris, but so far nothing has punched through the outer walls. In October 2001, engineers began to drill wells around the outside of the bathtub wall to lessen the load on the wall by pumping down the water level outside the wall.[38]

Another serious problem at Ground Zero has been a series of illnesses among the workers there caught in plumes of dust and debris. Many have persistently complained about coughs and sinus infections. A few have suffered acute lung traumas, including severe asthma treated by mechanical respiration. Experts suspect that these symptoms have been triggered by the release of toxic chemicals and metals into the environment around the site. The levels of benzene, dioxins, PCBs, lead, and chromium have been found to exceed federal standards. The data is troubling since the air, the water, and the soil have all been contaminated.[39]

Nonetheless, the work of removing the debris went on,

twenty-four hours a day, seven days a week. As time went by, operating engineers were the ones doing most of the actual work. These 300 men and women from International Operating Engineers, Locals 14 and 15, operated and maintained the cranes, excavators, and other heavy equipment. Also working at the site were ironworkers and carpenters. The firefighers stood by to retrieve any bodies that might be uncovered. The operating engineers had to strike a delicate balance between working fast enough to get the job done and slowly enough to retrieve any bodies. Working seventy and eighty hours a week on the job, workers said the smell of the bodies has gotten to some of them, and they have been having nightmares. Still, they kept going.[40] New York Fire Marshal Joseph McMahon, who worked morgue duty since September 11, said, "I want to be here until the very last body or body part is pulled out of the pile, when somebody steps up to the podium and says there is no more to recover. That's when I'll take my break. That's when I'll think about everything I've seen and put some closure on it."[41]

To understand the full implications of the September 11th attacks, we have to look to popular culture to see how the landscape of everyday life in the United States has been affected. Nearly anyone who witnessed the collapse of the Twin Towers on television said that the event reminded them of a big-budget Hollywood action movie. Suddenly, there were similarities between real life and *Die Hard*, where a skyscraper was held hostage. And we remember all those films with airplanes in trouble such as *Air Force One* and *Turbulence* and *Con Air*. Not to mention those films where national landmarks are attacked, such as *Independence Day* and *Godzilla*. The difference on September 11th was that there was no superhero, no Bruce Willis, to save us at the last minute.[42]

We should take a brief look at developments in the comic book field. We are all familiar with the superheroes, those powerful characters with buffed bodies dressed in colorful, skintight costumes. The superheroes, because they are possessed of fantastic abilities, are usually able to battle evildoers and turn the tide against all villains. Understandably, the readers of these comics began to ask themselves and the publishers, "Where were our superheroes on September 11?" Readers posed this question with special urgency to Marvel Comics, which features, among others, X-Men,

Captain America, and Spiderman. The writers and artists at Marvel believed that the readers deserved an answer, especially from Spiderman. Loyal readers remembered that Spidey, underneath that costume, was a New Yorker, a Jewish kid from Queens.

So Marvel devoted the next twenty-two-page issue entirely to the World Trade Center disaster. It is a high-quality, multicolor production, with no advertisements. Though the cover of this comic book is almost entirely black, the inside is full of drawings with abundant color. Indeed, the story is largely told in pictures since Spiderman speaks only four times for a total count of eighteen words. The storyline depends more on Spidey's inner thoughts than on his spoken words. Issue #36 of "The Amazing Spiderman" opens right after the attack with the hero, high on the roof of a nearby building, looking down at the ruins of the Twin Towers. Of course, Spidey feels guilty because he failed to prevent the attack. He tells himself, "How do you say we didn't know? We couldn't know. We couldn't imagine. . . . We could not see it coming. We could not be here before it happened. We could not stop it."[43] In the months that followed the attack several other Marvel Comics on the Twin Towers disaster appeared, with all the proceeds going to the Twin Towers Fund, which provides assistance to the families of New York uniformed service personnel who were killed or injured in the September 11 attack.[44]

In the aftermath of the attack on the World Trade Center, there has been considerable public debate on what to do about rebuilding. The one thing that everyone seems agreed upon is that the infrastructure must be rebuilt promptly. There is much to do. Below the streets are service lines for phones, electricity, steam, and transportation. As a temporary measure, Verizon and Con Edison have restored telephone and electric service by running cables above ground, but this is not a permanent solution. In the long term, one of the biggest projects is restoring transportation on the No. 1 and No. 9 subway tunnels and stations, not to mention the PATH facilities. The whole process is complicated by the lack of accurate underground maps. Digging becomes dangerous when workers run the risk of electrocution from high-voltage lines or burns from steam pipes. Says Bruce Wiproud, a utilities specialist,

"No other city has so many pipes, wires, and subways underneath it. There are twists and turns that you have no idea about, abandoned pipes that have been there for years, and you can hardly be sure of the maps unless you dig it up and take a look."[45]

When it comes to the question of rebuilding the Twin Towers, there is no consensus. There are no technical or engineering reasons why it cannot be done. Indeed, some experts say that it should be done. One of them is Ric Stoll, professor of international relations at Rice University, who says, "You want to send the message that we won't allow this to permanently change our society."[46] But it is hard to imagine tenants who would sign up for a building that has already twice been a target. And who would want to insure such a building?

Predictably, there are others who want the site to become strictly a memorial to the dead. Arguing for a park is Theodore Kheel, who was opposed to building the World Trade Center three decades ago. Kheel argued back then that the Port Authority should have been coordinating transportation, not putting up office buildings. Kheel passionately urged the Port Authority to help subsidize mass transit, something that Austin Tobin vigorously opposed. Kheel now says, "This building should not have been built in the first place—it was a mistake; it was too big. It was an easy target for the crazy people who blew it up."[47]

But Kheel's position is not widely shared. In a survey taken of New York, New Jersey, and Connecticut residents in November 2001, seven out of ten people wanted another commercial office building of some kind to be built on the site. The majority favored something less than 100 stories. Yet, surprisingly, a substantial minority of 42 percent wanted the new building to be as high, if not higher, than the original. But clearly those surveyed were ambivalent because more than half of them were worried about working in a skyscraper. Understandably, people wanted America to defy the terrorists, but they did not want to place themselves at risk.[48]

As the public debated the matter, real estate professionals wasted no time in forming a study group to come up with a plan. The American Institute of Architects, the New York City Partnership, and the Real Estate Board of New York were the key players in putting together a coalition with an ambitious name employing a military metaphor. Initially, they called their group the NYC Rebuild Task Force. Later it was strategically renamed NYC Infrastructure Task Force, since, of course, everyone is in favor of infrastructure. Whatever the name, Herbert Muschamp of the *New York Times*, with tongue in cheek, calls them "people with bow ties." There seems to be a consensus among these professionals not to build another tower, or set of towers, in a park. Instead, they appear to favor some multiple-use complex with cafés, shops, movie theatres, and a museum. All of these will incorporate the latest in old-fashioned paving stones, period street lights, security barricades, and an array of colorful flags.[49]

In the weeks and months following the attack, the Internet list-serves for planners and architects were abuzz with suggestions. When all is said and done, most of the suggestions fell into one of four broad categories: 1) Do nothing other than clean up the site and make the whole thing a memorial to the victims; 2) Rebuild the World Trade Center exactly as it was; 3) Rebuild it as Twin Towers, higher than ever; 4) Rebuild the same amount of office space, but in four towers of fifty stories each.[50] Reviewing these four options is a bit like taking a multiple-choice test when you do not know the answer. As this chapter is being written, no one knows what the outcome will be, but I do have a guess: It is likely to be some variant of number four. Of course, the plan will have to allocate some space for a memorial and perhaps a museum as well. And it is likely to be a plan of mixed use, allowing for some apartments as well as retail and entertainment facilities.

Certainly, the Lower Manhattan Redevelopment Corporation, chaired by former Goldman Sachs executive John C. Whitehead, will hold public hearings on these choices, since it is important to listen to the various constituencies. No doubt tough decisions will have to be made.[51]

Like most important questions of public policy, the matter of rebuilding is exquisitely complex and controversial. Each of the four positions outlined above has a fierce constituency, and each is convinced that they alone are correct. First, the families of the victims have the strongest moral case when they argue that the site is a burial ground, and some of them want the whole sixteen acres dedicated to memorialize the tragedy. Second, those who argue for rebuilding the Twin Towers exactly as it was before invoke the powerful historical example of the Campanile of St. Mark's Basilica in Venice, which collapsed and sank into the lagoon in 1902. Though it took ten years, the town elders rebuilt it exactly as it had been before.[52] Third, rebuilding the Twin Towers even higher than before is technically feasible, and some argue that it's the most patriotic way to defy the terrorists. If the Twin Towers are to be resurrected as a symbol of America, then more height is a positive thing. Finally, the most likely option of four towers of fifty stories each is the preference of Larry Silverstein, the lease owner of the World Trade Center. His proposal is affordable and practical, based on consultations with experienced architects and planners. Moreover, such buildings could, and should, be designed to be more resistant to fire and more accessible to firefighters.

In the fall of 2001, corporate architects and intellectual planners all offered suggestions. Highbrow design buffs scheduled open forums and meetings. In the past, developers and politicians, following the dictates of capitalism, often met with architects, who then delivered their plans as a fait accompli to the public, who had nothing to say about it. This time, Herbert Muschamp advises us, the powers that be must listen to the public. Architects, he tells us, have no special mandate; instead, "survivors, philosophers, firefighters, shopkeepers, musicians, window dressers, and dentists have at least as much right to the public's attention."[53] This attention to democracy is bound to be messy, but hopefully in the end it will result in a better product.

However, as this chapter is being written, authorities announced that the process of removing debris from Ground Zero has progressed much faster than anyone anticipated. Some thought the job would take two years, but it now appears that it will be completed in nine months, by June 2002. The result is greatly increased pressure to make decisions about the future of the site. So there will be little time for extended democratic debate. John C. Whitehead said, "We don't want that hole to be sitting there with nothing going on. That would be the worst thing. So we are going to try to have plans lined up as quickly as possible to permit construction to begin as soon as possible."[54]

In making plans for the site, the one thing that everyone is agreed upon is that the some kind of memorial must be constructed to commemorate the tragedy and to preserve the memory of those who died. Interestingly enough, the people of New York and New Jersey did not wait for a formal monument to be erected. Instead, they immediately came together in informal and communal ways to create what I have called "ephemeral memorials." People would gather at a significant place, creating homemade altars by bringing photocopied photographs of the dead and missing, children's drawings, holy cards, candles, cut flowers, ribbons, and flags to be left at the memorial site. The mourners who bring these objects realize that the tribute will last only a short time, but it serves the important purpose of giving people something immediate and tangible with which to express their grief. One of the first of these sites was Union Square Park in Manhattan at the base of an equestrian statue of George Washington. People gravitated to the park as a social gathering place.[55]

As time went on, more and more of these sites sprang up. At St. Paul's Chapel on Broadway, a block to the east of Ground Zero, there is a block-long iron fence, which was covered with flags, banners, letters, and T-shirts.[56] Impromptu memorials were created at St. Vincent's Hospital, Grand Central Station, Penn Station, the PATH station in Jersey City, and nearly every firehouse in New York City.[57] Alongside the Garden State Parkway, a set of large plywood letters spelling out "AMERICA" was set up, so people could pull over and write out messages or just sign their names.[58] Another shrine was built at a large rock formation in West Essex Park right at the border between Essex and Morris Counties in New Jersey. People placed candles at the base of the rock and, higher up, attached pictures with duct tape.[59] These temporary expressions of grief have attracted many visitors, many of whom take photographs of the shrines to help remember the experience.

Scholars like myself have struggled to explain the significance of these temporary memorials to journalists who have asked about them. In a letter to me, fellow folklorist Steve Zeitlin of New York City told me how difficult it was for him to interpret these things for a reporter from the *Los Angeles Times*: "I spoke about how these informal, spontaneous practices of creating memorials reveal the spirit. They are rituals of remembrance that are about the care and nurturing of a human spirit not as it approaches heaven but as it dwells among the living in story, memory, family history, and tradition."[60] I wrote back and told him that I was unable to improve on what he had said.

We all struggle with preserving the memory of those who have been lost, to make sure they are not forgotten. However valuable the makeshift and impromptu memorials may be, we all want something more permanent. Of more lasting significance than the ephemeral memorials are what I call "memorial projects." These are usually carried out within some kind of institutional framework with a view toward permanently archiving a body of data. For example, the Library of Congress has launched a project to archive Internet materials pertaining to the aftermath of the attacks of September 11, 2001.[61] In the same vein, the telephone company, Verizon Communications, offered to copy voice-mail messages onto an audiocassette for any of its users who wanted a more permanent copy of items in their voice-mail boxes on September 11.[62] Right after the attack, the New Jersey Historical Society announced that it would launch an oral history project, interviewing people about the New Jersey response to the tragedy.[63]

Still another example of a memorial project is the photographic exhibition that opened at the New-York Historical Society on Central Park West and 77th Street. Called "New York September 11 by Magnum Photographers," the photographs make up the first of six planned exhibits which the society calls its "History Responds Project."[64] Memorial projects of this kind are usually carried out by institutions, but in Tinton Falls, New Jersey, a full-time police officer and volunteer firefighter, Jared Stevens, took it upon himself to create an eight-foot-tall model of the World Trade Center out of plywood. The carefully constructed model was put on display at the Tinton Falls firehouse to honor the uniformed emergency service workers lost on September 11.[65]

But what about the Ground Zero site itself? In the short term, it simply was not possible to build a monument, which would require much public discussion and planning. What was needed was a way to provide the crowds of visitors with an unobstructed view of the site. The solution was to construct a thirteen-foot-high wooden viewing platform on nearby Fulton Street. The design was simple, basically two plywood ramps, one to ascend to the viewing platform and another to exit. Herbert Muschamp of the *New York Times* praised the concept. He wrote, "It had to be easy and cheap, sturdy, and flexible. It had to come in without arousing opposition and with the mayor's blessing. It didn't have to deal with complexities of meaning."[66]

The platform was so popular that the city had to come up with a scheme of issuing free tickets at nearby South Street Seaport for scheduled times in order to reduce the crowds. Thousands of people lined up every day to view the site.[67] An unexpected result of the tremendous success of the viewing platform was something of a revolt among the families of the victims. Most of the families felt that all the human remains of the victims should have been removed before putting up the platform. They tend to see the site as a grave, something that should not be open to public view. Antoinette Rubino, the mother of one of the victims, said, "It is like a freak show, these people passing by curious to see if they find a body or head or something. It is horrible. That is supposed to be a sacred place now. My child's body is all over that place."[68]

In the end, of course, a permanent monument will have to be constructed. There has been no shortage of ideas and suggestions. Some have suggested a park with walkways, benches, trees, and flowers. Others have suggested an eternal flame. Still others have suggested twin beams of light shining up in the sky to replicate the Twin Towers. A recurring suggestion has been to incorporate a large piece of the facade of one of the Twin Towers. This piece of steel, simply known as "the shroud," stood four stories tall, and it was the last standing piece of the Twin Towers until it was taken down and set aside for possible later use. James E. Young, an expert on memorials, has said that fragments of ruins have real value because they are the actual material of the past, preserving the narrative that comes with them. Young explained, "Ruins gesture to the moment of attack."[69]

I approach the matter of designing the permanent monument with some trepidation. Shortly before leaving office, Mayor Rudolph W. Giuliani said in his farewell address at St. Paul's Chapel, "I really believe we shouldn't think about this site out there right here, as a site for economic development. We should think about a soaring, monumental, beautiful memorial that just draws millions of people here that just want to see it. If the memorial was done correctly, you'll have all the economic development you want, and you can do the office space in a lot of different places."[70]

I think the mayor was sincere in his desire to turn the site into a memorial, but that outcome is improbable. What is far more likely is some kind of smaller memorial within a complex of office, residential, and retail towers. But then the pressing question remains: What will the monument look like? It is probably unwise to try to design it by committee. In trying to please everyone, we may end up pleasing no one. The matter will probably be decided by a design competition. Michael Kimmelman has convincingly argued that the winning design is likely to be Minimalist, the unofficial expression of memorial art. In the *New York Times*, Kimmelman wrote, "What used to be men on horses with thrusting swords has morphed more or less into plain walls and boxes."[71]

In other words, the World Trade Center memorial is likely to become as culturally important as the Lincoln and Jefferson memorials or the Tomb of the Unknowns in Arlington National Cemetery. But it will not look like any of these. There will be no colonnades or representational statuary. Minimalist sculpture originated as a rejection of subjectivity and romanticism, and it embraced precise, elemental geometric forms and pure colors. So the final product is unlikely to be a statue of three firemen raising a flag over a pile of twisted steel. Instead, it is far more likely to bear a resemblance to Maya Lin's Vietnam memorial, which is basically a Minimalist sculpture combined with a list of names.[72]

The attack on the Twin Towers of September 11, 2001, was an occurrence which inflicted widespread destruction and distress. The most catastrophic aspect, of course, was the unfathomable loss of more than 2,800 lives, almost more than we can bear. As we mourn the dead, we realize that our way of life has been threatened and our institutions have been challenged. The short-run impact of the attack is to impair the economy of the New York and New Jersey region. Obviously, one of the hardest hit institutions has been the Port Authority.

The once-proud agency that had built the Twin Towers in the first place was already reeling from the downsizing that took place in 1995 and 1996. Many long-term, loyal employees had been bought out or fired. Key executives, discouraged by the disruptions, took early retirement or resigned. Just prior to September 11, 2001, the Port Authority occupied 900,000 square feet of space in the North Tower for its flagship headquarters, where 2,000 of its employees worked. With the loss of this space, the displaced workers were temporarily squeezed into other agency buildings at the airports, the seaports, and in Jersey City. Senior officials who once had corner offices in the region's premier skyscraper found themselves in a nondescript building at the entrance to the Holland Tunnel in Jersey City. The agency, used to playing the role of landlord, now had to go out and compete on the open market to lease new space in midtown Manhattan and in downtown Newark. So the Port Authority, now just another tenant, will end up paying an average rent of $43 per square foot for the new space, compared with the $22 it was paying at the World Trade Center.[73]

Far worse than the loss of office space was the fact that the Port Authority now had to reorder its priorities. Important major projects had to be postponed in order to increase security at airports, harbors, bridges, and tunnels. Suddenly, money had to be found to pay state police and national guard soldiers who were patrolling Port Authority facilities. In the near future, the Port Authority police force will have to be expanded. Plans call for the purchase of new security equipment, including two harbor patrol boats and an armored personnel carrier. Sadly swept aside, perhaps for years, were plans to purchase a new fleet of PATH cars, plans to build new marine terminals in Jersey City and Brooklyn, and plans to construct a new terminal at John F. Kennedy International Airport. Ronald Shiftan, acting executive director, grimly explained, "We're not close to losing money, but we are in a situation where the large surpluses we had previously forecast have vanished. The impact will mostly be on the ability to fund the capital plan."[74]

The Port Authority's heartrending loss of its most important building, once the symbol of its dominance of the region, reminded some of the poem "Ozymandias," written by Percy Bysshe Shelley in 1817. The poem tells the story of Ozymandias, a tyrannical Egyptian king. Proud and vain, the king commissioned a statue to be made of himself. A traveler of modern times comes along through the desert and finds the statue amidst the ruins of the an-

cient kingdom. The traveler reads the words on the pedestal and re-
acts to them:

> "My name is Ozymandias, king of kings;
> Look on my works, ye Mighty, and despair!"
> Nothing beside remains. Round the decay
> Of that colossal wreck, boundless and bare
> The lone and level sands stretch far away.[75]

At the time that the inscription was written, it taunted earlier
readers by calling attention to the king's many accomplishments
and his dazzling, prosperous city. But many years later, after the
grand kingdom has fallen into ruins, the inscription takes on a new,
and ironic, meaning.

What are the long-term implications of the loss of the Twin
Towers? At this point, no one can answer the question with cer-
tainty. However, in the introduction to the hardcover edition of this
book, I made a prediction. Back then, I predicted that the Twin
Towers would be *the last tallest skyscraper in New York*. I pointed
out that by the early 1970s the culture was already changing in favor of smaller buildings. Now, more than ever, skyscrapers have
fallen out of fashion because they are seen as arrogant. No one has
expressed this idea better than Michael J. Lewis, chairman of the
art department at Williams College. In the past, we saw skyscrapers as lofty and majestic. Built with engineering ingenuity at spectacular cost, these buildings excited our imagination as they
reached for the sky. But now Lewis calls them "swagger buildings—arrogant, proud and strutting objects that are physical man-
ifestations of America's competitive culture."[76]

Not only is the future of the skyscraper in doubt, the whole
idea of centering a financial district in downtown has been called
into question. It now seems clear that some companies may never
return to Lower Manhattan. Studies have shown that 13.4 million
square feet of office space were destroyed in the World Trade Center attack, and financial services firms have occupied 4.4 million
square feet outside New York City since September 11. We may
have lost the financial district itself along with the loss of the Twin
Towers. M. Meyers Mermel, a commercial real estate expert, said,

"The financial district is dispersed, post 9-11. The question remains whether it can be reassembled. Tenants are indicating that there is little enthusiasm for returning downtown."[77]

But the attack on the World Trade Center has implications beyond the future of the skyscraper and the future of the financial district. We may go further and address the larger issues of war and peace, of the priorities of our nation in matters of security and social justice, of seeing the world as others see it, and of progress toward world peace. The lessons of September 11th are humbling ones. We have lost our illusion of immortality. Indeed, we could all benefit from rereading English historian Edward Gibbon's *The Decline and Fall of the Roman Empire*. That book reminds us that civilizations can perish, though we Americans are uncomfortable with that notion. James Atlas recently wrote, "Our national habit of optimism resonates in our triumphal phrases: the City on the Hill, Manifest Destiny, the New Deal. In this almost touchingly hopeful narrative, history is a progressive continuum from barbarism to liberation, a passage on our mission from darkness into light. What it fails to grapple with is the darker reality that civilizations, like all else, have a beginning and an end."[78]

In trying to find the larger meaning of the destruction of the Twin Towers, I am convinced that the most important thing we have lost is our innocence. We always believed, like Minoru Yamasaki, that globalization would bring world trade and world peace. We did not realize that globalization would also bring terrorism to our shores. Reading an op-ed essay in the *New York Times* by Daniel Born, editor of *The Common Review*, I was reminded of the relevance of F. Scott Fitzgerald's novel *The Great Gatsby* as it speaks to our predicament. In that novel, Nick Carraway, the young protagonist, had left the hardware business of his family in the Midwest to seek his fortune in the business world of New York. At the end of the novel, after suffering tragic experiences, Nick realizes his own loss of innocence as he watches the blinking green light at the end of a dock in Long Island. He thinks about the promise of those early navigators: "Gradually I became aware of the old island here that flowered once for Dutch sailors' eyes—a fresh, green breast of the new world."[79]

Notes

INTRODUCTION

1. Jim Dwyer and David Kocieniewski, Deidre Murphy, and Peg Tyre, *Two Seconds under the World* (New York: Crown Publishers, 1994).
2. Douglas Jehl, "A Tool of Foreign Terror, Little Known in the U.S.," *New York Times*, 27 February 1993.
3. Angus Kress Gillespie and Michael Aaron Rockland, *Looking for America on the New Jersey Turnpike* (New Brunswick, N.J.: Rutgers University Press, 1989).
4. Michael Aaron Rockland, interview with the author, New Brunswick, N.J., 25 October 1998.
5. For more on the idea of sublimity, see David E. Nye, *American Technological Sublime* (Cambridge, Mass.: M.I.T. Press, 1994).
6. Daniel Hudson Burnham, quoted by Austin Tobin in Roger Cohen, "Casting Giant Shadows: The Politics of Building the World Trade Center," *Portfolio* (Winter 1990–1991): 14.
7. Dwyer et al., *Two Seconds under the World*.
8. Ibid., 298.
9. Dennis Sweeney and Jules Roinnel, "Case Study, Windows on the World: Leasee Selection Process," Cornell University, Hotel Administration 731, Spring 1998.
10. Ibid.
11. Ibid.
12. Guy T. Baehr, "World Trade Center Hopes Fair Will Bring Folks to the Top When It's Foul," *Star-Ledger* (Newark), 10 March 1995.
13. Dolores Bauer of Lehigh University, telephone interview with the author, 8 September 1998.
14. E. F. Schumacher, *Small Is Beautiful: Economics as If People Mattered* (New York: Harper and Row, 1973).

15. Allen R. Myerson, "The Great Asian Steeple Chase," *New York Times*, 25 June 1995.
16. Jameson W. Doig, "To Claim the Seas and the Skies: Austin Tobin and the Port of New York Authority," in Jameson W. Doig and Erwin C. Hargrove, eds., *Leadership and Innovation: A Biographical Perspective on Entrepreneurs in Government* (Baltimore: Johns Hopkins University Press, 1987).
17. Robert DiChiara, interview with the author, 25 May 1995.
18. John Tierney, "What's New York the Capital of Now?" *New York Times Magazine*, 20 November 1994.
19. Al Frank, "P.A. Puts World Trade Center on the Market," *Star-Ledger* (Newark), 25 September 1998.

Introduction to the Paperback Edition

1. Parts of this introduction originally appeared as an essay, "Now What?", in *New Jersey Monthly*, November 2001, 151–152.

Chapter 1
Political Background: The Uneasy Alliance
between New York and New Jersey

1. A typical day in the life of Austin Tobin based on several conversations with different Port Authority officials who knew him well. Particularly helpful was a telephone conversation with Lloyd D. Schwalb, retired manager of Media Programming and Planning, on 15 November 1995 and a letter of 20 December 2001 from Carl K. Panero to the author.
2. Facts on the historical development of the Port of New York based on notes taken by the author on the New York Metropolis Exhibition at the New York State Museum, Albany, New York, on 27 January 1996.
3. James Morris, *The Great Port: A Passage through New York* (New York: Harcourt, Brace, and World, 1969), 142.
4. Ibid.
5. Factual information about the early history of the Port Authority is drawn from the scholarly work of others, especially Erwin Wilkie Bard, *The Port of New York Authority* (New York: Columbia University Press, 1942); Frederick L. Bird, *A Study of the Port of New York Authority* (New York: Dun and Bradstreet, 1949); Jameson W. Doig, *Metropolitan Transportation Politics and the New York Region* (New York: Columbia University Press, 1966); John I. Griffin, *The Port of New York* (New York: City College Press, 1959); Robert A. Caro, *The Power Broker: Robert Moses and the Fall of New York* (New York: Alfred A. Knopf, 1974); and

Joe Mysak with Judith Schiffer, *Perpetual Motion: The Illustrated History of the Port Authority of New York and New Jersey* (Santa Monica, Calif.: General Publishing Group, 1997). Additional helpful information comes from anonymous official publications of the Port Authority itself, ranging from the dated but valuable *The Port of New York Authority: A Monograph* of 1936 to the contemporary pamphlet *What We Do . . . At a Glance* by the Government and Community Affairs Department of 1994.

6. Bard, *The Port of New York Authority*, 24.
7. Ibid., 25.
8. *The Port of New York Authority: A Monograph*, 49–52.
9. Griffin, *The Port of New York*, 71.
10. Caro, *The Power Broker*, 615.
11. Bard, *The Port of New York Authority*, 333.
12. Caro, *The Power Broker*, 616.
13. *The Port of New York Authority: A Monograph*, 49–52.
14. James J. Flink, *The Automobile Age* (Cambridge, Mass.: MIT Press, 1988), 188–189.
15. L.T.C. Rolt, *Victorian Engineering* (New York: Penguin, 1970), 240.
16. *The Port of New York Authority: A Monograph*, 52.
17. Ibid., 59.
18. John Van der Zee, *The Gate: The True Story of the Design and Construction of the Golden Gate Bridge* (New York: Simon and Schuster, 1986), 81.
19. Port of New York Authority, *First Progress Report on Hudson River Bridge at New York*, 1 January 1928.
20. John A. Kouwenhoven, *The Arts in Modern American Civilization* (New York: W. W. Norton, 1948), 206.
21. Caro, *The Power Broker*, 616.
22. *Port of New York Authority: Monograph*, 55–56.
23. Ibid., 62–64.
24. Jameson W. Doig, "To Claim the Seas and the Skies: Austin Tobin and the Port of New York Authority," in Jameson W. Doig and Erwin C. Hargrove, eds., *Leadership and Innovation: A Biographical Perspective on Entrepreneurs in Government* (Baltimore: Johns Hopkins University Press, 1987), 139.
25. Cohen, "Casting Giant Shadows," 14.
26. Doig, "To Claim the Seas and the Skies," 143.
27. Joseph C. Goulden, *The Best Years, 1945–1950* (New York: Atheneum, 1976), 3–13.
28. Ray Monti, interview with the author, New York City, 1 January 1995.

29. Cohen, "Casting Giant Shadows," 16.

30. Port of New York Authority, *Weekly Report to the Commissioners from the Executive Director for the Week Ending March 13, 1961*, by Austin Tobin.

31. "Transport Is His Life," *New York Times*, 8 September 1961.

32. Editorial, *New York Herald Tribune*, 14 March 1961.

33. Editorial, *New York Journal American*, 14 March 1961.

34. Editorial, *Newark Evening News*, 13 March 1961.

35. *Weekly Report*, 13 March 1961.

36. "Days of Glory for H. & M. Featured Silk-Hatted Riders," *The Bergen Record*, 8 February 1962.

37. Ibid.

38. "H & M Bankruptcy," *New York Journal American*, 21 June 1962.

39. Editorial, *Newark Evening News*, 15 February 1962.

40. Editorial, *Bergen Record*, 21 March 1961.

41. *Weekly Report*, 20 March 1961.

42. "Rockefeller's Big Risk," *New York Times*, 3 April 1961.

43. "Governor Derides Attack by Meyner," *New York Times*, 31 March 1961.

44. In a letter of 29 November 2001, to the author, Richard C. Sullivan wrote that the idea to replace, rather than rehabilitate, the Hudson and Manhattan terminal building originated with Sidney Schacter, a member of the WTC study group staff. Schacter reported to Sullivan that the WTC and the PATH projects could be combined on the west side of Manhattan. Sullivan reported the new concept to Roger Gilman, who immediately arranged a meeting with Austin Tobin.

45. Cohen, "Casting Giant Shadows," 19–21.

46. "Meyner and Hughes—A Contrast," *Newark Evening News*, 16 January 1962.

47. Cohen, "Casting Giant Shadows," 21.

48. Editorial, *Bergen Record*, 27 December 1961.

49. Editorial, *Newark Sunday News*, 31 December 1961.

50. Cohen, "Casting Giant Shadows," 22.

51. "A Senate Lesson in How to Kill Time," *Sunday Star-Ledger* (Newark), 25 February 1962.

52. *Weekly Report*, 19 February 1962.

53. *Weekly Report*, 12 February 1962.

54. Guy Tozzoli, interview with the author, New York City, 15 November 1994.

55. "Biggest Buildings in World to Rise at Trade Center," *New York Times*, 19 January 1964.

56. Tozzoli, interview.

57. *Weekly Report*, 27 March 1962.

58. "N.Y. Casting Cold Eye on World Center Plan," *Newark Sunday News*, 31 December 1961.

59. *Weekly Report*, 19 February 1962.

60. *Weekly Report*, 5 March 1962.

61. *Weekly Report*, 16 April 1962.

62. "Small Merchants Protest Trade Center," *New York World-Telegram*, 30 March 1962.

63. Ibid.

64. "Small Guys Finish Last," *New York Herald Tribune*, 2 May 1962.

65. "Shabby Liberty St. Store Place for PA Relocations," *Newark Evening News*, 29 May 1962.

66. "A Challenge for the Port Authority," *New York Herald Tribune*, 14 July 1962.

67. "Downtown New York Merchants Fight World Trade Center Plans," *Bergen Record*, 16 August 1962.

68. Ibid.

69. Cohen, "Casting Giant Shadows," 23.

70. "Unified Customs House Sought," *Journal of Commerce*, 3 April 1962.

71. *Weekly Report*, 17 December 1962.

72. "State Will Rent at Trade Center," *New York Times*, 14 January 1964.

73. Guy F. Tozzoli, interview with the author, New York City, 15 November 1994.

74. Ibid. But according to Carl K. Panero in a letter of 20 December 2001 to the author, Richard Sullivan, Tozzoli's deputy director, was firmly opposed to the twin tower concept. He wanted several smaller buildings similar to Rockefeller Center. Sullivan wisely reasoned that buildings should be built as tenants were identified and the market could absorb the space. In this he was opposed by Levy, and Sullivan lost the fight.

75. Ibid.

76. "Biggest Building in World to Rise at Trade Center," *New York Times*, 19 January 1964.

77. Ibid.

78. Ibid.

79. "Real Estate Men Fight Port Agency," *New York Times*, 1 April 1964.

80. Ibid.

81. Ibid.

82. Ibid.

83. Ibid.

84. *Weekly Report*, 2 May 1966.

85. "Questions on the Trade Center," *New York Times*, 24 December 1966.

86. "Hearing Is Held on Trade Center," *New York Times*, 3 May 1966.

87. "City-Port Authority Talks on Trade Center Enter Crucial Stage," *New York Times*, 7 June 1966.

88. "Mayor Rebuffed on Trade Center," *New York Times*, 13 July 1966.

89. "Lindsay Assails Charge by Tobin," *New York Times*, 16 July 1966.

90. "He Broke a Stalemate," *New York Times*, 4 August 1966.

91. "City Ends Fight with Port Agency on Trade Center," *New York Times*, 4 August 1966.

92. *Weekly Report*, 8 August 1966.

CHAPTER 2
IT CAN'T BE DONE: OVERCOMING OBSTACLES IN BUILDING TALL TOWERS

1. Ray M. Monti, interview with the author, New York City, 4 January 1995. Monti's experience with the expense account showed the Port Authority's willingness to trust its executives. However, Carl K. Panero points out in a letter to the author of 20 December 2001 that years later some employees abused this trust, leading to a scandal which tarnished the agency's reputation.

2. "Construction's Man of the Year: World Trade Center's Ray Monti," *Engineering News Record*, 11 February 1971.

3. Ibid.

4. Ibid.

5. Kerby Saunders, "What the World Trade Center Means to the Local Economy," *Westsider* 29 (Fall 1964): 45.

6. Marc A. Weiss, "Tishman, David," in Kenneth Jackson, ed., *The Encyclopedia of New York City* (New Haven: Yale University Press, 1995), 1188.

7. Port of New York Authority, *Weekly Report to the Commissioners from the Executive Director for the Week Ending March 2, 1967*, by Austin Tobin.

8. Ray M. Monti, interview with the author, New York City, 4 January 1995.

9. "Trade Center Site Razing Under Way," *New York World-Telegram*, 25 March 1966.

10. "Demolition for Trade Center Reaches Half-Way: Utility Reloca-tion a Giant Problem," *World Journal Tribune*, 13 November 1966.

11. Ray Monti, "A Tall Order," *Portfolio* 3 (Winter 1990–91): 26.

12. Ibid.

13. The Port Authority of New York and New Jersey, "The World Trade Center: A Building Project Like No Other," February 1990, Publication no. 890711, 6–7.

14. "John Kyle, Aide in Port Authority," *New York Times*, 1 October 1970.

15. "Optimism Is Main Brace of Engineer's Life," *Star-Ledger* (New-ark), 22 November 1970.

16. "$61.1 Million in Trade Center Construction Contracts Let," *Newark Sunday News*, 20 November 1966.

17. "Young Engineers on Tough Job," *Newark Sunday News,* 4 De-cember 1966. In a letter to the author of 20 December 2001, Carl K. Panero wrote that it was necessary to import Italian operators for the excavation equipment. In the finest New York tradition of featherbedding, the union allowed this on the condition that its members were hired to watch as the job progressed.

18. Ray M. Monti, interview with the author, New York City, 4 Jan-uary 1995.

19. John M. Kyle, "Slurry Wall Process for Foundations," *Military Engineer*, June 1969, 315–317.

20. Charles J. Maikish, interview with the author, New York City, 11 November 1994.

21. *Weekly Report*, 3 January 1967.

22. "Estimate Raised for Trade Center," *New York Times*, 29 Decem-ber 1966.

23. Ibid.

24. "Questions on the Trade Center," *New York Times*, 24 December 1966.

25. Ray M. Monti, interview with the author, New York City, 21 De-cember 1994.

26. Ray M. Monti, "A Tall Order," 29.

27. "New York Gets $90 Million Worth of Land for Nothing," *Engi-neering News Record*, 18 April 1968, 515–517.

28. Ray M. Monti, interview with the author, New York City, 4 Jan-uary 1995.

29. "Trade Center Workers Dig Up the Past," *New York Post*, 27 De-cember 1966.

30. *Weekly Report*, 18 September 1967.

31. *Weekly Report*, 30 October 1967.

32. *Weekly Report*, 16 April 1969.
33. "Artifacts Are Dug Up at Trade Center Site," *New York Times*, 10 June 1968.
34. "A Section of the Hudson Tubes Is Turned into an Elevated Tunnel," *New York Times*, 30 December 1968.
35. Ray Monti, "A Tall Order," 29.
36. Ibid.
37. Discussion of the elevator problem based on Guy Tozzoli interview with the author, New York City, 15 November 1994, and on Carl K. Panero letter to the author of 20 December 2001.
38. Richard C. Sullivan, "New Concept in Vertical Transport," *Westsider* 29 (Fall 1964): 56–58.
39. "$61.1 Million in Trade Center Construction Contracts Let," *Newark Sunday News*, 20 November 1966.
40. Malcolm P. Levy, "Building the World Trade Center," *Westsider* 29 (Fall 1964): 50–58.
41. Robert Byrne, *Skyscraper* (New York: Atheneum, 1984).
42. Port Authority, "A Building Project Like No Other," 10.
43. "Unsettling Effects in the Room at the Top," *London Engineering News*, 18 May 1967, 446.
44. Jim Dwyer, David Kocieniewski, Deidre Murphy, and Peg Tyre, *Two Seconds under the World* (New York: Crown, 1994), 13.
45. Glenn Collins, "Notes on a Revolutionary Dinosaur," *New York Times Magazine*, 6 August 1972, 15.
46. "Unsettling Effects," 446.
47. "Supermarket for the World," *Christian Science Monitor*, 17 May 1969.
48. "The Wind, Fickle and Shifty, Tests Builders," *New York Times*, 5 May 1974.
49. *Weekly Report*, 4 April 1966.
50. *Weekly Report*, 29 August 1966.
51. Ibid.
52. Ray M. Monti, "A Tall Order," 30.
53. "New York Port Agency's $30 Million Saving on Steel Work Prompts Antitrust Inquiry," *Wall Street Journal*, 16 July 1969.
54. Port Authority, "A Building Project Like No Other," 12.
55. Ray M. Monti, interview with the author, 4 January 1995.
56. "Notes on a Revolutionary Dinosaur," *New York Times*, 6 August 1972.
57. Karl Sabbagh, *Skyscraper: The Making of a Building* (New York: Viking-Penguin, 1989), 293–294.

CHAPTER 3
ERECTING THE TOWERS: IT'S ONE STORY AFTER ANOTHER

1. "Trade Center Is Doing Everything Big," *New York Times*, 6 June 1969.
2. Ibid.
3. "World Trade Center's Construction Chief Wrestles to Keep Huge Project on Target," *Wall Street Journal*, 20 August 1969.
4. Ray M. Monti, interview with the author, New York City, 4 January 1995.
5. *Weekly Report*, 23 March 1970.
6. "Copter Drops 7 Tons of Steel into Kill van Kull," *Staten Island Advance*, 8 March 1970.
7. *Weekly Report*, 17 October 1968.
8. Port Authority, "A Building Project Like No Other," 16.
9. "The New Pyramids," *Newark Sunday News*, 13 October 1968.
10. Joseph Mitchell, "The Mohawks in High Steel," in Edmund Wilson, *Apologies to the Iroquois* (New York: Farrar, Straus, and Giroux, 1959), 5.
11. Ibid., 14–15.
12. Ibid., 20–23.
13. "Wall Street Congestion Becomes More Intense as New Buildings Rise," *Wall Street Journal*, 10 September 1968.
14. *Weekly Report*, 4 December 1967.
15. "Work on Trade Center Is Moving into Higher Gear," *New York Times*, 6 July 1967.
16. "PA to Continue Query Services at Trade Site," *Hudson Dispatch*, 8 July 1969.
17. Ray M. Monti, interview with the author, New York City, 21 December 1994.
18. "A Trade Center Street Is Missing in Action," *New York Post*, 16 April 1968.
19. "Trade Center Rolling Despite Council Pleas," *Newark Evening News*, 24 January 1967.
20. *Weekly Report*, 11 August 1968.
21. *Weekly Report*, 13 March 1969.
22. Ray M. Monti, interview with the author, New York City, 4 January 1995.
23. For more on the structural integrity of skyscrapers, see Mario Salvadori, *Why Buildings Stand Up: The Strength of Architecture* (New York: W. W. Norton, 1980), 107–125.
24. For more on the Hyatt Regency Hotel disaster, see Steven S. Ross, *Construction Disasters: Design Failures, Causes, and Prevention* (New York: McGraw-Hill, 1984), 388–404.

25. "Trade Center Safety Chief Depends on the Hard Hats," *Star-Ledger* (Newark), 29 November 1970.

26. "$500,000 for a Fall," *New York Times*, 4 December 1976.

27. "Trade Center Assailed for Buying Japan Steel," *World Journal Tribune*, 5 May 1967.

28. *Weekly Report*, 20 March 1967.

29. "Trade Center Assailed for Buying Japan Steel," *World Journal Tribune*, 5 May 1967.

30. *Weekly Report*, 20 March 1967.

31. *Weekly Report*, 9 December 1968.

32. For more on the problems of unionized labor in New York City, see Sabbagh, *Skyscraper*, 92–93 and 270–271.

33. "The $94,000 Hardhat," *Time*, 18 September 1972.

34. "$76,000 Pay in Overtime Indicated in Contract," *New York Times*, 3 September 1972.

35. The four steps in the construction of the towers are summarized from Port Authority, "A Building Project Like No Other."

36. Ray M. Monti, interview with the author, New York City, 4 January 1995.

37. *Weekly Report*, 16 September 1968.

38. *Weekly Report*, 22 August 1969.

39. *Weekly Report*, 20 October 1969.

40. *Weekly Report*, 17 November 1969.

41. *Weekly Report*, 13 December 1969.

42. *Weekly Report*, 30 April 1970.

43. "Sprayed-asbestos Fireproofing Work Halted," *Engineering News Record*, 7 May 1970. In a letter of 20 December 2001 to the author, Carl K. Panero wrote that the contractor Lou DiBono was found shot to death in the parking garage of the World Trade Center in 1990. There is a rumor that John Gotti was responsible because DiBono ignored his request for a meeting.

44. Ray Monti, "A Tall Order," *Portfolio* 3, no. 4 (Winter 1990–91): 31.

45. *Weekly Report*, 26 January 1970.

46. Sabbagh, *Skyscraper*, 302.

47. "Trade Center Quietly Becomes No. 1," *Star-Ledger* (Newark), 21 October 1995.

48. *Weekly Report*, 2 January 1973.

49. *Weekly Report*, 21 December 1970.

50. I interviewed Robert Kelley, son of Thomas Edward Kelley, on 27 November 1995 in Newark, New Jersey. Though Robert Kelley himself was not present for the move into the World Trade Center, his recollection of his father's experiences were clear and

vivid.

51. "Trade Center Gets Message," *Morris County Daily Record,* 17 December 1970.

52. "Tenants Settle in Trade Center," *New York Times,* 17 December 1970.

53. Robert Kelley, interview with the author, Newark, N.J., 27 November 1995.

54. Karl Sabbagh, *Skyscraper,* 311.

55. *Weekly Report,* 23 December 1970.

56. "New Challenges Facing the P.A.," *Star-Ledger* (Newark), 25 April 1971.

57. *Weekly Report,* 19 July 1970.

58. Port Authority, "A Building Project Like No Other," 16.

59. "Austin Tobin to Quit New York Port Agency He Headed for 30 Years," *Wall Street Journal,* 13 December 1971, and "Austin J. Tobin, Executive Director of Port Authority for 30 Years, Dies," *New York Times,* 9 February 1978.

60. *Weekly Report,* 11 September 1972.

61. The game metaphor was devised by reporter William E. Burrows in his article, "World Trade Center's Construction Chief Wrestles to Keep Huge Project on Target," *Wall Street Journal,* 20 August 1969.

62. Ibid.

63. *Weekly Report,* 2 October 1972.

64. "Our Most Towering Task," *Newark Sunday News,* 3 August 1969.

65. Guy Tozzoli, telephone interview with the author, 28 June 1995.

66. "Trade Center Is Dedicated," *Daily News* (New York), 5 April 1973.

67. "After the Fact: P.A. Gets Around to Dedicating the Trade Center," *Star-Ledger* (Newark), 5 April 1973.

68. "Cahill Hails Trade Center as Historic," *Asbury Park Evening Press,* 5 April 1973.

69. "Tobin, Citing the Rain, Passes Up Dedication," *New York Times,* 5 April 1973.

70. Guy Tozzoli, interview with the author, New York City, 15 November 1994.

71. Jameson W. Doig, "To Claim the Seas and the Skies: Austin Tobin and the Port of New York Authority," in *Leadership and Innovation,* ed. Jameson W. Doig and Erwin C. Hargrove (Baltimore: Johns Hopkins University Press, 1987), 166.

Chapter 4
Winning Acceptance:
How a White Elephant Became Prime Real Estate

1. Guy Savine, "Port Authority Is Viewed as Victim of Its Own Image," *Newark Sunday News*, 30 November 1969.
2. Eric Nash, *New York's 50 Best Skyscrapers* (New York: City and Company, 1997).
3. "Reviewing the World Trade Center," *New York Times*, 12 April 1967.
4. Theodore W. Kheel, "How the Port Authority Is Strangling New York," *New York* magazine, 17 November 1969.
5. Report of the Executive Director to the Board of Trustees, 3 January 1967.
6. Ibid.
7. Don Sheard, "Trade Center Assailed for Buying Japan Steel," *World Journal Tribune*, 5 May 1967.
8. Owen Moritz, "Port Authority's Trade Center Opening as Office Demand Falls," *New York Sunday News*, 1 November 1970.
9. Owen Moritz, "Trade Center Opens on a Many-Storied Day," *Daily News*, 17 December 1970.
10. Roger Harris, "P.A. Revenue: Trade Center Propped Up by Other Agency Facilities," *New York Times*, 12 November 1974.
11. "Trade Center Pollution," *Asbury Park Evening Press*, 11 July 1971.
12. "Seek to Bar Trade Center over Sewage," *Hudson Dispatch*, 10 May 1972.
13. Report of the Executive Director to the Board of Trustees, 19 July 1971.
14. Ray M. Monti, "Trade Center Lights," *New York Times*, 9 August 1971.
15. Robert Carroll, "Trade Center Computer Is Told Watt's Watt," *Daily News* (New York), 31 July 1972.
16. Frederick C. Klein, "Wall Street Congestion Becomes More Intense as New Buildings Rise," *Wall Street Journal*, 10 September 1968.
17. Don Sheard, "Trade Center Will Harm TV Reception Here," *World Journal Tribune*, 13 February 1967.
18. Clayton Knowles, "Big Trade Center Called Bird Trap," *New York Times*, 16 March 1967.
19. Wolf von Eckardt, "Scraping the Top With Arrogance," *Washington Post*, 13 January 1973.
20. David M. Sokol, "American Art and Architecture: Imaging America," Session 89, American Culture Association, Philadelphia, Pennsylvania, 13 April 1995.

21. Vincent Scully, *Architecture: The Natural and the Manmade* (New York: St. Martin's Press, 1991).

22. E. D. Hirsch, Jr., Joseph F. Kett, and James Trefil, *The Dictionary of Cultural Literacy* (Boston: Houghton Mifflin, 1988), 155–189.

23. Robert McG. Thomas, Jr., "King Kong Plunges as Thousands Gasp," *New York Times*, 22 June 1976.

24. Ada Louise Huxtable, "A Skyscraper Fit for a King (Kong)?" *New York Times*, 1 February 1976.

25. Grace Lichtenstein, "Stuntman, Eluding Guards, Walks a Tightrope between Trade Center Towers," *New York Times*, 8 August 1974.

26. "Trade Center Tightropist Will Do Penance for Kids," *Star-Ledger* (Newark), 8 August 1974.

27. Lee Dembart, "Queens Skydiver Leaps Safely from Roof of the Trade Center," *New York Times*, 23 July 1975.

28. Ibid.

29. "Fleeting Fame," *New York Times*, 15 February 1976.

30. "Flying Young Man," *New York Times*, 27 July 1975.

31. Edith Evans Asbury, "Toymaker, 27, 'Never Scared' on the Way Up," *New York Times*, 27 May 1977.

32. Mary Breasted, "Climber Conquers 110-Story Tower," *New York Times*, 27 May 1977.

33. Ibid.

34. Ibid.

35. Murray Schumach, "Fly Pays $1.10, a Cent a Floor; City Drops Suit," *New York Times*, 1 June 1977.

36. John P. McNett, "Letter to the Editor," *New York Times*, 1 June 1977.

37. "Lookout Unveiled at Trade Center," *Star-Ledger* (Newark), 16 December 1975.

38. Al Pettenati, retired manager of the Observation Deck, interview with the author, New York City, 27 December 1994.

39. Paul J. C. Friedlander, "New York's New View from the Top," *New York Times*, 9 April 1972.

40. Philip H. Dougherty, "Trade Center to Promote at Top," *New York Times*, 9 December 1975.

41. Report of the Executive Director to the Board of Trustees, 22 December 1975.

42. Frank Mazza, "PA Has an Upbeat Pitch," *Daily News* (New York), 16 December 1975.

43. Pettenati, interview.

44. Paul Goldberger, "From 110 Stories Up: A Silent City Far Below," *New York Times*, 15 December 1975.

45. "World Trade Center Honors New Jersey Woman as Millionth Visitor," *New York Times*, 5 November 1976.

46. Frederick V. Boyd, "An Event Worthy of Observation," *Star-Ledger* (Newark), 8 November 1979.

47. "After 2,412 Visits to Top, the View is Still New," *New York Times*, 3 September 1984.

48. Pettenati, interview.

49. Ibid.

50. Ibid.

51. Ibid.

52. Ibid.

53. Ibid.

54. Morris Miller, interview with the author, New York City, 12 December 1994.

55. Ibid.

56. Report of the Executive Director to the Board of Trustees, 30 June 1975.

57. Jules Roinel, interview with the author, New York City, 1 July 1998.

58. Kathleen Duffy, "Joseph Baum, Chairman," press release, undated, New York City.

59. Pamela Parseghian, "Joe Baum," *Nation's Restaurant News*, February 1996.

60. James Vilas, "The Impresario of Eating Out," *Town and Country*, October 1995.

61. Ibid.

62. Parseghian, "Joe Baum."

63. Thomas P. Ronan, "Port Unit Scored on Trade Center," *New York Times*, 9 October 1975.

64. Frank Mazza, "Call Trade Center Cafe Plan Undigestible," *Daily News* (New York), 9 October 1975.

65. Roger Harris, "P. A. Stands Firm on Post Trade Center Club," *Star-Ledger* (Newark), 30 October 1975.

66. Frank Mazza, "PA Spending Probe Seated on Posh Chair Stories," *Daily News* (New York), 25 October 1975.

67. Howie Kurtz, "Port Authority Fighting Claims of Extravagance," *Bergen Record*, 12 November 1975.

68. "Ronan Sees Profit in Trade Center Club," *Star-Ledger* (Newark), 3 December 1975.

69. Frank Mazza, "If PA Eatery Bars Public, SLA May Bar Bar," *Daily News* (New York), 22 December 1975.

70. Frank Mazza, "PA Club Won't Serve Pie in the Sky Today," *Daily News* (New York), 12 April 1976.

71. Report of the Executive Director to the Board of Trustees, 3 May 1976.
72. James Villas, "The Impresario of Eating Out," *Town and Country*, October 1995.
73. Greene, "The Most Spectacular Restaurant."
74. Frank Mazza, "Try to Get PA's Eatery in Sky Off the Ground," *Daily News* (New York), 13 April 1976.

Chapter 5
Architecture: Beloved by All Except the Experts

1. Pierre Bourdieu, *The Logic of Practice* (Stanford, Calif.: Stanford University Press, 1990), 137.
2. Any detailed account of the architectural history of the World Trade Center must rely on the work of Anthony W. Robins, who is the director of survey at the New York City Landmarks Preservation Commission. See his *Classics of American Architecture: The World Trade Center* (Englewood, Fla.: Pineapple/Omnigraphics, 1987). Although this book is only sixty-four pages in length, it is comprehensive in its focus on the architecture of the building. It will be very difficult for scholars in the future to do a more thorough job since the Port Authority Library was closed for economic reasons in September 1995; and some of the key figures interviewed by Robins, including Minoru Yamasaki, have since died.
3. Ibid., 26.
4. Ibid., 27, 31.
5. Ibid., 29.
6. For the basic facts of Minoru Yamasaki's life, see Ann Lee Morgan and Colin Naylor, eds., *Contemporary Architects* (Chicago: St. James Press, 1987), 1013–1015. For a brief critical appraisal, see Paul Heyer, *Architects on Architecture* (New York: Walker and Company, 1966), 185–195. However, the best single source is his own autobiography. See Minoru Yamasaki, *A Life in Architecture* (New York and Tokyo: Weatherhill, 1979).
7. Yamasaki, *A Life in Architecture*, 27–36.
8. Robins, *Classics of American Architecture*, 33.
9. Yamasaki, *A Life in Architecture*, 115.
10. Ibid., 117. Also in a letter of 20 December 2001, Carl K. Panero points out a little-known hazard to occupants of tall buildings. The Battelle Institute conducted a study of the varying pressure between the interior and exterior of tall buildings. A column of dense cold air next to a column of less dense hot air causes this phenomenon. In a tall building a person within two feet of the exte-

rior wall could be ejected because of rapid equalization resulting from the loss of glass barrier.

11. Ibid. Also, according to Panero, the curtain wall was purchased with a performance specification. The bidders were given wind loads, profile, and color but no details. The manufacturers did the engineering. Jim Davis, the chief engineer for the Cupples Corporation (Alcoa's manufacturing partner), designed a skin without gaskets or caulking by employing a pressure equalized system very much like laying up shingles. This plan simplified erection and gave them an advantage over their competition. A full-scale mock-up went to the Sakinoski's testing facility in Miami and was subjected to a rigorous testing program.

12. Ibid., 114–118.

13. Robins, *Classics of American Architecture*, 112–113.

14. Ibid., 40.

15. John Tauranac, *The Empire State Building: The Making of a Landmark* (New York: Scribner, 1995), 28.

16. Norris D. McWhirter, *The Guinness Book of Records* (London: Guinness Superlatives, Ltd, 1985), 106.

17. David Bennett, *Skyscrapers: Form and Function* (New York: Simon and Schuster, 1995), 62–63.

18. Robins, *Classics of American Architecture*, 41.

19. Yamasaki, *A Life in Architecture*, 114.

20. Faye Hammel, *Frommer's Comprehensive Travel Guide to New York* (New York: Prentice Hall, 1994), 223.

21. Robins, *Classics of American Architecture*, 49–58.

22. Ada Louise Huxtable, "Biggest Buildings Herald New Era," *New York Times*, 26 January 1964.

23. Ada Louise Huxtable, "A New Era Heralded," *New York Times*, 19 January 1964.

24. Ada Louise Huxtable, "Engineering Feat," *New York Times*, 2 February 1964.

25. Editorial, *New York Times*, 21 January 1964.

26. Wolf von Eckardt, "Manhattan Towers Are to Be Topped," *Washington Post*, 1 March 1964.

27. Wolf von Eckardt, "New York's Trade Center: World's Tallest Fiasco," *Harper's* magazine, May 1966, 94–100.

28. Ada Louise Huxtable, "Who's Afraid of the Big Bad Buildings," *New York Times*, 29 May 1966.

29. Ibid.

30. Ada Louise Huxtable, "Big but Not So Bold," *New York Times*, 5 April 1973.

31. Ibid.

32. Elliot Willensky and Norval White, *AIA Guide to New York City*, 3d ed. (New York: Harcourt Brace Jovanovich, 1988), 48.
33. Paul Goldberger, *The City Observed: New York, a Guide to the Architecture of Manhattan* (New York: Vintage Books, 1979), 10–11.
34. Robert Venturi, *Complexity and Contradiction in Architecture* (New York: Museum of Modern Art. Distributed by Doubleday, Garden City, N.Y., 1966).
35. The discussion of how the World Trade Center is neither completely in the International Style nor the Postmodern is drawn from the author's interview with Gaylord Richardson at the annual meeting of the American Culture Association on 26 March 1996, Las Vegas, Nevada.
36. Following my presentation on "The Architecture of the World Trade Center" at a panel on American Art and Architecture at the American Culture Association on 26 March 1996, several participants commented on their pleasant experiences of seeing the sculptural effects of the Twin Towers from a moving platform at a distance.
37. Gaylord Richardson, interview with the author, Las Vegas, Nev., 26 March 1996.

CHAPTER 6
THE WORLD TRADE CENTER CONCEPT:
NOT JUST ANOTHER OFFICE BUILDING

1. Roger E. Axtell, *The Do's and Taboos of International Trade: A Small Business Primer* (New York: John Wiley and Sons, 1989), 10–11.
2. Ibid., 52–53.
3. Austin J. Tobin, "The World Trade Center . . . Symbol of Future Leadership," *Westsider* 29 (Fall 1964): 86.
4. George Rossi, Assistant Director, World Trade Center, interview with the author, New York City, 14 November 1994.
5. Hutton, *The World of the International Manager*, 7–8.
6. Rossi, interview, 14 November 1994.
7. Guy F. Tozzoli, "Telling the World the Story," *Westsider* 29 (Fall 1964): 38–41.
8. Rossi, interview, 14 November 1994.
9. Joseph P. Fried, "World Trade Center Still in Shadow," *New York Times*, 31 May 1979.
10. George T. Rossi, telephone conversation with author, 3 July 1997.
11. Ibid.
12. Fried, "World Trade Center."

13. Rossi, conversation, 3 July 1997.
14. Ibid.
15. Advertisement, *Journal of Commerce*, 14 March 1996.
16. Guy Tozzoli, interview with the author, New York City, 15 November 1994.
17. Robert T. Kelley related the Baker story in his course "Introduction to World Trade" on 11 September 1995, at the World Trade Institute of the World Trade Center, New York City.
18. Information about the Evening School of World Trade, the World Trade Institute at the World Trade Center New York, was drawn from catalogs as well as discussions with school officials.
19. Ibid.
20. "World Trade Institute Is Labeled 'Heart' of Center," *New York Times*, 5 April 1973.
21. Eunice Coleman, interview with the author, New York City, 7 December 1994.
22. Peter Yerkes, Port Authority Media Relations, telephone interview with the author, 13 October 1998.
23. Albert Cohen, interview with the author, New York City, 1 February 1996.
24. Ibid.
25. For more on values toward work, wealth, consumption, and achievement, see Vern Terpstra and Kenneth David, *The Cultural Environment of International Business*, 2d ed. (Cincinnati: South-Western Publishing, 1985), 126–128.

CHAPTER 7
A CITY WITHIN A CITY; OR, A DAY IN THE LIFE . . .

1. Eugene Raggio, General Operations Supervisor, interview with the author, New York City, 21 November 1994.
2. My description of operations is based on observations made on 21 November 1994, on a tour of duty arranged by Robert C. DiChiara, then assistant director of the World Trade Center.
3. Robert DiChiara, interview with the author, New York City, 17 July 1998.
4. Robert DiChiara, interview with the author, New York City, 5 November 1997.
5. Robert DiChiara, interview with the author, New York City, 14 July 1998.
6. Peter Balma, electrical engineer, telephone interview with the author, 15 September 1998.
7. Ibid.
8. Sergeant Charles O'Neill, "Port Authority Police," 40-page

booklet, Port Authority Police Headquarters, Jersey City, N.J., 1993.

9. Captain Joseph Martella, Port Authority Police (retired), interview with the author, New York City, 13 December 1994.

10. David Sawyer, interview with the author, New York City, 19 November 1997.

11. Deidre Carmody, "A City Unto Itself," *New York Times*, 28 May 1984.

12. Anthony Dowd, interview with the author, New York City, 22 November 1994.

13. Report of the Executive Director to the Board of Trustees, 10 July 1972.

14. Roko Camaj, interview with the author, New York City, 15 March 1995.

15. Arthur Del Bianco, interview with the author, New York City, 15 March 1995.

16. Jerry Jacobs, *The Mall: An Attempted Escape from Everyday Life* (Prospect Heights, Ill.: Waveland Press, 1984), 95–109.

17. Ibid., 104.

18. Robert DiChiara, interview with the author, Hoboken, N.J., 26 October 1997.

19. Thomas J. Lueck, "Traffic Jams the Sidewalk," *New York Times*, 29 November 1997.

20. Martella, interview.

21. Sal Marciante, interview with the author, New York City, 7 November 1997.

22. Dena Kleiman, "Negotiations Are Under Way to Construct Hotel at World Trade Center," *New York Times*, 15 January 1978.

23. Dorothy J. Gaiter, "Hotel in the Trade Center Greets Its First 100 Guests," *New York Times*, 2 April 1981.

24. Claudi H. Deutsch, "20 Months after Bombing, Vista Hotel to Finally Reopen," *New York Times*, 31 October 1994.

25. I attended the event, held on the 2nd-floor lobby, on 15 November 1994, New York City.

26. Thomas J. Lueck, "Vista Hotel for Sale, Port Authority Says," *New York Times*, 10 May 1995.

27. My observations and those of Sal Marciante were confirmed by articles in *Cosmopolitan* in the mid-1990s.

28. Steve Goldstein, "Trade Center Sets Date for Hotel Work," *Daily News* (New York), 22 March 1978.

29. I was given a complete tour of the New York Marriott World Trade Center and its facilities on 14 July 1998 by Carmen Cruz, international program manager.

30. Mark Finston, "New Hotel Will Grow in Downtown Manhattan," *Star-Ledger* (Newark), 27 March 1979.
31. Robert DiChiara, interview with the author, New York City, 21 November 1994.
32. Robert DiChiara, interview with the author, New York City, 26 October 1997.
33. Eugene Raggio, interview.
34. I had the opportunity to observe the roll call of security guards at the World Trade Center in the company of Robert V. Debellis, Operations Group Supervisor, at 11:00 P.M. on a Monday evening, 21 November 1994, New York City.
35. Ibid.
36. Tina Rosenberg, "Helping Them Make It through the Night," *New York Times*, 12 July 1998.
37. O'Neill, "Port Authority Police."
38. Bruce Lambert, "Croissants? A Clam Bar? Is This the Port Authority Terminal?" *New York Times*, 6 August 1995.
39. Robert DiChiara, interview with the author, New York City, 21 November 1994.
40. I attended the dedication of the memorial on the plaza of the World Trade Center, New York City, 25 May 1995.

CHAPTER 8
DESTRUCTION:
THE TERRORIST ATTACK AND ITS AFTERMATH

1. Minoru Yamasaki, cited in Robert Sullivan, ed., *Life: One Nation: America Remembers September 11, 2001* (Boston: Little Brown and Company, 2001), 12.
2. John A. Kouwenhoven, *The Beer Can by the Highway: Essays on What's American about America* (Baltimore: The Johns Hopkins University Press, 1961), 43-50
3. Chronology of the events of September 11, 2001, are from Sullivan, *One Nation*, 25-60. For more on the motives of the terrorists and on airport security, see James F. Hoge, Jr., and Gideon Rose, eds., *How Did This Happen?: Terrorism and the New War* (New York: Public Affairs, 2001).
4. Michael J. Crosby cited in Kevin Matthews and B.J. Novitsky, "World Trade Center Destroyed," *Architecture Week*, No. 66, 12 September 2001.
5. John A. Jones cited in British television documentary "How the Twin Towers Collapsed," Darlow Smithson Productions, broadcast in Great Britain on Channel 4, 13 December 2001, produced by Philip Wearne and directed by Ben Bowie.

6. Evan Thomas, "Horror and Heroes of a Day That Changed America" (cover story), *Newsweek,* 31 December 2001, 50.

7. Ibid., 54.

8. Vincent A. Dunn cited in Wearne and Bowie, "How the Twin Towers Collapsed."

9. David Blankenhorn cited by Patricia Leigh Brown, "Heavy Lifting Required."

10. Mike Kehoe cited by Jodie Morse, "Glory in the Glare," *Time* 31 December 2001, 98.

11. Chronology of the attack on the Twin Towers is from Sullivan, *One Nation*, 19–63.

12. Michael J. Crosbie, "Engineering Forensics of Collapse," *Architecture Week* 71 (17 October 2001).

13. James Glanz and Eric Lipton, "Experts Urging Broader Inquiry in Towers' Fall," *New York Times*, 25 December 2001.

14. Philip Wearne, British investigative journalist, telephone interview with the author, 15 December 2001.

15. Interview with W. Gene Corley is from "Special Report: Falling Down," *IEEE Spectrum Online*, September 2001. See http://www.spectrum.ieee.org.

16. Ibid.

17. James Glanz, "From Torn Steel, Cold Data of Collapse," *New York Times*, 9 October 2001.

18. Crosbie, "Engineering Forensics."

19. Wearne and Bowie, "How the Twin Towers Collapsed." See also James Glanz with Michael Moss, "Faulty Fireproofing Is Reviewed as Factor in Trade Center Collapse," *New York Times*, 13 December 2001; and James Glanz with Michael Moss, "Trade Center's Fireproofing Had a Questionable History," *New York Times*, 14 December 2001.

20. Ibid. See also James Glanz, "In Collapsing Towers, a Cascade of Failures," *New York Times*, 11 November 2001; and James Glanz, "Demand Rises for Widening Investigation into Collapse," *New York Times*, 15 December 2001.

21. The Poynter Insitute, *September 11, 2001* (Kansas City: Andrews McMeel Publishing, 2001) 58. This book is a collection of newspaper front pages published immediately after the disaster.

22. Sullivan, *One Nation*, 80–101.

23. Ibid., 122–123; and N. R. Kleinfeld, "In Stopping to Save Woman, Rescuers Saved Themselves," *New York Times*, 28 September 2001.

24. Susan Sachs, "At the Site, Little Hope of Uncovering Survivors," *New York Times*, 19 September 2001.

25. Dan Barry, "At the Scene of Random Devastation, a Most Orderly Mission," *New York Times*, 24 September 2001.

26. John Keats cited by Amy Ellis Nutt, "Let's Be Grateful for Lessons Learned," *Star-Ledger* (Newark), 22 November 2001.

27. Peter Genovese, "Site Seers," *Star-Ledger* (Newark), 28 September 2001.

28. Paul Goldberger, "Building Plans: What the World Trade Center Meant," *The New Yorker*, 24 September 2001, 78.

29. Matt Zoller Seitz, "The View from Ground Zero," *Star-Ledger* (Newark), 4 November 2001.

30. Jim Dwyer, "Happy New Year, Same as the Old One," *New York Times*, 30 December 2001.

31. Associated Press, "WTC Victims from All Walks of Life," *Home News Tribune* (New Brunswick, New Jersey), 27 October 2001.

32. Janny Scott, "In Neckties or Fire Helmets, Victims Shared a Work Ethic," *New York Times*, 4 November 2001.

33. Ibid.

34. Eric Lipton and James Glanz, "Slowed by Site's Fragility, the Heavy Lifting Has Only Begun," *New York Times*, 13 October 2001.

35. Feature, "America's Deepest Wound, and the Round-the-Clock Effort to Heal It," *Star-Ledger* (Newark), 21 November 2001.

36. Lipton and Glanz, "Slowed by Site's Fragility."

37. Dan Barry and Amy Waldman, "At Landfill, Tons of Debris, Slivers of Solace," *New York Times*, 21 October 2001.

38. Dennis Overbye, "Under the Towers, Ruin and Resilience," *New York Times*, 9 October 2001.

39. Juan Gonzalez, "A Toxic Nightmare at Disaster Site," *Daily News* (New York), 26 October 2001, and David France, "Now, WTC Syndrome," *Newsweek*, 5 November 2001, 10.

40. Charlie LeDuff, "As Dig Goes on, Emotions Are Buried Deep," *New York Times*, 18 November 2001.

41. Steve Chambers, "A Steely Resolve Fills This Crumpled House," *Star-Ledger* (Newark), 30 December 2001.

42. Matt Zoller Seitz, "Myth and Mayhem: How Terrorists Use Our Own Pop Culture Against Us," *Star-Ledger* (Newark), 23 September 2001.

43. "The Amazing Spider Man," Vol. 2, No. 36, (New York: Marvel Comics, 2001). My attention to this item was drawn by Amy Ellis Nutt, "A Web of Sorrow," *Star-Ledger* (Newark), 13 November 2001.

44. "*Heroes* Third Printing, *Moments of Silence* Ship This Week," *Diamond Dateline*, 9 January 2002, 2.

45. Jayson Blair, "In an Urban Underbelly, Hidden Views of a Terror's Toll," *New York Times*, 14 October 2001.

46. Michael D. Lemonick, "The Twin Towers: Should They Be Rebuilt?" *Time*, 24 September 2001, 66.

47. Craig Wilson and Maria Puente, "Should the Twin Towers Rise Again?" *USA Today*, 25 September 2001.

48. Kevin Coughlin, "Public Now Ambivalent about Skyscrapers' Role," *Star-Ledger* (Newark), 19 November 2001.

49. Herbert Muschamp, "A Rush to Complete Plans for Downtown," *New York Times*, 14 October 2001.

50. The author presented these four options in an interview with Zain Verjee of CNN International, which aired on 8 January 2002.

51. Raymond Gastil, an urban planner at the Van Allen Institute, explained the public hearings, during the same interview with Zain Verjee.

52. Amy Ellis Nutt, "New York City Should Look to Venice and Rebuild the Twin Towers," *Star-Ledger* (Newark), 19 December 2001.

53. Herbert Muschamp, "The Deadly Importance of Making Distinctions," *New York Times*, 30 December 2001.

54. Eric Lipton, "Cleanup's Pace Outstrips Plans for Attack Site," *New York Times*, 7 January 2002.

55. Michael Kimmelman, "In a Square, a Sense of Unity: A Homegrown Memorial Brings Strangers Together," *New York Times*, 19 September 2001.

56. Kathleen O'Brien, "WTC Memorials Thrive at Church," *Star-Ledger* (Newark), 11 January 2002.

57. Dan Bischoff, "Towering Tribute: Artists, Officials, Ponder How to Memorialize the Events of Sept. 11," *Star-Ledger* (Newark), 5 October 2001.

58. Dith Pran, photographer, "Painted Plywood Letters Spell Out AMERICA," *New York Times*, 30 December 2001.

59. Dith Pran, photographer, "A Rock Formation in West Essex Park," *New York Times*, 6 January 2002.

60. Steve Zeitlin, letter to the author, 20 November 2001.

61. See Library of Congress, Internet Archive, at September 11.archive.org., (http://150.156.112.3). See also the Internet Archive at www.archive.org and the WebArchivist at www.webarchivist.org.

62. Lisa Guernesey, "Digital Memories of Terror's Victims," *New York Times*, 13 December 2001.

63. Jennifer D. Braun, "Sept. 11, from the Jersey side," *Star-Ledger* (Newark), 26 November 2001.

64. Jonathan Mandell, "History Is Impatient to Embrace Sept. 11," *New York Times*, 18 November 2001.

65. John A. Harnes, "Firefighter-cop Displays 8-foot Trade Center Model," *Home News Tribune* (New Brunswick, New Jersey), 30 December 2001.

66. Herbert Muschamp, "With Viewing Platforms, a Dignified Approach to Ground Zero," *New York Times*, 22 December 2001.

67. Stephanie Gaskell, "Tickets to Ground Zero," *Home News Tribune* (New Brunswick, New Jersey), 13 January 2002.

68. Dean E. Murphy, "As Public Yearns to See Ground Zero, Survivors Call a Viewing Stand Ghoulish," *New York Times*, 13 January 2002.

69. Sarah Boxer, "A Memorial Is Itself a Shaper of Memory," *New York Times*, 27 October 2001. See also Herbert Muschamp, "The Commemorative Beauty of Tragic Wreckage," *New York Times*, 11 November 2001; and Dean E. Murphy, "Toppling of 'Shroud' Stirs Emotions," *New York Times*, 16 December 2001. There is a robust tradition of incorporating ruins into landscape architecture for parks and gardens. See Kenneth Clark, *The Gothic Revival* (London: John Murray, 1973), chapter 3, especially 48–50.

70. Michael Kimmelman, "Out of Minimalism, Monuments to Memory," *New York Times*, 13 January 2002.

71. Ibid.

72. Ibid.

73. Al Frank, "Once a Landlord, Now P.A. Is Tenant," *Star-Ledger* (Newark), 27 October 2001.

74. Al Frank, "The P.A.'s Largest Plans Are in Doubt: $9.5 Billion Agenda Swept Aside by Crisis," *Star-Ledger* (Newark), 11 December 2001; and Al Frank, "Attacks Hasten 'Do-able' P.A. Projects: $864 Million Will Fund Ferry and PATH Upgrades and More Security Following Sept. 11," *Star-Ledger* (Newark), 7 November 2001.

75. Percy Bysshe Shelley, "Ozymandias," in Laurence Perrine, *Sound and Sense: An Introduction to Poetry* (New York: Harcourt, Brace, and World, 1963) 97–98.

76. Michael J. Lewis, "Building with Attitude: The 'Look at Me' Strut of a Swagger Building," *New York Times*, 6 January 2002.

77. Associated Press, "Some Companies May Not Return to Lower Manhattan Addresses," *Home News Tribune* (New Brunswick, New Jersey), 30 October 2001.

78. James Atlas, "Among the Lost: Illusions of Immortality," *New York Times*, 7 October 2001.

79. Daniel Born, "Innocence Toppled and Lost," *New York Times*, 22 September 2001. F. Scott Fitzgerald, *The Great Gatsby* (New York: Charles Scribner's Sons, 1925), 227.

Index

About the Author

A graduate of Yale University and a Fulbright Scholar, Angus Kress Gillespie is professor of American Studies at Rutgers University. Author of several books and numerous articles, Dr. Gillespie has an interest in architecture, engineering, and transportation. He is frequently consulted and quoted by the news media. He has often shared his findings with radio listeners on National Public Radio, and he has appeared on the ABC television show *Good Morning America*.

Gillespie has studied ships, superhighways, and skyscrapers. As a researcher, he likes to take a monumental work of engineering and "tease" it for its cultural implications. At Rutgers University, he is well known for his courses in maritime culture, which survey international shipping and the history of seaports in New York and New Jersey. Gillespie is listed in the reference series *Who's Who* as one of "the best teachers in America."